Lake Superior to Rainy Lake:
Three Centuries of Fur Trade History

A Collection of Writings

Edited and Introduced by

Jean Morrison

Thunder Bay Historical Museum Society
2003

©2003, The Thunder Bay Historical Museum Society, except as otherwise noted
ISBN 0-920119-48-4

All rights reserved. No part of this publication may be reproduced, stored in a retrieval system, or transmitted in any form or by any means, electronic, mechanical, photocopying, recording, or otherwise (except for brief passages for purposes of review) without prior written permission of the coyright holders.

Publisher: The Thunder Bay Historical Museum Society Inc.
425 Donald St. E., Thunder Bay, Ontario P7E 5V1.
tel: (807) 623-0801; fax: (807) 622-6880; e-mail: *tbhms@tbaytel.net*

Funding for the printing of this book was provided by
The Thunder Bay Historical Museum Society's Publications Fund

Cover and page design, and layout: Thorold J. Tronrud

Printed by: Friesens Corporation
One Printers Way
Altona, Manitoba, R0G 0B0
Canada

Printed in Canada on acid-free paper

National Library of Canada Cataloguing in Publication

Lake Superior to Rainy River : three centuries of fur trade history : a collection of writings / edited and introduced by Jean Morrison.

Includes bibliographical references and index.
ISBN 0-920119-48-4

1. Fur trade—Ontario, Northern—History. I. Morrison, Jean, 1926-
II. Thunder Bay Historical Museum Society III. Title.

FC3094.5.L33 2003   380.1'4397'0971311   C2003-905569-8

Prologue

The year 2003 is a landmark in the annals of Thunder Bay and District. It is the 200th anniversary of the founding of Fort Kaministiquia, the North West Company's inland headquarters at the Kaministiquia River's exit into Thunder Bay on Lake Superior's northwest coast. Re-named Fort William in 1807 for William McGillivray, the company's principal director, the Fort became famed as the centre of a vast fur trade empire which, at its peak, stretched from the St. Lawrence River beyond Lake Superior to the Arctic and Pacific Oceans.

After the merger in 1821 of the North West and Hudson's Bay companies, Fort William had a reduced status as an ordinary trading post. Its function as the gateway to the west via the Kaministiquia River, however, continued throughout the era of the birchbark canoe. While a decline in the fur trade led to the post's closure in 1883, the fort's site continued to serve as Canada's gateway to the west in the age of steam transportation by water and by rail. The name Fort William also endured in the municipality of Fort William which joined Port Arthur in 1970 to form the City of Thunder Bay.

2003 then is the 200th anniversary of unbroken non-Native habitation at the mouth of Kaministiquia River and thus can be considered the bi-centennial of the municipality of Thunder Bay and environs.

2003 has another significance for Thunder Bay. It is now thirty years since Her Majesty, Queen Elizabeth II officially opened Old Fort William (now Fort William Historical Park). Since 1973, this superb reconstruction has made important contributions to Northwestern Ontario by imparting a deeper awareness of this region's crucial role in Canada's fur trade history. To honour this dual anniversary the Thunder Bay Historical Museum Society decided to mark the occasion by publishing a tribute to the original Fort William and to its reconstruction.

As stipulated by the Society, *Lake Superior to Rainy Lake: Three Centuries of Fur Trade History* goes beyond Fort William to include the fur trade in Northwestern Ontario. Much has been published on various aspects of the Canadian fur trade but few works have treated the Northwestern Ontario trade as distinct entity. Although a number of published articles and research reports have dealt with specific aspects of the Northwestern Ontario fur trade, these are scattered in journals or government files and are often quite inaccessible to the general reader. The Society deemed that a sampling of this material gathered under one cover would rescue many worthy studies from obscurity while at the same time make a noteworthy contribution to the literature of the fur trade.

Geographically, Northwestern Ontario is divided by the Height of Land between the Lake Superior and Hudson Bay watersheds. Within its limits, however, the Hudson Bay watershed is divided into two lesser drainage systems, one whose waters drain directly into James Bay and Hudson Bay, and the other whose waters take a circuitous route to salt water via Lake Winnipeg and its northeast tributaries. Along the southern fringes of this lesser Hudson Bay system, the waters flow westward to Lake Winnipeg from the Height of Land through Lac La Croix, Rainy Lake, Rainy River, Lake of the Woods and the Winnipeg River.

From 1670 to 1869, the Hudson's Bay Company held monopoly control over all lands draining into Hudson Bay by virtue of its royal charter granted by Charles II of Great Britain. Meanwhile, before the end of its North American tenure in 1763, France claimed much of the continent's interior, thanks largely to its traders out of Montreal who ventured deep into the northwest perhaps as far as the Rocky Mountains and down the Mississippi River to the Gulf of Mexico. West of Lake Superior, they followed rivers and erected *postes* within that part of the Hudson Bay basin drained by the Winnipeg River, lands included in the Hudson's Bay Company's charter.

With the British Conquest of New France, the Anglo-Scots who took over the Montreal trade used the old French route up the Ottawa River and crossed Lake Superior to its western shore. To reach the interior they then ascended the Pigeon River or, after 1803 the Kaministiquia, crossed the Height of Land and proceeded west along waters within the Hudson Bay watershed and therefore within the jurisdiction of the Hudson's Bay Company. On the basis of exploits by their French predecessors in that region, Montreal's traders also claimed

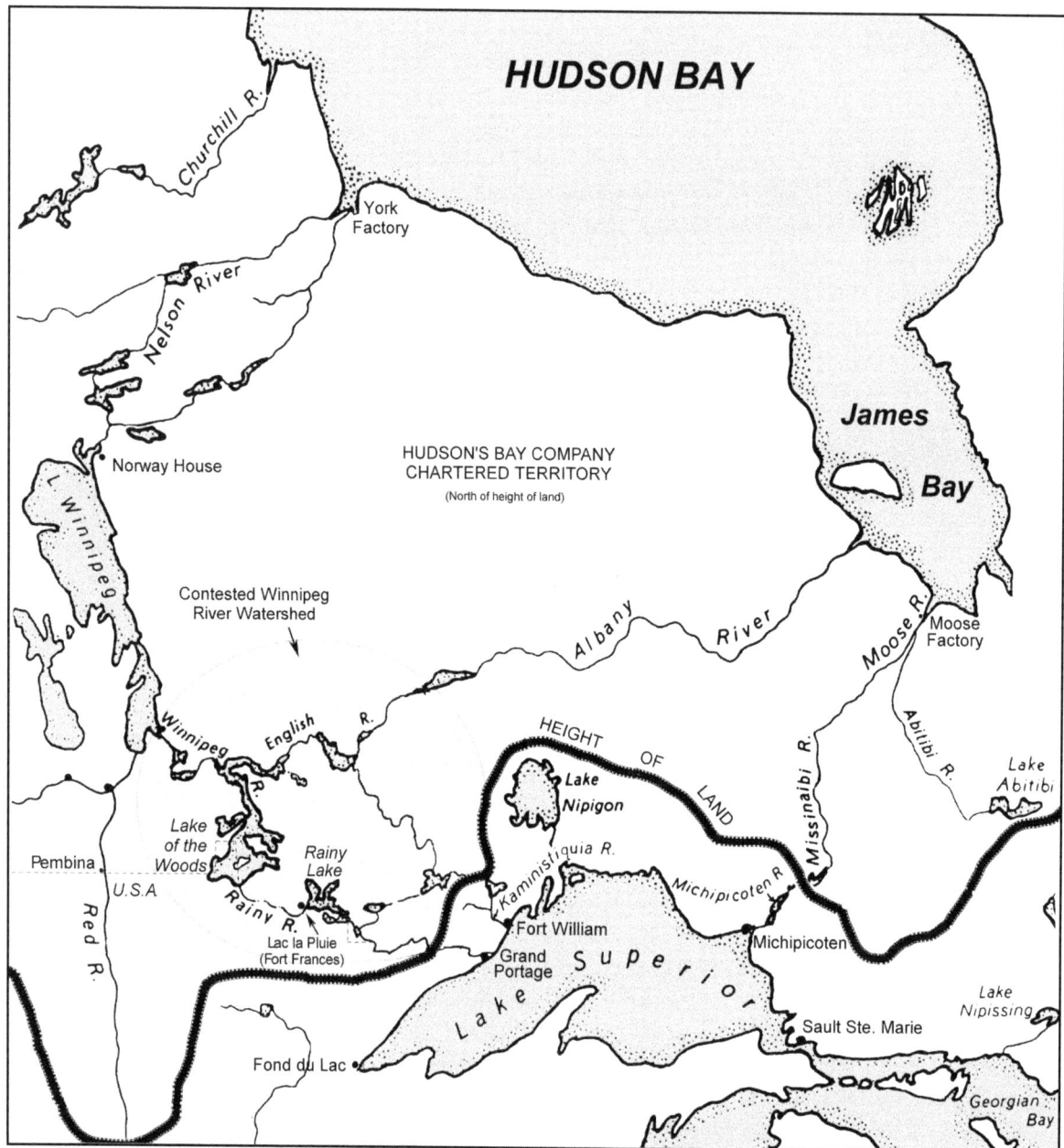

THE GEOGRAPHY OF NORTHWESTERN ONTARIO'S FUR TRADE.

Montreal's fur traders considered the Lake Superior watershed as their domain. North of the Height of Land were the Hudson's Bay Company's chartered territories within which lies the Winnipeg River system. This system together with Lake Superior and its tributaries formed the Montreal-based fur trade's east-west corridor. Map by Thorold J. Tronrud.

transportation and trading rights in this now contested part of the Hudson Bay drainage basin.

Lake Superior to Rainy Lake will emphasize Northwestern Ontario's southern margins, that strip of land which encompasses the Lake Superior drainage basin and the portion of the Hudson Bay basin drained by the Winnipeg River. Together these regions formed the crucial east-west corridor in the Montreal fur trade's transportation system during both the French and British regimes.

(The fur trade in lands draining directly into Hudson Bay had a northern orientation, one quite distinct from the east-west orientation of the southern trade. Its history, the subject of Victor P. Lytwyn's excellent *The*

Fur Trade of the Little North: Indians, Pedlars, and Englishmen East of Lake Winnipeg, 1760-1821, does not come within the purview of this book except where it and that of the southern corridor intersect.)

Three establishments along the Voyageurs' Highway between Sault Ste. Marie and today's Ontario-Manitoba border had vital roles in the transcontinental fur trade out of Montreal. On Lake Superior's northeastern coast Michipicoten linked Superior to James Bay via the Michipicoten, Missinaibi and Moose Rivers; after 1821 it served as headquarters and depot for the Superior trade. Midpoint on the southern corridor was Fort William, portal to the interior via the Kaministiquia River and the North West Company's inland headquarters and transshipment point. To the west, Lac la Pluie (or Rainy Lake) functioned as the turn-around point for the Athabasca trade while giving easy access to the Albany River in the north and the Mississippi River to the south.

Lord Selkirk had a good grasp of the strategic importance of Michipicoten and Rainy Lake. Following his occupation of Fort William in 1816, he ordered detachments of his De Meuron mercenaries to seize these key points on the North West Company's east-west trade route.[1] *Lake Superior to Rainy Lake* takes it title from the significance of this long but narrow strip of land to the history, not only of Northwestern Ontario but also to Canada.

The articles in this book have been written by a diversity of authors – academics, post-graduate students, professional researchers and keen amateurs. It is hoped that it will appeal to a diversity of readers as well.

Jean Morrison, editor
Thunder Bay, Ontario
2003

NOTES

[1] [Wilcocke, Samuel Hull], *A Narrative of Occurrences in the Indian Countries of North America since the Connexion of the Right Hon. the Earl of Selkirk with the Hudson's Bay Company, and his Attempt to Establish a Colony on the Red River* (London, 1817), pp. 111-13.

Contributors

The former historian at Old Fort William (1975-1990), **Jean Morrison** has written on local fur trade and labour history for the *Dictionary of Canadian Biography, The Beaver,* the Thunder Bay Historical Museum Society *Papers and Records* and other publications. Her most recent work is *Superior Rendezvous-Place: Fort William in the Canadian Fur Trade* (Toronto: 2001).

The late **Dr. Elizabeth Arthur** (1920-1997) taught history at the Fort William Collegiate Institute (1952-1964) and at Lakehead University (1964 to 1985). Her many publications include *Thunder Bay District, 1821-1892: A Collection of Documents* (Champlain Society, 1973) and several items for the *Dictionary of Canadian Biography, Ontario History* and the Thunder Bay Historical Museum Society's *Papers and Records*. She also served the Society as member of the board, as honorary president and as first editor of the revived *Papers and Records*.

Theodore Catton is a historian with Historical Research Associates in Missoula, Montana, where he specializes in Native American and environmental history. He is the author of *Inhabited Wilderness: Indians, Eskimos, and National Parks in Alaska,* and numerous articles and book-length reports. His second book, *National Park, City Playground: Mount Rainier through the Twentieth Century*, is forthcoming from University of Washington Press.

Ed Jerome lives in Hallock, Minnesota and is a direct descendant of the Fort William canoemaker, Antoine Collin through his grandmother, Marie Jeanne Collin, granddaughter of Jean Baptist Collin, the canoemaker's son and Jean Baptiste's wife Betsy Henry, daughter of Alexander Henry the Younger. He has a B.A. from Bemidgi State University in Minnesota and conducts research on his ancestors in the Hudson's Bay Company Archives, the Minnesota Historical Society and Provincial Archives of Manitoba. He is a Red River cart maker like his Métis ancestor, André Jerome, and co-writes articles on Pembina Métis history with Ruth Swan.

David Kemp is Professor of Geography at Lakehead University and a climatologist who teaches and writes about environmental issues. He has a particular interest in the fur trade and the impact of weather and climate on the logistics of the trade and the people involved in it.

Dr. Victor Lytwyn is an independent consultant specializing in the field of Aboriginal and Treaty rights. He has worked with First Nations and government agencies throughout Ontario to resolve land, water and other resource issues. His publications include *Muskekowuck Athinuwick: Original People of the Great Swampy Land* (2002), and *The Fur Trade in the Little North: Indians Pedlars and Englishmen East of Lake Winnipeg, 1760-1821* (1986).

Marcia Montgomery is a professional historian in Seattle, Washington. Her work includes numerous cultural resource reports and evaluations for federal and state agencies. She is co-author of *Hard Drive to the Klondike: Promoting Seattle During the Gold Rush*, a book published for the National Park Service.

Judy Petch is a part-time student at Lakehead University and a fan of local Thunder Bay history. She serves on the Editorial Committee, Thunder Bay Historical Museum Society *Papers and Records*.

Ian T. Stuart was a free-lance historical researcher at the time he prepared "Fur Trading at St. Joseph Island and Beyond: from the French regime to 1821" for Parks Canada.
John Weiler is a heritage consultant.

Joe Winterburn has been the tinsmith and an historical interpreter at Old Fort William since 1984 and was assistant curator at the Thunder Bay Historical Museum Society from 1976 to 1983. He is a member and past-president of the Canadian Corps of Voyageurs, a volunteer group at Old Fort William which re-enacts the Corps of Canadian Voyageurs raised by William McGillivray in the War of 1812 and the de Meuron Swiss Regiment in British pay, some of whose members Lord Selkirk hired in 1816 as soldier-settlers for his Red River Settlement.

A native of Montreal, **Ruth Swan** received her BA from Bishop's University, Lennoxville, Quebec. Her MA thesis from the University of Winnipeg dealt with ethnicity and the administration of the Hon. Robert Atkinson Davis, her great-great uncle and second Premier of Manitoba (1874-78). She has written six articles on Métis history and has submitted her doctoral thesis to the University of Manitoba on " The Crucible: Pembina and the Origins of the Red River Valley Métis". She hopes to find a job in a history-related field.

Acknowledgements

From Lake Superior to Rainy Lake needed the help of many people to bring it to fruition. For a good part of its contents the following are gratefully acknowledged. Authors Victor P. Lytwyn, Ted Catton and Marcia Montgomery, Joe Winterburn, David Kemp, Ruth Swan and Edward Jerome and Judy Petch agreed to use of previously published papers, some with editorial changes. Dennis Carter-Edwards, Ontario Region, Parks Canada arranged for permission to publish selections from Ian T Stuart's "Fur Trading at St. Joseph Island and Beyond". For Catton's "The Rainy Lake Region in the Fur Trade", permission to publish was also sought from the National Park Service. The referral of Tim Cochrane, Grand Portage National Park to Mary Graves, Voyageur National Park led to Don Stevens, Senior Historian, Midwest Region, Omaha, Nebraska who informed me that the report in the public domain. Various suggestions by several employees in the Ontario public service as to which government branch had authority to grant approval for use of John Weiler's report on Michipicoten finally led to the Ministry of Consumer and Business Services, Publications Ontario Copyright Unit and the kind permission of the Queen's Printer of Ontario. As well, several people, too many to name, gave (unsuccessful) leads to the late Elizabeth Arthur's executor.

Arden Ogg, Managing Editor, Papers of the Algonquian Conference, University of Manitoba gave permission to reprint the Swan/Jerome article on Antoine Collins while Julie Arnold (for Ken Bird Executive Manager), Ontario Genealogical Society accepted Jean Morrison's request to use her article on fur trade families "as you see fit". Dr. Ernie Epp, Lakehead University brought my attention to Dean L. Anderson's paper, "The Flow of European Trade Goods into the Western Great Lakes Region, 1715-1760" while Steve Nielsen, Reference Associate, Library, Minnesota Historical Society sent the correct citation to the Montreal Merchants Records. Kaireen Morrison and Johanna Rowe of the Township of Michipicoten Heritage Committee provided material and illustrations, on various aspects of Michipicoten history including Louisa MacKenzie Bethune's grave and Anne Morton, Head, Research & Reference, Hudson's Bay Company Archives supplied information about the Hudson's Bay Company's Michipicoten post. The many individuals who offered help and advise on the modern fur trade are acknowledged in the introduction to the final chapter.

Several worthwhile articles were considered for publication but sadly could not be used for various reasons. Scott Hamilton's "Over-Hunting and Local Extinctions: Socio-Economic Implications of Fur Trade Subsistence", *Culture and Environment*, R.W. Jamieson et al., eds. (University of Calgary Archaeological Association, 1993) has a northern plains rather than Northwestern Ontario orientation and his "Dynamics of Social Complexity in Early Nineteenth-Century British Fur-Trade Posts," *International Journal of Historical Archaeology*, Vol. 4, No. 3, 2000, compares Fort William with York Factory but is too lengthy for this publication. Space did not permit inclusion of David Chapman's edited version of "Fur Trade Rivalry on the Rainy River, 1793-1797" by Alma E. Henry (TBHMS *Papers and Records*, (2000)). This condensation of Henry's version of the journals of Donald 'Mad' McKay and of John McKay, however, could well be read in conjunction with Catton's "The Rainy Lake Region". David Arthurs' "Rediscovering Red Rock House: The History and Archaeology of a Late 19th Century Fur Trade Post", a paper presented to the TBHMS 4th Annual McKirdy Lecture (1986) unfortunately was not available for publication.

Others who helped in many ways include Peter Boyle, Marty Mascarin and Shawn Patterson at Fort William Historical Park, staff at Lakehead University Library and the Thunder Bay Public Library as well as local historian Elinor Barr. The unexpected complexity of this undertaking as well as personal factors delayed completion of this project for at least one year more than at first anticipated. The patience of the TBHMS Publications Committee thus deserves special recognition. The committee's chair, Beth Boegh, and members Mark Chochla, David Kemp, Wayne Pettit and Tory Tronrud all made notable contributions to this project by offering editorial advice, selecting illustrations and proof-reading.

One of the great divides in this world is between the users of Macs and PCs. Transmission of material between my Mac and the Museum's PC seemed frustratingly impossible until Shawn Allaire stepped in and by some miracle, which I still don't understand, was able to use her computer to relay my material to the museum.

I would especially like to thank the Thunder Bay Historical Museum Society for undertaking the publication of *From Lake Superior to Rainy Lake* and thereby steering me into hitherto unknown aspects of Northwestern Ontario's fur trade history. Much credit for the final outcome of this publication, however, goes to Tory Tronrud, who is not only the society's director but its desktop publisher, designer, cartographer and computer whiz *par excellence*. And a big final thank to my best critic and proof-reader, my always indulgent husband, Ken Morrison.

Jean Morrison, editor
Thunder Bay, Ontario
2003

Table of Contents

Prologue 2
Contributors 6
Acknowledgements 8
Table of Contents 10
Illustrations 11

Part One - **The French Fur Trade** 12
    Introduction 13
    Ian T. Stuart . "The Organization of the French Fur Trade, 1650-1760". 15

Part Two - **From 1650 to 1900: Two overviews** 23
    Introduction 24
    Victor P. Lytwyn, "The Anishinabeg and the Fur Trade" 25
    Theodore Catton, "The Rainy Lake Region in the Fur Trade" 46

Part Three - **Transportation and Logistics** 57
    Introduction 58
    Joe Winterburn, "Lac la Pluie Bills of Lading, 1806-1809" 59
    David Kemp, "The Impact of Weather and Climate on the Fur Trade in the
        Canadian North-West" 68

Part Four - **Fur Trade Rivalry and Relationships** 76
    Introduction 77
    Theodore Catton , "The Fur Trade Experience in the Rainy Lake Region" 78
    Ian T. Stuart, "The Indians and the Lake Superior Trade" 88

Part Five - **À la façon du pays** 91
    Introduction 92
    Jean Morrison, "Some Fur Trade Families from Lake Superior to Rainy Lake" 93
    Ruth Swan and Edward A. Jerome. 1998. "The Collin Family at Thunder Bay: A Case
        Study of Métissage" 105
    Elizabeth Arthur, "Angelique and her Children" 117

Part Six - **After 1821: The Sway of the Hudson's Bay Company** 124
    Introduction 125
    John Weiler ,"The Hudson's Bay Company's Michipicoten Post, 1821-1904" 126
    Judy Petch, "Fort William Post Journals of the 1820's and 1830's: Some Extracts" 139

Postscript - **The Modern Fur Trade** 152
    Introduction 153
    Jean Morrison, "Ups and Downs in the Modern Fur Trade" 155

Some Relevant Readings 167

Index 169

Illustrations

Ojibwa elder (TBHMS 972.4.17) *12*
Fort William, 1871 (TBHMS 976.100.1M) *23*
Chippewa Wigwams, Kaministiquia *26*
William McGillivray with wife and child *33*
Front view of Fort Kaministiquia, June 15, 1805 ...... *34*
Fort William, 1871, by William Armstrong *35*
The Mission of the Immaculate Conception at Fort William, circa 1800 ...... *40*
Fort Frances, 1857, by Henry Youles Hind *47*
Thomas Selkirk, fifth Earl of Selkirk. From a portrait ascribed to Raeburn *50*
Canoes and boats awaiting cargo (TBHMS 972.2.333) *57*
Lac La Pluie Bills of Lading *61*
Voyageur re-enactor carrying bales of marked trade goods *64*
Grant of Arms to William and Simon McGillivray *66*
"An Early Nip" by Charles Graham *73*
Engraving by H.A. Ogden, from: *Canada Illustrated: The Art of 19th-Century Engraving* (Toronto: Dreadnought, 1982) *76*
Hudson's Bay Company Post at Rat Portage, 1857 ...... *82*
Ojibwa family (TBHMS 972.2.34) *91*
Louisa MacKenzie Bethune headstone *100-101*
Daniel McKenzie tombstone *101*
Memorial stones to Susan McGillivray *103*
Marie Jeanne Collin and Alexandre Jerome with children at their farm *106*
Family of Alexander Jerome and his wife, Marie Jeanne Colin Jerome *108*
Hudson's Bay Company post at Nipigon *118*
Fort at Michipicoten (TBHMS 972.4.31) *124*
Michipicoten Hudson's Bay Company post, from a painting by William Armstrong *131*
Steamship Algoma *132*
Fort William, 1858 ...... *140*
Hauling Nets on Lake Nipigon, by Charles Graham *148*
Modern fur traders (TBHMS 979.1.892) *152*
Fur press at Long Lake (or Long Lac), early 1900s *157*
The latest fashions in fur, 1910-11 ...... *158*
Hudson's Bay Company store on Simpson Street, Fort William, circa 1910 ...... *162*

Maps

The Geography of Northwestern Ontario's Fur Trade *4*
"Sketch of the entrance of the River Kamanistigua and Sketch of Thunder Bay, 1802", by Captain R.H. Bruyère *16*
Main trade routes of the North West Company *69*
Rainy Lake Region *85*
Lake Superior District and Surrounding Area, 1821-1887 ...... *127*

Part One
The French Fur Trade

The French Fur Trade - Introduction

In 1731, a birchbark canoe carried the famed Pierre Gaultier de Varennes, sieur de la Vérendrye, from Fort Kaministiquia to a bay just south of the Pigeon River's exit into Lake Superior. From there he and his party crossed a nine-mile "grand portage" to a navigable section of the river and proceeded inland. The Grand Portage, instead of the Kaministiquia River, would be the Montreal fur trade's route into the interior until 1803 when the North West Company moved its inland headquarters north from Grand Portage to the mouth of the Kaministiquia.

To mark the 250th anniversary of La Vérendrye's first crossing of the Grand Portage, the Fourth North American Fur Trade Conference met in 1981 at Grand Portage, Minnesota and Thunder Bay, Ontario under the auspices of the U.S. National Park Service, the Minnesota Historical Society and Old Fort William.

In his keynote address entitled "La Mer de l'Ouest: Outpost of Empire", Professor W. J. Eccles (1917-1998) placed La Vérendrye's explorations within the context of French imperial ambitions: to discover a land route to the western sea and to contain the British foe on the Atlantic seaboard (as well as on Hudson Bay). Until the Seven Years' War, it seemed that this ambition was realized, for as Eccles noted, with less than a thousand men, France held down the North American interior, a stunning accomplishment made possible through the fur trade. Not only did the trade help defray the expenses of French explorers and soldiers, but it ensured Indian loyalty with the merchandise Natives obtained as presents or in exchange for furs.[1]

French dominion over much of the continent, however, proved to be ephemeral, dependent entirely on Indian good will. "In fact," Eccles argued, "French sovereignty in the west existed only within French posts, beyond no farther than the range of French muskets. ... The French were not sovereign in the west, the Indian nations were." The French North American empire may be deemed a failure and not only because it met defeat by British forces in 1759. Its explorers never did discover a Northwest Passage to the Pacific Ocean. One reason was chronic government underfunding and another was the interminable warfare between hostile Indian tribes whom the French had armed. (An offshoot of the Indian wars was the taking of prisoners as slaves for trade to the French who then sold them in Montreal or Quebec.)

Much has been written about the exploits and explorations of New France's trader-explorers and the forts they established in Northwestern Ontario. Little attention, however, has been given to the actual conduct of the local trade. In 1984, this lack was partly remedied by Lakehead University's publication of *Les Pays d'en Haut, 1620-1900: Explorateurs, voyageurs, missionnaires, dans le Nord-Ouest de l'Ontario*. Edited and introduced by Alain Nabarra, *Les Pays d'en Haut* includes extracts, in the original French, from written observations of the area by such traders as Greysolon DuLhut, Jacques de Noyon and Gabriel Franchère.

At the Sixth International Fur Trade Conference in 1991, Dean L. Anderson drew attention to the area north and west of Lake Superior in his paper "The Flow of European Trade Goods into the Western Great Lakes Region, 1715-1760". Although returns in furs and market fluctuations figure largely in works about the French fur trade, not as much is known about the quantity and types of goods shipped inland to maintain the trade. Anderson addresses this oversight by examining invoices of sales to traders at Michipicoten, Nipigon and Rainy Lake as well as at Detroit, Michilimackinac and on Lake Michigan.[2]

Anderson's figures give not only an indication of the relative strength of the Upper Lakes posts but also the complexity of fur trading relationships suggested by the variety of goods traded or given to the Indians. The relative insignificance of Northwestern Ontario in the overall French trade is shown by the extant records for the various posts between 1715 and 1760. While Detroit and Michilimackinac had fifteen and fourteen posts respectively, Rainy Lake had eight, Nipigon three, and Michipicoten only one.[3]

Anderson listed the goods in order of expenditure and categorized them by function, thirteen in all. Clothing (and materials to make clothing) made up an impressive over sixty percent of the total expenditures for the Western Great Lakes region, followed by seventeen percent for hunting related articles, over five percent for cooking and eating supplies and, surprisingly, just below five percent for alcohol use. As seen, a slight variance pertained to the three Northwestern Ontario posts Anderson examined:

Category	Rainy Lake	Nipigon	Michipicoten
Clothing	55.28	65.89	59.82
Hunting	15.46	13.34	10.36
Alcohol Use	6.92	3.56	9.02

The high figures for clothing, he suggests, has "implications for understanding the part that Native women played in the fur trade." With imported textiles to wear, women now prepared animal skins for trade not personal use. The Natives soon became discerning judges of quality and when given a choice between the French or English product, the superiority of the English eventually won out. As Harold A. Innis may have overstated, "The English woollen industry was of fundamental importance to the fur trade, and eventually to the control of Canada by England."[4]

In both the French and British fur trade much of the cloth shipped inland was destined, not for trade to Indians but for use by company personnel and their "country" families. Traders and voyageurs in both regimes acquired cloth, clothing and other commodities by purchase or as *equipments* as stipulated by their contracts or *engagements*. The value of European textiles to the fur trade can hardly be over-emphasized. Cloth and clothing were important status symbols for Native men and women and also for traders and voyageurs who dressed in the Indian country according to current fashions.[5]

Besides the significance of textiles in the French fur trade, the roles of women and mixed-blood progeny in the *pays d'en haut* deserve more attention as do such issues raised by Eccles as Ojibwa-Sioux wars, the taking of slaves, the use of alcohol and the influence of the Church. "The Organization of the French Fur Trade" below addresses some of these topics by looking at French activity in the Upper Lakes at both the local level and the wider context of French imperial policy.

The following article by Ian T. Stuart is one of several in this book by a public historian, public history broadly defined as directed at a popular audience for public purposes and usually, though not always, under public auspices. This particular piece is taken from a much larger report which Parks Canada commissioned in 1986 as an interpretive aid for its Fort St. Joseph National Historic Site.[6] Founded in 1796, Fort St. Joseph was destroyed by U.S. forces in the War of 1812. As suggested by its title "The Fur Trade at St. Joseph Island and Beyond: From the French regime to 1821", the report covers a time period and geographical area much beyond those of Fort St. Joseph. The following excerpts give a good indication of the contribution public history can make to broaden public knowledge of the past.

NOTES

[1] W. J. Eccles, "La Mer de l'Ouest: Outpost of Empire", in Thomas G. Buckley, ed., *RENDEZVOUS: Selected Papers of the Fourth North American Fur Trade Conference*, 1981 (St. Paul: 1984), pp. 1-14.

[2] Dean L. Anderson, "The Flow of European Trade Goods into the Western Great Lakes Region, 1715-1760," in J. S. H. Brown, W.J. Eccles, and D. P. Heldman, eds., *The Fur Trade Revisited: Selected Papers of the Sixth North American Fur Trade Conference, Mackinac Island, Michigan, 1991* (East Lansing and Mackinac Island: Michigan States University Press and Mackinac State Historic Parks, 1994), pp. 93-115.

[3] Anderson, p. 98.

[4] Harold A. Innis, *The Fur Trade in Canada*, rev. ed. (Toronto: University of Toronto Press, 1956), pp. 79-80.

[5] Jean Morrison, *Superior Rendezvous-Place: Fort William in the Canadian Fur Trade* (Toronto: Natural Heritage Books, 2001), pp. 46-8.

[6] St. Joseph's Island is in St. Mary's River near its outlet into Lake Huron some 30 miles (45 km) southeast of Sault Ste. Marie, Ontario.

The Organization of the French Fur Trade, 1650-1760*

by Ian T. Stuart

The Origins of the French Fur Trade

It has been argued that the French fur trade began with Cartier's first voyage to the St. Lawrence River in 1534. Once there, the trade was guided by the geography of the St. Lawrence River system. Indians carried their furs down the rivers flowing into the St. Lawrence while settlers and traders gradually moved up river, onto the lakes and into the continental interior. It was in the fur-rich northwest that the trade realized its potential.

Traditionally, the French relied upon native allies to collect and carry furs to the settlements on the St. Lawrence. First Algonquin and later Huron Indians acted as middlemen for the French by re-trading European goods for the furs of distant hunting tribes in the northwest. While this system was in operation, the merchants of New France gained access to the fur-rich northwest without having to invest heavily in transportation and labour. By the mid-17th century, however, competition between the Huron and Iroquois nations for the lucrative position of middlemen resulted in inter-tribal war.

The destruction of the Huron villages disrupted orderly trade and resulted in the wholesale reorganization of the French fur trade after 1650. The seeds of this reorganization were already in place prior to 1650. Since Champlain's time, adventurers, known as *coureurs de bois*, had organized their own trading expeditions to the northwest, carrying their goods to wilderness settlements such as Sault Ste. Marie and Michilimackinac.

Colonial merchants were forced by the activities of the *coureurs de bois* to engage their own agents to trade directly with the Indians. Attempts by the colonial administration to regulate or deter the *coureurs de bois* failed. By the 1670s the merchants of New France or their agents were trading directly to the Indian country and had developed their own finance, marketing and transportation system.[1]

Early Exploration and Settlement in the Northwest to 1671

The work of early explorers and missionaries was of immeasurable importance to the eventual expansion of the fur trade from the St. Lawrence River valley into the northwest. These men, accompanied by native guides, traced long-established Indian canoe routes and learned the techniques of that specialized mode of transport. They made direct contact with the hunting tribes of the interior and introduced them to European trade goods. Also, in concert with missionaries, explorers and traders established the first permanent settlements in the region.

The first European to reach the outlet of Lake Superior was probably Etienne Brulé, an interpreter employed by Governor Samuel de Champlain. Brulé travelled from his posting among the Hurons of Georgian Bay in 1622 in search of a trade route west and skirted the Lake Huron shoreline until he came to the present day site of Sault Ste. Marie. He was followed over a decade later by another one of the Governor's young recruits, Jean Nicolet, who in 1634 journeyed by canoe with the assistance of seven native guides from Lake Huron past the modern day site of Mackinac and out onto Lake Michigan.

In 1641 two young Jesuit missionaries, Isaac Jogues and Charles Raymbault, visited the rapids that separated Lakes Huron and Superior. They named the site Sault de Sainte Marie, preached the gospel to about 2000 natives who had gathered and learned of tribes who lived to the west of the great lake before them. These travels in the

---

*Extracted from Ian T. Stuart, "The Fur Trade at St. Joseph Island and Beyond: From the French regime to 1821", Part 1 (Environment Canada, Parks, 1986), pp. 8-38; Manuscript on file, Parks Canada, the Ontario Service Centre, Cornwall, Ontario. © Parks Canada. Permission to publish kindly granted.

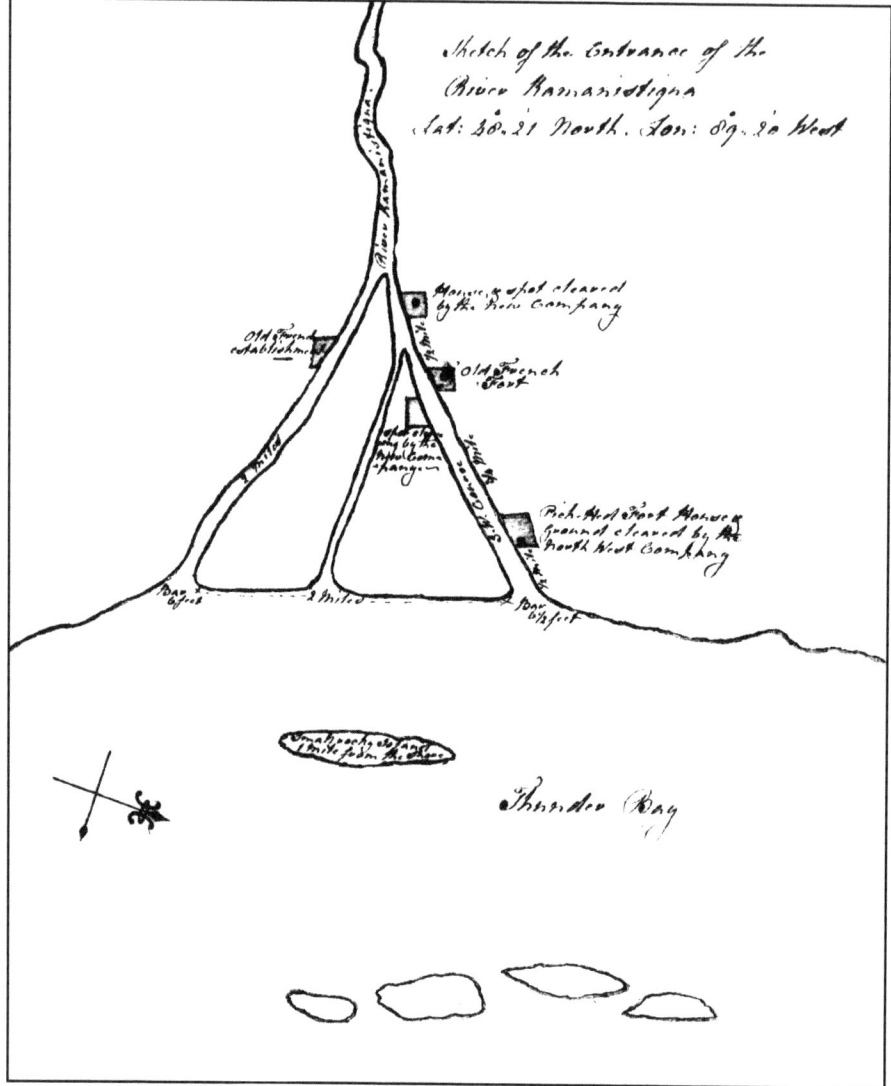

Sketch of the entrance of the River Kamanistigua and Sketch of Thunder Bay, 1802, by Captain R.H. Bruyère. The locations of the two French forts are seen as well as those of the planned XY and North West Companies. (NAC, National Map Collection, C 85839)

northwest are indicative of France's interests in the region prior to 1650; that is, missionary work among the Indians, the discovery of a passage to the west and the establishment of territorial control. At the outset, trade was strictly regulated and placed in the hands of large chartered companies. Profits were to be used to promote colonization, exploration and the missionary effort. However, as knowledge of the wealth of furs in the northwest spread, the system envisioned by colonial administrators in France broke down.[2]

The first men known to have travelled on Lake Superior were the famous adventurers Pierre Esprit Radisson and Médard Chouart, Sieur des Groseilliers. They travelled to the northwest in 1658 returning two years later with a rich cargo of furs and the knowledge that the best furs could be obtained to the north and west of Lake Superior. After their return exploration began in earnest. One of the most important individuals during this stage of development was a Jesuit missionary Jean Claude Allouez. Accompanied by the famous explorer and trader Nicolas Perrot, he travelled west in 1665 in the Indian canoes returning from Montreal. Leaving Perrot at the Sault, Allouez continued onto Lake Superior where, with the assistance of Indian guides, he skirted the entire shoreline, finally arriving at Chequamegon Bay where he established a small mission post. Two years later Allouez, abandoned his Chequamegon Bay mission and with Fathers Jacques Marquette and Claude Dablon founded the first permanent mission at the Sault de Sainte Marie.[3]

The post at the Sault would become the Jesuit headquarters in the northwest, but it almost immediately assumed an important place as a centre for fur traders. In fact, a year after the establishment of the mission in 1668 there were twenty five voyageurs residing at the site.[4]

Trading in the Interior

Climatic and geographic factors imposed a certain order on the fur trade despite attempts by the government to regulate commercial activity beyond the boundaries of New France. In 1650, prior to the breakdown of regulatory measures, merchants gathered on the plains near the gates of the Montreal settlement in the early summer and waited for the arrival of flotillas of western canoes laden with furs. Here, they set up their booths displaying the various trade goods demanded by the natives: knives, kettles, blankets, mirrors and ornamental goods including beads and silver. The importance of these fairs was reduced by the activities of the *coureurs de bois* and government officials who, under the guise of military or exploratory expeditions to the Indian country, engaged in fur trading. Both brought the French into direct contact with the Indians in their villages. For example, when Nicolas Perrot visited an Indian encampment in Wisconsin in the 1660s the natives could not comprehend why a stranger had travelled so far to obtain their worn out robes. Moreover, Perrot proposed to exchange the robes for a variety of goods which they regarded as extremely valuable. "They adored him like a God", wrote La Potherie. "When he left the room, they insisted on carrying him upon their shoulders; the way over which he passed was made clear; they did not dare look in his face; and the women and children watched him from a distance."[5] A ready market and ample supplies of furs held out the prospect of excellent profits for those adventurous enough to invest in or undertake a journey to the interior.

A staple of the trade was French brandy although its sale was frowned upon by the Jesuits and responsible traders owing to the dangers involved. These dangers were described graphically by one chronicler:

> The village or the cabin in which the savages drink brandy is an image hell: fire [coals] flies in all directions, blows with hatchets and knives makes the blood flow on all sides; and all the place resounds with frightful yells and cries. They bite off each other's noses, and tear away their ears; wherever their teeth are fixed, they carry away the morsel. The father and mother throw their babes upon the hot coals or into the boiling kettles. They commit a thousand abominations - the mother with her sons, the father with his daughters, the brothers with their sisters. They roll about on the cinders and coals, and in blood.[6]

The Indians generally awoke to find that they had traded away their furs as well. Liquor was essential to the trade. "It is the Commandants, it is the Garrisons, who, uniting with the brandy traders have completely desolated the missions by almost universal Drunkenness and Lewdness", wrote one Jesuit missionary stationed at Michilimackinac.[7] Despite almost continual complaints about the use of liquor among the tribes it remained an essential part of the trader's outfit.

The extension of the trade to the distant tribes demanded attention to organization. For example, traders were dependent upon reliable supplies of food which, in the interior, could be obtained at Michilimackinac and the Sault. Equally important was securing financial support for trading expeditions. A reliable supply of trade goods and a ready market for returns was essential to the success of any venture. In response an elaborate system evolved where specific responsibilities of the Indian trader and the merchant were defined.

Goods for the trade were imported from France by Montreal merchants on consignment and supplied to license holders or illegal traders on credit or for a share of profits. The license holder was responsible for purchasing the goods, supplying the canoe, hiring the canoemen and provisioning the trip. Responsibility for the success of the venture was usually entrusted to a *bourgeois* or proprietor who, if he did not hold a share in the license, was hired by the Montreal merchant. The goods were packaged in Montreal for transport on one of three main routes, the Ottawa River, the Great Lakes route via Detroit and Michilimackinac and the less important Toronto portage. Canoes were navigated by up to five men.

Those traders who wintered with the Indians in their villages usually spent two to three years in the country before returning. Those who only travelled as far as the depots, carrying goods to exchange for the furs of those French and Indians who would venture no further, spent just a single season inland, their canoes departing in the early spring and returning before navigation closed in late October.

Any merchant might purchase a license and enter the trade but ultimately all pelts were sold to whomever held the monopoly on exports, for instance, the Company of the Farm. The Farmers paid 350,000 livres in 1675 for this privilege and agreed to accept a government set price structure based on livres 10 sols for *gras*, or the best quality beaver, 4 *livres* 10 *sols* for *veule*, medium quality, and 3 *livres* 10 *sols* for *dry* or the poorest quality beaver. When the merchants brought their beaver to the Company's warehouses in Quebec the furs were sorted, graded and weighed. From the value agreed upon the Company deducted its commission and issued bills of exchange worth 50% in two months time and the balance in an additional 120 days. Under this system there was very little exchange of hard currency, the merchant generally being obliged to accept bills of exchange on Paris because colonial money was undervalued by twenty-five percent.[8]

The French fur trade was organized along occupational lines. There were a variety of occupations involved, each performing a specific function in the system. There were those individuals who operated within several of the occupational groups at once but, generally, it is possible to identify and classify them as follows:

INDIVIDUAL OR GROUP	FUNCTION
Merchants in France	-purchase and shipment of trade goods
	-financial support of Montreal and Quebec merchants
	-eventual marketing of fur returns
Montreal Merchants	-financial support and supply of license holders
	-responsible to their French suppliers
Inland merchants	-travel to the depots to trade
	-limited risks compared to the Montreal merchants
	-responsible to the supplier
License Holders	-often a trader or Montreal merchant but could be simply an inter-mediary
	-control the legal permission to trade to the interior
	-responsible to the government for observing regulations
Bourgeois	-the merchant's agent
	-responsible for the success of the venture
	-hired by the merchant
Indian Traders	-responsible for making contact and trading with the Indians
	-hired by the bourgeois or the merchant
Indians	-gather the furs and consume the trade goods
Monopoly Company	-control over marketing of returns
	-responsible to the Crown in France

Trade relations developed in this way between the manufacturer and merchant in France, the Quebec and Montreal merchants, the license holder, the *bourgeois*, his *engagés*, and the Native fur trappers. It was a system that functioned well and remained largely remained intact after the Conquest.

Great Lakes Posts After 1713

The strategy of focusing the fur trade on Montreal by regulating the numbers of canoes travelling west had been a clear failure; Natives would not undertake the long journey down to the St. Lawrence because *coureurs de bois* were able to carry trade goods inland and return and still reap a substantial profit. Prices rose steadily after 1713, even for lower quality furs, making the trade accessible to marginal operators. Consequently, licensing continued to be the regulation of preference among administrators because in theory it enabled the government to screen out undesirables and limit supply. In practice it did nothing to control the numbers of illegal traders operating in the west. The policy of outright prohibition by abandoning every trading post beyond Montreal had been ineffective. Iroquois hostility and war with England led to a re-evaluation of past restrictive practices and a movement toward recovering a degree of French influence among the Indians in the interior.

This represented a major policy departure for the French administration based on the realization of the unique demands of the trade, the strategic necessity of maintaining Indian alliances and the the continuing imperial rivalry with the English.

A series of raids had been carried out against the Hudson's Bay Company posts during the late 1600s effectively reducing its ability to interfere with the Indians of the interior. The terms of the Treaty of Utrecht, 1713, had returned the Hudson's Bay Company posts to British control. However, Governor Vaudreuil decided that "in order to Keep the Savages attached to us; to maintain peace and union among the Nations; to keep in order the French traders who should go there with Licenses to trade...." a series of *postes du nord* should be established and maintained.[9]

This led, in 1717, to the establishment of a fort at the mouth of the Kaministiquia River by Zacharie Robutel, Sieur de la Noue and two others at Rainy Lake and Lake Winnipeg.[10] The prosecution of the *postes du nord* policy coupled with the discoveries of Pierre Gaultier de Varennes, Sieur de la Vérendrye, gave the French access to the fur trading tribes of the west at a time when Indian war to the south had reduced supplies of beaver from that region. These posts were ultimately leased or "farmed out" to favourites who, in turn, sub-let the post to merchants anxious to prosecute the fur trade. In this manner the settlement patterns of the Great Lakes posts were established prior to the Conquest.

La Vérendrye is one of those major figures in Canadian history whose fame, ironically, has clouded our understanding of his life and career. Admired for his heroic quest to discover the overland route to the western sea, his equally important activities as a fur trader and military commander have been overlooked. La Vérendrye began his career as a fur trader in 1715 at his family estate near Trois Rivières on the St. Maurice River. A failed attempt to secure a commission in the French army led to an effort to obtain advancement in the colony. This effort was ultimately successful with his appointment in 1727 as commandant of the *postes du nord* along the north shore of Lake Superior at Kaministiquia, Lake Nipigon and Michipicoten. The principal reason for establishing the posts was not commercial but rather to provide a staging ground for explorations to the interior which would extend French interests to the western sea. The fur trade would operate to defray the expenses of establishing the posts.

La Vérendrye's conduct as commander was criticized for it was said he paid too much attention to trading. In fact, profits on the three posts exceeded 32,000 livres in 1730 and, in the main, were gained at the expense of the Hudson's Bay Company. Established on the shores of Lake Superior, La Vérendrye turned his attention turned to the region between Lake Superior and Lake Winnipeg. In 1731 he set out from the Grand Portage for the interior. The expedition established a chain of eight posts, founded a trading relationship with the resident Crees and Assiniboines and improved known inland portages, trails and canoe routes. The French government was reluctant to commit itself financially to the enterprise and this forced La Vérendrye to turn to colonial merchants for capital. It is little wonder certain attention was paid to profit.

In 1731 La Vérendrye built Fort Saint-Pierre at Rainy Lake, the first in a series of eight posts. In the spring of 1732 the expedition pushed on to the Lake of the Woods where they built Fort Saint-Charles which served as his headquarters. Fort Maurepas, named for the then Minister of Marine, was established at Red River in 1734, followed by Fort La Reine at present day Portage la Prairie in 1738 and, between 1741 and 1743, Forts Dauphin, Bourbon, and Paskoya on Lake Winnipegosis, near Lake Winnipeg, and near Cedar Lake respectively. By 1743 he had opened the region between Lakes Superior and Winnipeg to the fur trade. The posts on Lake Superior played an important role in this development as staging points for the journey inland. In this manner La Vérendrye's expeditions to the west mirrored the structure and organization of the fur trade in the post-conquest period.[11]

KAMINISTIQUIA

Located at the mouth of the Kaministiquia River at present day Thunder Bay, the first fort was probably constructed in 1679 by Daniel Greysolon, better known as Duluth, to act as a staging post for his explorations in the west. This post was abandoned after the Edict of 1696 and re-established by Sieur de la Noue in 1717 because it commanded the portage route inland. Trading was carried on with the Cree and Assiniboine Indians nearby. The first commander was de la Noue from 1717 to 1721 and later Sieur Deschaillons, 1721 to 1723 and Sieur de Verchères, 1724 to 1727. La Vérendrye wintered at Kaministiquia in 1731. In 1743 the Sieur La Corne du Breuil paid 3000 livres for the post and, in 1750, the Sieur de Beaujeu Villemonde assumed control. Bourgainville's Memoir of 1757 noted that "Kamanistigoya" had been leased most recently for 4000 francs to monsieur Cugnet who, in turn, sublet the post to Sieur Toussaint Portier [Pothier]. The name Toussaint Pothier turns up again in association with the North West and South West Fur Companies at St. Joseph Island. With the French defeat at Quebec in 1759, Kaministiquia was abandoned and burned to the ground. Its site remained unoccupied for some time after the Conquest.[12]

Michipicoten

Located at the south side of the Magpie River on Michipicoten Bay, Lake Superior, the French post was established shortly after 1717 as a result of the *postes du nord* policy. Sieur de Charvis' report on the State of Canada in 1730 remarked that a "profitable" trade was carried out there. In 1743 Michipicoten was leased for 3750 livres to Jean Baptiste Duplessis, Sieur Gatineau, a militia Captain. He was "induced" following the expiry of his lease in 1746 to renew the arrangement but was required to pay only 1000 livres and send only one canoe (likely because of Indian unrest in the area). In 1750 the Sieur de Beaujeu Villemonde was commanding at Michipicoten but evidence suggests that after that date the Sieur Repentigny exercised control over the post. It was he who sublet Michipicoten "free from the Charges of the lease" to the Sieur d'Eschambault in 1758. The post was occupied by British traders shortly after the Conquest.[13]

Sault Ste. Marie

First established as a Jesuit mission in 1668, it was abandoned in 1689 due to Iroquois aggression and re- established shortly thereafter. Its importance as a centre of trade was confirmed by its strategic location on the communication route separating Lake Superior and Lake Huron. The abundant supply of whitefish and the co-operative "Saulteur" Indians who fished the river made the Sault an important provisioning point on the journey west. Galinée explained in 1670: "This fish is so cheap that they give ten or twelve of them for four fingers of tobacco. Each weighs six or seven pounds.... This is the reason why the French go there, notwithstanding the frightful difficulties that are encountered."[14]

The Sault served primarily as a stopping off point on the journey west and there is no evidence that a substantial trade was ever conducted there. In 1750 the French government granted a seigneury to Louis Le Gardeur, Sieur de la Repentigny and Captain Louis de Bonne, Sieur de Mise1le, on the condition that they establish an agricultural settlement. Included in the grant was the right to trade; however, evidence suggests the post at the Sault was not profitable. According to Bougainville a picket fort was erected and 100 packages were collected yearly from the Saulteux nearby. Yet there was only one tenant, Trois Rivières native Jean Baptiste Cadotte, who was managing the estate when Alexander Henry arrived at the Sault in 1762. Cadotte's Sons Michel and Jean Baptiste were both associated with the North West Company at the Sault at a later period.[15]

Michilimackinac

Located at the straits separating Lakes Huron and Michigan, Michilimackinac, like the Sault, was founded as a mission site. The French fort was located on a large sandy cove across from the Island. It was the most important fur trading post in the region due to its position as a depot for those travelling to the southwest. It was administered by a military commander who was responsible for supervising licensed traders in the area. La Potherie described it as "the general meeting-place for all the French who go to trade with stranger tribes; it is the landing-place and refuge of all the savages who trade their peltries."[16] Lahontan explained that the settlement was "the Staple of all the goods that they truck with the South and the West Savages; for they cannot avoid passing this way, when they go to the Seats of the Illinese and the Oumanis.... The Skins which they import from these different places, must lye here some time before they are transported to the Colony."[17] Abandoned by the government in the late 1690s, it was reoccupied soon after and a fort was constructed. The French continued in possession of the post until 1761 when Charles de Langlade, the French Commander, surrendered the post to Lieutenant William Leslie of the 60th Regiment.[18]

The French Trade Prior to the Conquest

In the popular mind the fall of New France in 1760 can be explained by its immediate cause, the military defeat of the French on the Plains of Abraham. There were, of course, other circumstances which contributed to the downfall of the French. Not surprisingly the fur trade was an important factor in this event.

By the mid-1700s an elaborate and efficient trading organization had been developed in New France. Detroit and Michilimackinac had been become important depots for provisions. Inland posts and transportation routes to the interior had been discovered by La Vérendrye and other explorers. Contact with Indian tribes had been made and trading relationships established. In short, the foundations for the later development of the northwest by the English had been laid first by the French.

Expansion to the far west meant furs were gathered and trade goods distributed over a wider area which contributed to rising costs. This problem was addressed by greater specification of function among traders and merchants and the development of partnerships. The trader, experienced in dealing with Indians, and the Montreal merchant, with his ties to the commercial community of France, were supported by the government which authorized the erection of fortified trading posts and military expeditions against their competitors. The colony was completely dependent on the fur trade for its economic survival. Nothing, however, could solve the problems caused by the exhaustion of the supply of beaver in known territory. Indian wars during the first half of the century also disrupted the French trade. War contributed to rising costs which in turn weakened the economic stability of the colony. As Harold Innis has concluded, "Heavier drains were made on the resources of the home government, and more especially on the resources of the colony. The French power in New France collapsed of its own weight. Institutional development characteristic of the fur trade was not adequate to the new economic conditions."[19]

Conclusion

The fur trade of the French era is significant for three principal reasons. First, French explorers and missionaries were the earliest Europeans to penetrate into the lands north of Lake Superior and establish contact with the Indians residing there. Second, French fur traders known as *coureurs de bois* laid the groundwork for the trade of the interior, that is, established trading relationships with the Indians, determined the type of goods to be used and the methods of financing, transportation, and provisioning. Finally, Scottish and English merchants who moved to Quebec after 1760 made use of French fur trading techniques. The government too adopted methods of regulating the northwest trade such as licensing which had been developed by French administrators over the previous century. In short, in order to understand how the fur trade operated it is necessary to see how it evolved through its various stages.

NOTES

[1] Louise Phelps Kellogg, *The French Regime in Wisconsin and the Northwest* (New York: Cooper Square Publishers, 1968; lst pub. 1925), pp. 59-60, 101; Harold A. Innis, *The Fur Trade in Canada* (Toronto: University of Toronto Press, rev. ed. 1956), pp. 36-42; E. E. Rich, *Montreal and the Fur Trade* (Montreal: McGill University Press, 1966), pp. 3-18.

[2] The term "northwest" referred to the lands drained by the Upper Lakes, as well as the territory beyond Lake Superior. The French called it *le pays d'en haut* or the "upper country". See E.E. Rich, *The Fur Trade and the Northwest to 1857* (Toronto: McClelland and Stewart, 1967), pp. 1-23; Louise Phelps Kellogg, ed., *Early Narratives of the Northwest, 1634-1699* (New York: Charles Scribner's Sons, 1917), pp. 11-16; Reuben Gold Thwaites, ed., *The Jesuit Relations and Allied Documents, 1610-1791* (Cleveland: Burrows, 1896-1901), Vol. 23: pp. 223-227, 175-19.

[3] G.D. Scull, ed., *Voyages of Peter Esprit Radisson* (Boston: Prince Society, 1885), pp. 134-172; R.G. Thwaites, ed., *Collections of the State Historical Society of Wisconsin*, Vol. 16 (1902), pp. 31-2, 59-62.

[4] Thwaites, ed., *Jesuit Relations*,Vol. 50, pp. 249-311, Vol. 51, pp. 21-69; Edward H. Capp, *The Story of BAW-A-TING, Being the Annals of Sault Sainte Marie* (Sault Star Presses, 1904), p. 43.

[5] Thwaites, ed., *Wisconsin Historical Collections,* Vol. 16, pp. 33-5.

[6] Emma Helen Blair, ed., *The Indian Tribes of the Upper Mississippi Valley and Region of the Great Lakes*.(Cleveland: Arthur H. Clark, 1911), Vol. 1, pp. 208-9.

[7] S.R. Mealing, ed., *The Jesuit Relations and Allied Documents: A Selection* (Toronto: McClelland and Stewart, 1963), pp. 112-3.

[8] E.B. O'Callaghan, ed., *Documents Relative to the Colonial History of the State of New York* (Albany, 1855-1857), Vol. 9. pp. 152-3; Innis, *The Fur Trade in Canada* , pp. 59-63; W. J. Eccles, *Frontenac, The Courtier Governor* (Toronto: McClelland and Stewart, 1962), pp. 75-7; Robert Chalmers, *A History of Currency in the British Colonies* (London: 189.93), pp. 175-183: Kellogg, *French Regime*, pp. 367-385.

[9] Thwaites, ed., *Wisconsin Historical Collections*, Vol. 16, p. 437.

[10] *Wisconsin Historical Collections*, Vol. 16, p. 440; Innis, *The Fur Trade in Canada*, pp. 89-92.

[11] A.S. Morton, "La Vérendrye: Commandant, Fur Trader and Explorer", *Canadian Historical Review*, Vol. 9, no. 4 (December 1928), pp. 284-298. Lawrence J. Burpee, ed., *Journals and Letters of Pierre Gaultier de Varennes de la Vérendrye and his Sons* (Toronto: Champlain Society, 1927).

[12] See Innis, *The Fur Trade in Canada*, pp. 89-92; Ernest Voorhis, *Historic Forts and Trading Posts of the French Regime and of the English Trading Companies* (Ottawa: Department of the Interior), pp. 88, 113-4, 160-1; *Wisconsin Historical Collections*, Vols. 16, 17, 18, numerous references.

[13] Thwaites, ed., *Wisconsin Historical Collections*, vol. 17, pp. 434-435, 45-1; vol. 18, pp. 84-5, pp. 200-202; *Michigan and Pioneer and Historical Collections* (1904), Vol. 34, pp. 73-85; Michael J. Shchepanek, "Trading Posts of the Moose-Michipicoten Trade Route", *Canadian Geographical Review*, Vol. 82 (February 1971), pp. 66-9.

[14] Kellogg, ed., *Early Narratives*, p. 207.

[15] Thwaites, ed., *Wisconsin Historical Collections*, Vol. 18, pp. 141-2; Alexander Henry, *Travels and Adventures in Canada and the Indian Territories between the years 1760-1776,* ed. James Bain (New York, Burt Franklin, 1969), pp. 183-5; Graham MacDonald, "Commerce, Civility and Old Sault Ste. Marie", *The Beaver* (Autumn 1981), pp. 19-25.

[16] Blair, ed., *Indian Tribes*, Vol. 1, p. 282.

[17] Louis Armand de Lahontan, *New Voyages to North America*, ed. Reuben Gold Thwaites (Chicago: 1905), p. 146.

[18] Thwaites, ed., *Wisconsin Historical Collections*, Vol. 16, pp. 257-259; Vol. 17, pp. 424-430; pp. 432-3; pp. 444-5; Vol. 18, pp. 172-183. See also National Archives of Canada, MG 18 N 50, Ayer Collection, Ms 511, Order for Charles de Langlade, 30 September 1761.

[19] Innis, *The Fur Trade in Canada*, p. 114.

Part Two
From 1650 to 1900:
Two overviews

Part Two - From 1650 to 1900:
Two overviews

The authors of these historical surveys of Fort William and Rainy Lake are public historians. A self-employed consultant on Aboriginal and Treaty issues, Victor Lytwyn has applied his expertise to current Aboriginal issues ranging from the fishing rights of the Walpole Island First Nation on Lake St. Clair in Southern Ontario to Native land ownership issues in Northern Manitoba and Ontario. Theodore Catton, on the other hand, works for a large private public history firm in the United States whose employees include over a dozen historians and archaeologists and whose clients range from the National Park Service to Indian tribes and several public and private agencies. Both have careers which prove the relevance of university history degrees to fields outside the realm of academia.

Inevitably the contents of these articles and the preceding one on the French fur trade somewhat overlap. But while Stuart's focus was the Upper Lakes, Lytwyn's is the Kaministiquia and Pigeon Rivers and Catton's is the entire Rainy Lake region. As might be expected from one so versed in Aboriginal history, Lytwyn emphasizes the fur trade more from the Native perspective than from the European. Thus Anishinabeg, the word commonly used by the Ojibwa to describe themselves, appears not only in his title but also throughout his text.

Catton's report for Voyageurs National Park was located quite by accident on the Thunder Bay Public Library's website. The Park was established in 1975 by the United States Congress in order to preserve "the outstanding scenery, geological conditions, and waterway system which constituted a part of the historic route of the Voyageurs who contributed significantly to the opening of the Northwestern United States." Located on Rainy Lake's southern shores, it is close to International Falls, Minnesota across the United States-Canada border from Fort Frances, Ontario. Like so many studies prepared for National Park Service fur-trade related

The Anishinabeg and the Fur Trade*
By Victor P. Lytwyn, Ph.D

Introduction

The history of the fur trade in the Thunder Bay area has received considerable attention over the years mainly because of the important function of Fort William as an *entrepôt* for the North West Company during the period 1803 to 1821. Historians have been particularly fascinated by the men who directed the affairs of the North West Company, and in Fort William as their base of operations on Lake Superior. Hence, the portrayal of the fur trade in the Thunder Bay area has been typically cast in light of the exploits of men such as Simon McTavish and William McGillivray who were principal directors of the Company. This chapter seeks to broaden the time horizons beyond the affairs of the North West Company by tracing the fur trade history of the Thunder Bay area from pre-European contact times to the end of the Hudson's Bay Company era at the close of the nineteenth century. It will also place the Thunder Bay area within a much larger geographical framework, and examine the connections between Thunder Bay and the northwestern interior of North America.

This chapter also focuses on the role of Aboriginal people in the fur trade. Until recently, the participation of Aboriginal people has been overlooked in published works relating to Fort William and the fur trade period. However, recent studies such as Jean Morrison's book on Fort William and Carolyn Gilman's book about Grand Portage have successfully challenged previous held views of Aboriginal people as unimportant or nondescript actors in the fur trade story.[1] The following chapter will affirm that Aboriginal people were important participants in the fur trade and significant contributors to the development of the economy of the region.

Commerce in the Thunder Bay Area Before European Contact

The original people, or Anishinabeg,[2] who have lived in the Thunder Bay area "since time immemorial," established commercial relations with neighbouring indigenous peoples a long time ago. The antiquity and importance of commerce to the Anishinabeg way of life has been recorded in oral traditions and on birchbark scrolls. These iconographic records were used to symbolically portray significant events in Anishinabeg history prior to contact with Europeans in the seventeenth century. The oral traditions and birch bark scrolls indicate that interaction with neighbouring peoples was an integral part of the life of the Anishinabeg. Oral traditions speak of seasonal gatherings of large numbers of people from far away who came together at central places such as Thunder Bay to participate in important ceremonies and other events. William W. Warren, an Anishinabe historian, explained that the spiritual ceremony known as the "Me-da-we-win" was an annual "national gathering" of different groups of people."[3] Such gatherings promoted spiritual linkages among the widespread Anishinabeg Nation, and also facilitated social, political and economic networks among these people.

Although non-written records do not provide specific details about the economy, it is evident that commercial exchange networks linked the Anishinabeg of the Thunder Bay area with many other groups of people in the Lake Superior basin and beyond. Archaeological investigations have also shown that Aboriginal peoples developed complex and widespread trading relationships that crisscrossed the continent long before the arrival of Europeans. For example, copper tools and weapons originating in the western Lake Superior region about 6,000 years ago have been found in sites as far away as the St. Lawrence River in the east and the Saskatchewan River in the west.[4] It is evident that the Thunder Bay area was one of the primary hubs of commercial activity well before the arrival of the first Europeans.

Victor P. Lytwyn, "The Anishinabeg and the Fur Trade," in Thorold J. Tronrud and A. Ernest Epp, eds., *Thunder Bay: From Rivalry to Unity* (Thunder Bay: Thunder Bay Historical Museum Society, 1995), pp. 16-36. Revised October 2002.

Early European Contacts and Aboriginal Middlemen Traders

The European fur trade in North America probably began as an activity incidental to commercial fishing in the coastal waters of the eastern seaboard. As early as 1502, English fishing vessels were active in the Grand Banks off the coast of Newfoundland.[5] Portuguese and French fishermen were also working the area in the early sixteenth century, and it is evident from the written records that they were carrying on a trade in furs to supplement their harvest of fish. For example, a Portuguese report around 1540 claimed that, in addition to fish, thousands of animal pelts were also being shipped to France.[6] Jacques Cartier's visit of to Chaleur Bay in 1534 confirmed that the local Micmac people were already experienced in trading furs with Europeans.[7]

European goods that were traded to Aboriginal people along the eastern seaboard spread into the interior of North America along well-established trade routes[8]. The rate and geographical extent of this transmission was affected by relationships between neighbouring Nations. While some trade routes between allied Nations facilitated a rapid spread of European goods, others were blocked because of warfare or other sources of friction. The St. Lawrence River - Great Lakes route was blocked at the time of initial European contact because of hostile relations between Nations on either side of this strategic waterway. When Samuel de Champlain visited the area in the early seventeenth century, he found two powerful confederacies locked in warfare for control of the region. In the north, the Iroquoian-speaking Huron and Petun Nations were allied with a number of Algonquian-speaking Nations including the Montagnais, Kichesipirini, Weskarini, Onontchataronon, Matouweskarini, Nipissing, Ottawa and Ojibway Nations[9]. The southern alliance was made up of Iroquoian-speaking peoples, and included the Mohawk, Oneida, Onondaga, Cayuga and Seneca Nations, commonly known as the Five Nations Confederacy.

For the Thunder Bay Anishinabeg, the warfare that embroiled the lower Great Lakes Nations also blocked direct access to European goods. In order to circumvent these military blockades, secondary trade routes were used to move furs and European trade goods. Northern trade routes, some reaching as far north as James Bay, secured the flow of European trade goods to the Thunder Bay Anishinabeg during the time of war. One trade route connected Lake Superior to Tadoussac by way of Lake Nipigon, Albany River, James Bay and the Saguenay River. This northern trade route was first described in writing by Gabriel Druillettes, a Jesuit missionary in New France who interviewed Awatanik,

Chippewa Wigwams, Kaministiquia. This photograph, circa 1900, illustrates the blending of old and new ways. The men and women are wearing clothing bought from the Company store but their birchbark lodgings are of a type used since time immemorial. TBHMS (Carson Piper Collection), 972.2.34

a Nipissing leader of an Aboriginal trading party who came from Lake Nipigon to Tadoussac in 1660.[10] The success of trading ventures such as Awatanik's was tempered by increasing threats from Five Nations Iroquois warriors who raided deep into the northern regions in the latter half of the seventeenth century. Fear of Iroquois raids was strong even among the Aboriginal people who lived near the coast of James Bay.[11]

In 1701 a tremendous gathering of Nations took place at Montreal to negotiate an end to the long period of warfare that had plagued the Great Lakes region since the time of initial European contact. Over 1,000 delegates from numerous Nations gathered at Montreal in the summer of 1701, and they agreed to a peace treaty, commonly referred to as the Great Peace.[12] The 1701 Montreal Treaty laid the foundation for peaceful relations between the Aboriginal Nations of the Great Lakes region. A wampum belt signifying a dish with one spoon memorialized the agreement between the Nations to share hunting grounds.[13] Although conflicts between these Nations occasionally flared after 1701, they were minor in comparison with the pre-1701 warfare that was endemic in the region. After 1701, the economy of the Great Lakes region expanded rapidly, and the Thunder Bay Anishinabeg were situated in a strategic hub of the fur trade that expanded into the western interior of North America.

Early European Fur Trade Contacts in the Lake Superior Region

Aboriginal people who became middlemen traders were initially reluctant to allow European fur traders direct access to the sources of their fur supplies. French fur traders were anxious to visit the upper Great Lakes region, but they were prevented from doing so by Aboriginal Nations who jealously guarded their middleman position. For example, Samuel de Champlain was consistently rebuffed by Montagnais middlemen who controlled the Saguenay River trade route, and by Algonquin and Ottawa middlemen who guarded the access to the Lake Superior region.[14] The control over trade by the middleman Nations was weakened by the endemic warfare throughout much of the seventeenth century in the Lower Great Lakes region. It was also undercut by a series of devastating epidemic diseases that swept through the region in the seventeenth century. Smallpox, measles and influenza epidemics caused widespread death and suffering. Mortality rates of 50 per cent and higher have been estimated among all of the infected Nations.[15] These epidemics wrought havoc among the Nations closest to the Europeans, and prepared the ground for the subsequent expansion of European fur traders beyond the Aboriginal middlemen and into the interior of the continent

The gateway to Lake Superior was a narrow, rapid passage known as Bow-e-ting, and later named Sault Ste. Marie by the French. Bow-e-ting was a natural hub connecting Lake Superior and the other Great Lakes. Here, many Nations would gather during the summer for trade and other purposes. The productive fisheries at the rapids provided abundant sustenance for the seasonal gatherings of large numbers of people. When Jesuit missionaries first visited Bow-e-ting in 1648, they called the resident Anishinabeg Nation "Saulteurs," after the rapids. According to the Jesuits, the Saulteurs controlled the trade with other Aboriginal people who lived in the Lake Superior basin, and they warned that the French fur traders would have to first obtain rights of passage from them if they wished to visit these other Nations.[16]

In 1660, a group of Ottawa and Huron middleman traders took two Frenchmen, Pierre Esprit, sieur de Radisson and his brother-in-law, Medard Chouart, sieur des Groseilliers, to Lake Superior. They travelled widely throughout the Lake Superior region, and Radisson later claimed to have reached James Bay on his return trip to Quebec.[17] Radisson and Groseilliers were instrumental in opening up the fur trade in the Lake Superior region to French fur traders, but they were unable to convince the authorities in New France to commission a trading venture into James Bay. Radisson believed that the direct route into James Bay would be more lucrative because of cheaper transportation costs and also because it would by-pass the Aboriginal middlemen who controlled access into Lake Superior through the Great Lakes routeway. Disenchanted with the French authorities, Radisson and Groseilliers sold their plans to a group of English entrepreneurs who commissioned a trading venture into James Bay in 1668. The success of that venture led to the incorporation of the Hudson's Bay Company (hereinafter HBC) in 1670. Assisted by a Royal Charter granted by English King Charles II, the HBC established a monopoly over the fur trade into Hudson Bay.

While the English-based HBC was establishing a foothold in the Hudson Bay region, French fur traders continued to advance into the Lake Superior country and beyond. In 1679, Daniel Greysolon, sieur Du Lhut, established a trading post near the mouth of the Kaministiquia River.[18] At the same time, other French traders were swarming into the Upper Great Lakes region to capitalize on the huge profits that could be made on furs. Although the French authorities tried to stem the rapid expansion of fur trading activity by issuing exclusive licenses, or conges, they could not stop illegal traders from venturing into the licensed areas. The unlicensed traders, known as *coureurs de bois* (wood runners), established temporary trading posts or lived with Aboriginal people in their villages and camps. Nothing much is known about the activities of the *coureurs de bois*, but by 1680 it was reported that more than 800 were active in the Upper Great Lakes region.[19]

French Fur Trade in the Eighteenth Century

The rapid expansion of the fur trade in the latter decades of the seventeenth century by both English and French traders contributed to an over-supply of furs, especially beaver, on the European market. The French authorities sought to alleviate the glut by cancelling all trading licenses. As a result, the Kaministiquia post and others on the Great Lakes were closed in 1696. However, the closure of the trading posts proved to be ineffective because many *coureurs de bois* continued to operate with impunity, and the HBC held onto their posts despite several French attacks.

In 1715, the French colonial authorities in New France re-opened the trade in the *pays d'en haut*, or upper country, and in 1717 a new post was established at the mouth of the Kaministiquia River. The new post was managed by Zacharie Robutel, sieur de La Noue, who worked aggressively to win back the allegiance of Aboriginal people who had re-oriented their fur trading activity to the HBC during the absence of the French. The new French trading system also promoted westward expansion, and the Kaministikquia post became a springboard for fur trade settlements in the western interior.

Westward expansion from Kaministiquia was made possible by the Anishinabeg of the region who drew maps, guided, and provisioned the French fur traders. The Anishinabeg who lived between Lake Superior and Lake Winnipeg were closely allied, and this promoted a rapid expansion of the French fur trade settlement frontier. When the French leader Pierre Gaultier de Varennes de La Vérendrye first visited Lake of the Woods in 1731, he was greeted by Chief La Marteblanche[20] who stated that: "the Kaministiquia road will always be a smooth one for the French."[21] However, it may have been that Chief La Marteblanche was inviting the French on the one hand while trading furs with the English. HBC records from Albany Fort and York Factory indicate that a leader named "Martin" or "Wappestan" traded with the HBC during the 1720s and 1730s. He was usually described as a "French Indian" or a "Far Upland Indian," and it is possible that he was the same leader who greeted La Vérendrye at Lake of the Woods in 1731 (HBCA, B.3/a/9-20; B.3/d/29-47).

The French trading post at the mouth of the Kaministiquia River served the local fur trade and also acted as a break-of-bulk point for the posts in the western interior. It is apparent that the French favoured the Grand Portage canoe route as an avenue into the western interior, but it is not known if a post was in operation at the Grand Portage during that period.[22] The paucity of written records and archaeological artifacts from the French period make it difficult to reconstruct the activities of the traders. Similarly, the activities of the Thunder Bay Anishinabeg cannot be documented precisely for that time period. A report by Jesuit missionary Claude Coquart in 1742 indicates that there was an Anishinabeg village at Grand Portage, and Coquart described the Chief as: "very influential ...a man of decision whose intrepidity produces an impression on the others."[23]

A New British Order

While the French fur traders pushed ever westward to reach new territories, events in the east were transpiring which would soon change the course of fur trade history. In 1760, French forces in the St. Lawrence River valley succumbed to British troops and a new British order supplanted the old French regime. The British victory over the French was relatively quick, but the Aboriginal Nations who were allied to the French proved more formidable and resilient foes. British fur traders and troops were attacked by the French allies, the most famous being the Detroit uprising in 1763 led by Pontiac, war chief of the Ottawa Nation. After protracted conflict and negotiation, a peace treaty was reached in 1764.[24] The treaty was negotiated at "The Crooked Place" or Niagara Falls, and delegates from many nations were in attendance. William Johnson, who represented Britain, explained that King George III had issued a Royal Proclamation in 1763, and that the British recognized the territorial rights of the Aboriginal Nations. In return for peace, the British also promised to regulate the fur trade and protect the Aboriginal Nations in the possession of their hunting grounds.

The 1764 Treaty allowed newly arrived British fur traders in Montreal and other towns in the St. Lawrence valley to re-establish the network of posts and supply systems that had operated during the French regime. Often, the early British fur traders developed partnerships with French traders who had long experience in the field. Such was the case of Alexander Henry who formed a partnership with Jean Baptiste Cadotte and operated a successful trade in the Lake Superior region. In the early years the British colonial authorities attempted to control the trade in much the same manner as the French conge system of the seventeenth century, but this soon gave way to a more open market and many small companies and partnerships entered the fur business.

One of the earliest fur traders to operate in the Lake Superior region was Ezekiel Solomon, a Jewish trader who had supplied British troops from Albany, New York. After the war Solomon moved quickly to enter the northwestern fur trade, and established himself at Michilimackinac in 1761, even in advance of the British troops. In 1763, he was taken prisoner during the Michilimackinac uprising, and he was later ransomed at Montreal. By 1770, Solomon had re-established his business and focused his attention on developing the Lake Nipigon trade. By 1780, Solomon controlled the fur trade in a wide territory around Lake Nipigon and operated seventeen trading posts. Solomon's success, however, came to an abrupt end during the 1782-83 season, when a smallpox epidemic spread throughout the Lake Nipigon country, killing many Aboriginal people and temporarily ruining the fur trade.[25]

The Lake Nipigon fur trade under Solomon operated quite independently from the trade that developed in other parts of the Lake Superior region. At the western end of the lake, the old French trading post location at the mouth of the Kaministiquia River was abandoned in favour of Grand Portage, which offered easier access to the western interior. Grand Portage quickly became the *entrepôt* for the fur trade that developed in the area known as the "Great North." That term was used to designate the area along the canoe route to Lake Winnipeg and included the vast territory to the north and west of that lake. The term "Little North" referred to the area east of Lake Winnipeg, and included the territory around Lake Nipigon.

The fur trade that developed in the Grand Portage area in the 1760s was based on a complex set of relationships between suppliers of trade goods, buyers of furs, transportation crews and the men who conducted the trade in the interior. Gradually, the many Montreal firms initially involved in the fur trade business were reduced to a small number of companies. Smaller partnerships merged together and many were squeezed out of business by the intensive competition that developed as the fur trade expanded into the western interior. In 1779, nine powerful Montreal firms sent representatives to Grand Portage to negotiate an agreement to combine their interests rather than compete against each other. Central figures in this partnership agreement were Joseph and Benjamin Frobisher and Simon McTavish. The 1779 agreement laid the foundation for the future establishment of the North West Company.

THE NORTH WEST COMPANY

The smallpox epidemic of 1782-83 that led to the ruin of Ezekiel Solomon's trading empire in the Little North also had significant consequences for the fur trade in the Grand Portage area. The Anishinabeg who lived near the major fur trade transportation routes were exposed to the full force of the epidemic. The smallpox was transmitted quickly along these routes, and the mortality rates were extremely high. According to a HBC journal entry from Gloucester House on 22 June 1782, Anishinabeg visitors reported that: "there is a great mortality among the Indians and that most of the Indians in and near the raney [Rainy] Lake is dead."[26] The loss of so many people, both young and old, caused tremendous suffering and hardship for years after the epidemic. The participation of the Anishinabeg in the fur trade economy in the aftermath of the smallpox epidemic was significantly different from that in the pre-epidemic period. According to Carolyn Gilman:

> Smallpox changed the demographic ratio of whites to Indians, and the balance of power shifted. Hitherto, traders had been guests in a thriving society with its own systems of justice and control. Now, with Indian society reeling, the traders unleashed their own sense of justice and hierarchy... The trade, which in many ways had reached a mutually beneficial balance, began to show signs of exploitation and domination.[27]

The smallpox epidemic also caused major transformations in the non-Aboriginal fur trade economy. Prominent figures like Ezekiel Solomon faded from the scene in the Little North, and a small group of Montreal merchants consolidated their hold on the fur trade in the Great North. In 1784, the loose coalition that had formed at Grand Portage in 1779 took on a more permanent structure and the name North West Company (hereinafter NWC). Once again the Frobisher brothers and Simon McTavish were instrumental in organizing the company which was based on shares divided between Montreal merchants and fur traders in the interior, or so-called wintering partners. The fur trade territory was divided into areas called departments, and each area was managed by a wintering partner. Each spring, the NWC wintering partners would meet at Grand Portage to discuss the state of the fur trade in their respective departments. These annual meetings were also occasions for important discussions on the fur returns, price of goods, cost of country provisions, relations with Aboriginal peoples, and the competition with other fur traders, especially the HBC. Decisions to increase or decrease the number of men and the quantity of trade goods in each department were reached for the common good of the partners who shared in the annual profits accruing from the entire trade. These meetings also enabled them to cut costs and to concentrate on the most profitable areas within the fur trade territory. As a result, NWC trading posts expanded and shifted according to local fur resources and market conditions in Montreal and Europe.

The success of the NWC soon ruined many rival Montreal-based competitors. By about 1790, the NWC controlled much of the fur trade in the Great North through the Grand Portage *entrepôt*. The HBC responded by building its own inland trading posts, but the NWC managed to keep one step ahead of its London-based rivals throughout the latter decades of the eighteenth century. In 1796, the fur trade in the Little North, which had remained in the hands of independent fur traders, was brought into the NWC fold. Duncan Cameron, who then controlled the Little North fur trade, became a wintering partner in the NWC and remained in charge of the area that came to be known as the Nipigon Department in NWC parlance.

Grand Portage was the seasonal administrative headquarters for the NWC. It was the major break-of-bulk point where large Great Lakes-faring *canots de maître* (master canoes) unloaded trade goods from Montreal and picked up furs procured from the inland country. The transportation system was predicated on the birch bark canoe and the men who paddled and carried the canoes and goods over thousands of miles, often through rough waters and over dangerous terrain. The Great Lakes *canots de maître* were usually thirty-six feet long and weighed about 600 pounds. These large vessels were built to carry about 6,000 pounds of cargo. Smaller canoes, known as *canots du nord*, were used to navigate the inland waterways beyond the lakehead. These canoes were typically twenty-five feet long, weighed about 300 pounds and could carry 3,000 pounds of cargo.[28] Canoes of varying sizes were also employed around the posts for fishing, delivering mail and other jobs. The NWC also developed a schooner service on Lake Superior that was designed to carry more cargo and provide greater insurance against the unpredictable freshwater sea of Lake Superior. Beginning in 1793 the seventy-five ton *Otter* was employed on the route between Sault Ste. Marie and Grand Portage, making four trips each summer.

Each summer there was a great rendezvous when the men who worked on the Lake Superior *canots de maître* and schooners met the inland voyageurs at Grand Portage. By the 1790s over 1,000 men congregated for the rendezvous, and for a few weeks each summer Grand Portage was the scene of tremendous activity. Alexander Mackenzie enumerated the men employed by the NWC around 1798 as follows: "fifty clerks, seventy-one interpreters and clerks, one thousand and twenty canoe men, and thirty-five guides."[29] Rivalry between the inlanders and the Lake Superior voyageurs was keen during this brief period. Sometimes the activity boiled into abandoned merriment or vociferous conflict among the men, but the wintering partners who were also present were able to maintain order.

For much of the year, the activity at Grand Portage was concerned with the fur trade in the local department. This business was handled by a small corps of men, and reflected the relatively poor state of the fur resources in the local area. A list of NWC employees in 1799 shows only seven men in the Grand Portage Department. The list also gave the wages (in Grand Portage *livres* currency) of the following men: Doctor Munro - 1,200, Charles Hesse - 600, Zachary Cloutier - 750, Antoine Collin - 600, Jacques Vaudreuil - 600, Francois Boileau - 1,000, and Bruce – 300.[30]

Although the fur resources in the immediate vicinity of Grand Portage appear to have been depleted very early, the Anishinabeg who lived in the area prospered in the fur trade economy by supplying provisions and other goods to the NWC. Fresh fish, especially whitefish, lake trout and sturgeon were important trade items for immediate consumption at the trading post and cured fish was a critical provision year-round and also served as an essential portable food supply for the transport brigades coming to and from Grand Portage. Other less desirable fish species such as pike, pickerel, and suckers were bought by the traders mainly for dog food. Dogs were important work animals, especially in winter when sled transport was an essential means of conveyance over snow. Large animals such as moose, caribou and bear were hunted by the Anishinabeg and surplus amounts were traded at the NWC post. Supplies of meat and fat were important ingredients in the diet of the Anishinabeg and the fur traders. Other foods that were traded included berries, wild rice and Indian corn. Medicines prepared from plants were also valuable trade items. Other products such as birch bark canoes, snowshoes and sleds were also in high demand at Grand Portage. In addition, Anishinabeg men and women gained seasonal employment as guides and voyageurs. These non-fur activities promoted a diversified economy, and provided a comfortable livelihood for the Anishinabeg who were involved in this commerce.

The trade goods supplied by the NWC to the Anishinabeg covered a wide range of utilitarian and luxury goods. Metal goods such as pots, pans, kettles, knives and axes quickly replaced Aboriginal wares made of clay, bone and stone because the former were more efficient and durable. Cloth and woollen garments replaced fur and skin clothing because the former were cheap and easy to replace. Luxury items such as beads, ornaments, vermilion and lace supplemented Aboriginal decorations made of local resources such as porcupine quills and feathers. Tobacco, although originally a product of the Americas, was supplied by the NWC and valued by the Anishinabeg for its significance in spiritual and other ceremonies. Liquor was also initially used ceremonially, but addiction to alcohol led to physical and social problems in Anishinabeg communities.

The use of liquor in the fur trade became endemic as fur traders sought to increase profits with watered liquor, and many Aboriginal hunters and trappers became addicted to the intoxicating effects of rum, brandy and other alcoholic beverages. In 1793, HBC trader Joseph Colen remarked:

> These Canadian Traders are so artful, it is impossible to keep the few skins the Indians procure from them, as they attend their tents with liquor, and collect the produce of their hunt almost immediately on animals being killed... The number of Natives who have fallen victims to intoxication within these two years past are many, and should the Canadians continue their practice of carrying their strong spirits to the tents of Natives I much fear the whole country will soon be depopulated.[31]

Accidental deaths and other physical problems associated with the use of liquor was compounded by social stresses on families who were torn apart by the abuse of alcohol. Although the fur traders realized the negative consequences associated with liquor, they continued to use it as a competitive strategy to keep furs away from rival traders.

The NWC fur trade empire at the turn of the eigtheenth century was also beset by unrest among its own men and partners, and internal divisions threatened to break-up the Company. The central figure in the rebellion against the NWC was Alexander Mackenzie, the man who had gained fame as the first non-Aboriginal person to visit the Arctic Ocean in 1789 and cross North America in 1793 . Mackenzie, who would be knighted by King George III in 1802 for his journey of exploration, became dissatisfied with the way the NWC was being operated. In particular, he railed against the authority of Simon McTavish who presided over the affairs of the Company with growing autocracy. In 1799 a new fur trade company was formed that came to be known as the XY Company. In 1800, Alexander Mackenzie joined the XY Company and the stage was set for a brief period of intensive competition between the two fur trade companies.

The XY Company built beside the NWC at Grand Portage, and also constructed a network of trading posts in the interior at strategic locations beside established NWC and, in some cases, HBC trading posts. The close competition that followed this strategy saw the price of goods plummet and the cost of gifts and other incentives to Aboriginal hunters and trappers escalate to unprecedented levels. The use of liquor also increased to record levels throughout the fur trade country. In many places, rival fur traders sought to starve out their competition by buying up surplus country food supplies. Aboriginal hunters and trappers were threatened with death if they took their trade to another Company. Violent encounters on all sides increased dramatically, and for a few years much of the fur trade country was held in a grip of fear and confusion.

At Grand Portage, the large seasonal gatherings of NWC and XY Company men proved difficult for the officers of either company to maintain peace and order. Anishinabeg hunters and trappers were intimidated and threatened by the desperate traders. John Tanner described the difficulties faced by Anishinabeg people who visited Grand Portage during this period. In addition to threats of violence, Anishinabeg people often were bribed with liquor in order to make them trade their furs. Tanner observed:

> when we came to this side of the portage, Mr. McGilveray [McGillivray] and Mr. Shabboyea [Chaboillez], by treating her [Tanner's adoptive mother] with much attention, and giving her some wine, induced her to place all her packs [of furs] in a room, which they gave her to occupy. At first, they endeavoured, by friendly solicitation, to induce her to sell her furs; but finding she was determined not to part with them, they threatened her; and at length, a young man, the son of Mr. Shabboyea, attempted to take them by force; but the old man interfered, and ordering his son to desist, reproved him for his violence.[32]

Simon McTavish died in 1804 and the new head of the NWC, William McGillivray, was able to negotiate a merger with Sir Alexander Mackenzie & Company. The new NWC absorbed the business interests of its upstart rival and many of the men were taken into the fold of the re-organized company. Mackenzie's company was given one-quarter interest in the new company, but Mackenzie was prohibited from interfering in the operation of the business. Carolyn Gilman observed that: "it was a Pyrrhic victory for Mackenzie. The one stipulation McGillivray would not negotiate was that 'Sir Alexander Mackenzie is excluded from any interference in the company."[33]

Return to Kaministiquia

The Treaty of Paris signed in 1783 between British and American negotiators established the international boundary line which cut the Great Lakes in two and placed Grand Portage on the American side of the line. Anishinabeg leaders insisted that the boundary line was ineffective since they had not been consulted nor did they agree to the line running through their territories. Anishinabe historian William Warren observed

> They [Anishinabeg] could not be made to understand or acknowledge the right which Great Britain and the United States assumed, in dividing between them the lands which had been left to them by their ancestors, and of which they held actual possession.[34]

NWC officials also protested the boundary line because it left Grand Portage and some other trading posts in

William McGillivray with his second wife, Magdalen McDonald, and daughter Anne Marie. Portrait by William Berczy, c. 1806. McGillivray, a nephew of Simon McTavish, a founder of the North West Company, started his career as a clerk but rose to prominence in the late 1790s. In 1804, after the death of McTavish, he took control of the NWC. In 1807 Fort William was named in his honour. In 1821 he was instrumental in negotiating the merger with the Hudson's Bay Company but his career in the fur trade ended with the new order. TBHMS 977.113.443

American territory. Unresponsive to the concerns of the Anishinabeg and the NWC, the boundary line persisted on maps and official plans, and eventually the line was surveyed and the border became a reality on the ground.

Although the boundary line did not immediately become effective, the NWC understood that a new location would have to be found for its Lake Superior *entrepôt*. In the summer of 1784 the NWC sent Edward Umfreville to explore a new route through the Lake Nipigon country. Umfreville, a former HBC employee, engaged local Anishinabeg guides to take him through the canoe route from the Nipigon River to the confluence of the English and Winnipeg Rivers. At this junction, Umfreville had reached the main canoe route from Grand Portage to Lake Winnipeg. Umfreville's report to the NWC recommended the Nipigon route as an alternative to Grand Portage. However, the NWC was slow to abandon Grand Portage because there was no pressure from American or British authorities to enforce their respective jurisdictions within their borders until the signing of the Jay Treaty in 1794. Thereafter, the NWC made more serious plans, and in 1803 they vacated the Grand Portage post. Their destination, however, was not Nipigon. Instead, they chose to relocate about thirty miles (fifty kilometres) north at the mouth of the Kaministiquia River near the old French trading post.[35]

THE NORTH WEST COMPANY AT FORT WILLIAM

The move by the NWC to the mouth of the Kaministiquia River was resisted by the local Anishinabeg who viewed this development as an intrusion into their territory. William Warren commented that:

> The Indians could not, or would not, understand the necessity of this movement [from Grand Portage to Kaministiquia], as they claimed the country as their own, and felt as though they had a right to locate their traders wherever they pleased.[36]

In order to smooth over relations between the Company and the Anishinabeg an agreement was reached in 1798 that allowed the NWC to build a post at Kaministiquia. That agreement conveyed an area of ten by twelve miles at the mouth of the river to the NWC in return for three pounds provincial currency and "divers other good causes and valuable considerations." To signify the agreement a wampum belt was given and a parchment document was signed by eight officials from the NWC and ten chiefs and elders of the Kaministiquia Anishinabeg. With that agreement in hand, the NWC was ready to move to Kaministiquia. In 1803 they dismantled the Grand Portage buildings and constructed their new headquarters at the mouth of the Kaministiquia River. In 1807 the NWC named its post Fort William in honour of William McGillivray who had become the Company's chief director.

Work at the new post was conducted in much the same fashion as had previously been done at Grand Portage. With the merger between the NWC and XY Company in 1804, the volume of business increased significantly at Fort William. The annual summer rendezvous was attended by larger numbers of men as the ranks of the NWC swelled with the addition of many former XY men. The labour force at Kaministiquia also increased significantly as thirty-five men were employed in 1805 in comparison to seven in 1799.

In order to maintain profits, the wintering partners of the NWC needed to obtain more furs to pay the increased expenses of men and equipment in each of the departments. This proved very difficult because fur resources in many areas had been depleted by the early years of the nineteenth century. The period of intensive competition involving the XY Company had thinned out the fur resources in many areas, and the fur trade was on a more precarious footing after the merger. In addition, the HBC began to offer stiffer competition by expanding its operations into areas once held exclusively by the Canadian traders. In 1804, Duncan Cameron, the veteran NWC fur trader predicted that the fur trade could not last long under the current conditions. Cameron observed:

> even if there was no opposition at all in the country to spoil the trade, it is now getting so barren and poor that in a dozen years hence, the returns from it will be so trifling that, even if one company had the whole, on the cheapest terms, it will be little enough to pay the expenses of carrying on the business, for the hunt is declining very fast, and we are obliged every year to make new discoveries and settle new posts. Even with all that, we cannot keep the former average of returns, although the consummation of goods is increasing every year, and I believe that our discoveries are now about at an end, and that the trade cannot be extended much further than it is at present.[37]

Cameron's predictions proved to be very accurate as both the NWC and HBC struggled for control over the dwindling fur trade returns.

The HBC had avoided settling posts near the main canoe routes from Grand Portage and Kaministiquia until the nineteenth century. A small outfit from Albany Fort had been tried in the Rainy Lake district from 1793 to 1798, but the returns were small and the HBC found it too expensive to send men and supplies from James Bay to compete against the Canadians. However, in 1815 the HBC began to recruit men in the Montreal area and send these men and supplies directly into the interior by way of the Kaministiquia River route. This

Front view of Fort Kaministiquia, June 15, 1805, artist unknown. From the original oil painting in Dr. Vancortlandt's collection, Ottawa. Published in Father Aeneas McDonell Dawson, Our Strength and their Strength *(Ottawa, 1870). TBHMS, 972.2.194.*

Fort William, 1871, by William Armstrong. This painting depicts daily activities of the Anishinabeg at a camp on the Kam River across from Fort William. TBHMS 972.48.39.

was a significant development because it placed the HBC on the same transportation and communication lines with the NWC. The competition between the two companies was as close as that which had developed earlier between the NWC and XY Company.

The NWC attempted to remove the HBC from the Fort William transport route by appropriating country provisions along the route. Supplies of fish, game and wild rice along the line from Fort William to Lake of the Woods were bought up by the NWC. In the prairie region the NWC attempted to keep precious supplies of bison meat and pemmican away from the HBC. The establishment of an HBC-sponsored colony at the forks of the Red and Assiniboine Rivers in 1812 was, in part, a strategy designed to secure a reliable supply of bison and pemmican. The leader of this venture was Thomas Douglas, Earl of Selkirk, who was a prominent shareholder in the HBC. The colony, initially populated by Highland Scots, was a failure because of poor weather conditions and inadequate logistical support for the fledgling settlement. The colonists were also intimidated by NWC traders and Métis who lived in the area. In 1815 many of the settlers left the colony, and in 1816 a party of NWC and Métis raiders descended on the few who remained and killed 21 people near a place known as Seven Oaks. The incident, popularized as the Seven Oaks massacre, triggered an immediate response by the HBC. Selkirk had already been on his way to Red River with a contingent of mercenary soldiers known as the des Meurons regiment, and they proceeded to Fort William after learning of the Seven Oaks incident. Selkirk and his troops seized the fort from the NWC and imprisoned William McGillivray and others who were at the fort in the summer of 1816.

The HBC held onto Fort William during the winter of 1816-17, as complicated court proceedings unfolded in Montreal. Although the NWC eventually succeeded in re-occupying Fort William, the fur trade business had been severely damaged. Both the NWC and HBC found the post-1817 period impossible to continue under the same competitive conditions. With the death of Selkirk in 1820, negotiations between officials from each company led to an agreement to merge in 1821. Under this agreement the NWC was absorbed by the HBC in much the same manner as the NWC had earlier absorbed the XY Company. Some of the NWC traders were re-hired by the HBC, but the flag and colours of the old Nor'Westers was replaced by the HBC standard.

Hudson's Bay Company at Fort William

The fur trade after 1821 underwent major changes to the logistical network that supplied the interior trading posts. The old NWC system had been dependent on the Great Lakes transportation system, and Fort William was the major *entrepôt* for the trade that was carried on in the northwestern interior of the continent. The newly re-organized HBC chose to retain the transportation system that had been developed from Hudson and James Bay. In this system York Factory, located at the mouth of the Hayes River, was the most important *entrepôt* into the interior. The decision to abandon Fort William as a major break-of-bulk centre was effected quickly, and the fort was reduced to a minor district headquarters. The "grand rendezvous" became only a memory, and the hustle and bustle that had previously characterized Fort William was reduced to a slow-paced routine after 1821.

After 1821 the HBC implemented many cost-cutting measures that were designed to recoup losses and make the fur trade profitable once more. George Simpson, who became Governor of the Company's North American operations in 1826, directed the closure of many trading posts and trimmed the labour force. Fort William survived the cuts, but it was reduced to a rather minor post in the new order, and the once active *entrepôt* was the centre of only a small local trade. In the summer of 1830, Frances Simpson, wife of George Simpson, visited Fort William on her way west to the Red River settlement. Roderick McKenzie Sr., Chief Trader in charge of Fort William, greeted her and she observed that "This Establishment is of considerable extent, and some years ago, was the principal Depot of the North-West Company: but the buildings are going fast to decay, and it is now of very little importance in comparison to what it was then."[38]

An important reason for keeping Fort William open after 1821 was to keep a watch on American fur traders who were increasing in numbers south of the border. Competition from American fur traders across the border also caused increased expenses for the HBC as the Company was forced to cut prices and give extra gifts to keep the local Anishinabeg fur hunters loyal. The HBC also set up watch posts along the border to dissuade hunters from taking their furs to the Americans.

Efforts to reach an agreement on regulating the trade near the American-British border began in 1829 when William Aitkin, Chief Trader of the American Fur Company's (hereinafter AFC) Fond du Lac Department, visited HBC Chief Factor Angus Bethune at Sault Ste. Marie. These initial talks led to an agreement between the companies in 1833 by which the HBC agreed to pay 300 pounds sterling per year in return for the abandonment of the AFC posts along the boundary between Lake Superior and the Red River. The AFC continued to operate a post at Grand Portage, but it served as a commercial fishing station. The AFC advised the HBC that their men at Grand Portage were "expressly forbidden to trade one skin from your Indians."[39] The agreement between the HBC and AFC was effective for a decade until the failure of the AFC in 1842.[40]

In the post-1821 period, the work around the fort was varied. In addition to the fur trade business, every-day tasks included boat-building, cooking, baking, threshing grain, blacksmithing, cutting wood, road construction, clearing snow, repairing equipment and milking cows. In 1823 the Company farm produced 23 bushels of peas, 24 ½ bushels of oats, 23 bushels of barley and 10 ½ bushels of mixed oats and barley. In 1835, the harvest included 1,260 bushels of potatoes.

Some of the customs from the old NWC era continued long after the merger. For example, on January 1, 1836, the following was recorded in the Fort William journal:

> The people of the Establishment came to pay their Bourgeois the annual visit on this day according to the custom of the country - and they were treated as usual on that occasion - which is, as much Brandy and wine as they choose to drink and cakes etc. We also gave the Indians a regale and liquor as much as they reasonably could drink.[41]

Many of the employees of the trading companies at Fort William had married local Anishinabeg women and they had families with close connections to the Anishinabeg community. Jennifer Brown observed that:

"By 1821, when the companies merged, practically all officers of the Hudson's Bay and North West Companies, and many lower-ranked employees as well, were allied with women born in the Indian country."[42] In 1828, there were five families living at Fort William as well as two elderly people who were dependent on the fort. Some of the HBC and former NWC employees who were let go after 1821 chose to remain near Fort William. These men were usually called "freemen," a term that was used to describe men who had been released from fur trade contracts[43]. Other names such as "halfbreed" and "Métis" were also used to describe these men and their children. Prominent freemen in the Fort William area included Antoine and Michel Collin. Antoine Collin, who was described as "Old Collin" in 1824, was likely the same man who was employed by the NWC at Grand Portage in 1799. Michel Collin was one of Antoine's sons, and both men gained their livelihood by fishing and hunting part-time for the HBC. In the fall of 1823, Antoine's fishery produced thirty-one casks of salted fish and Michel's fishery yielded twenty casks.

The distinction between "freemen," "half breeds," "Métis" and "Indians" was often blurred in the records of the HBC at Fort William. For example, a man named Louis Ross was employed by the HBC in 1824-25, and referred to as a "half breed."[44] In 1835, Louis Ross was called an Indian, and hunted with other Anishinabeg in the Fort William area, and in the spring of 1836 he was associated with a group of freemen led by Michel Collin.[45]

Although the freemen were not permanently employed by the Company, the HBC did not tolerate them selling furs to others. For example, in the winter of 1823-24, HBC Chief Factor John Haldane reprimanded visiting surveyor Lieutenant Henry Bayfield for trading furs with the freemen. The HBC daily journal entry on December 1, 1823, illustrates the Company's position:

> although these freemen were not in the Company's permanent employ, they derived the whole of their support from the Company; and that in every estimate made for the supply of the Indians, the necessaries required by these people were always included - in consequence of which they were to be considered as on the same footing with the Indians; and any clandestine trade carried on with them, as an infringement of the Company's rights.[46]

Some of the freemen were paid on a monthly basis, while others sold their produce directly to the Company like their Anishinabeg neighbours. The freemen who lived near Fort William were skilled fishermen, hunters, trappers and canoe-builders.

THE FORT WILLIAM ANISHINABEG IN THE FUR TRADE AFTER 1821

The Anishinabeg population in the vicinity of Fort William appears to have declined in the period immediately following the 1821 merger, but rebounded in later years. In 1824, John Haldane, Chief Factor in charge of the HBC's Lake Superior Department, commented

> The Indians about Fort William are not so numerous as they were some years ago - some having gone to Nipigon, others to Fond du Lac, and a small portion to St. Mary's. The number still frequenting this establishment, generally, may amount to 28 men and lads.[47]

However, by 1829, the population had apparently increased as Roderick McKenzie Sr., Chief Trader, provided a census count of 49 men, 51 women and 96 children.[48]

Table 1: HBC Fur Returns from Lake Superior District, 1825-63 (select species)
Source: HBCA, B.135/h/1

date	beaver	lynx	marten	mink	muskrat
1825	2,779	923	6,956	1,788	24,287
1826	3,097	1,263	7,532	2,883	26,142
1827	2,495	1,493	7,460	2,649	28,598
1831	2,266	2,296	2,430	1,245	17,231
1834	1,712	835	5,043	2,873	39,959
1835	1,567	1,181	7,132	3,655	29,620
1836	1,469	1,494	7,925	3,312	21,437
1837	1,451	2,266	5,524	2,325	16,098
1838	1,111	2,289	3,074	1,317	15,920
1841	936	542	2,692	1,056	13,667
1842	923	431	3,639	2,486	16,581
1843	920	383	3,784	1,256	18,243
1844	1,020	583	3,645	4,984	20,026
1847	662	1,827	3,619	3,321	10,593
1848	670	2,770	4,655	3,154	11,400
1849	903	3,768	4,343	3,930	9,458
1850	1,051	2,963	5,226	3,717	10,073
1851	890	1,047	4,072	2,110	10,934
1852	1,136	505	4,875	1,723	15,738
1853	1,093	426	2,968	2,056	19,562
1854	1,414	360	2,957	1,876	14,159
1855	1,576	395	5,520	2,476	15,173
1856	1,838	802	4,525	3,202	21,842
1857	1,881	1,343	5,686	3,121	15,913
1858	2,911	2,133	4,689	3,026	14,354
1859	2,986	1,775	3,964	3,181	8,474
1860	3,369	1,154	3,474	1,767	5,569
1861	3,898	418	3,131	2,040	10,051
1862	5,107	225	3,482	1,673	8,532
1863	5,275	232	4,485	2,914	17,267

In 1821 there was one principal chief among the Fort William Anishinabeg. His name was "Espagnol," and John Haldane explained that it was "the only name he goes by, even with the Indians."[49] Espagnol, or "the Spaniard" as he was often called by the HBC, hunted with his band in the area south of Grand Portage, but he remained loyal to the HBC even after the American Fur Company established a post nearby at Grand Marais in 1823. In the summer of 1824, the Spaniard arrived at Fort William with one of his sons-in-law and their winter hunt in furs.[50] As usual, he was given a new suit of clothing, a large keg of mixed rum and other gifts. On his leaving the fort, the Spaniard received other gifts, including ammunition, a bag of corn and 2 kegs of mixed rum.[51] In 1829, Roderick McKenzie Sr. commented that the Spaniard "was the principal Indian leader of this fort, and had a great deal of influence amongst his tribe."[52] In 1830, the Spaniard met Frances Simpson, who visited Fort William on her way to the Red River Settlement. Simpson noted that the Spaniard, although old, was "the most lively, good-tempered looking Indian, I had met with." She described his attire as very gaily dressed in a Scarlet Coat, with black velvet cuffs and collar, edged with gold lace - a White Calico Shirt ornamented with a frill about 1/2 a yard in depth - cloth Stockings worked with beads, an immense Sword dangling by his side, an enormous cocked hat, surmounted by a profusion of different coloured feathers.[53] A younger man who was described as his son-in-law accompanied the old chief. The Spaniard visited Fort William to trade furs and receive presents of liquor, tobacco, beads and cloth.

The HBC records from Fort William identified other leading men among the Anishinabeg population. These included: Little Rat, who was the leader of a group who lived near Lac de Milles Lacs ;[54] Grand Coquin and his brother Peau de Chat whose winter hunting grounds were located near Whitefish Lake;[55] L'Illinois who wintered at Black Bay;[56] L'Homme du Sault whose hunting grounds were near a place called Portage la Prairie; and the Little Englishman and his band who wintered with the Spaniard near Grand Portage.[57]

The Anishinabeg women also performed important roles in the fur trade around Fort William. John McLoughlin was impressed by the work done by the women who lived near Fort William, and he wrote that: "The Provence of the women is dressing the furs, draging [sic] her family furniture in the Campments, and in short all that is to be done about the lodge."[58] Women were often employed during the winter at snaring rabbits. They were also active in making maple sugar in late winter and early spring. The women claimed ownership of their respective "sugar bushes."[59] Some women were employed in cultivating and harvesting potatoes and other crops in the Company's fields, and others were expert in building and repairing canoes.[60]

Men and women participated in fisheries near Fort William, with the men usually engaged in fishing and the women working in processing the fish. An important fishing station was at the rapids in the Kaministiquia River where sturgeon were speared and caught in seine nets. Sturgeon were also caught with nets in Sturgeon Bay. In winter, "loches" or burbot were speared through holes in the ice. Lake trout were also speared in winter, and set-lines baited with suckers were also used to catch lake trout in winter. The HBC traded fish with Anishinabeg and freemen who established active commercial fisheries that also supplied the American market. Fishing stations were located at Rabbit Island, Pattie Island, Point Brule, Sheep Island, Welcome Islands, the Rapids, Point au Pierre, Grand Portage, Point au Tonnore, Black Bay, Sturgeon Bay and Shagionas Island.

After 1821, the HBC officially discouraged the sale of liquor to Aboriginal people but, in practice, liquor was sold and given away free to Anishinabeg hunters near Fort William. Sometimes the HBC traders would take pains to conceal the distribution of liquor when government agents or other travellers were nearby. Such was the case in the summer of 1824 when British and American survey parties were at Fort William. The daily journal entry on July 24, 1824, illustrates the Company's business practice regarding liquor:

> The Main Poque, L'Homme de Sault, Little Englishman, Najob and families arrived from Isle Royale, they say there are no carribou there this summer and supposed them all crossed to the main land last winter. They brought nothing but fish, principally dried whitefish, which they wished to trade for liquor but Mr. McKenzie told them he could not let them have any liquor to drink at the fort but he would trade the fish if they went off some distance to drink.[61]

The diminished activity around Fort William after 1821 seems to have stabilized fur bearer populations in the region. The HBC also implemented a number of policies after 1821 that were designed to conserve fur resources, especially beaver,[62] but these may not have been as effective in areas such as Thunder Bay which was exposed to competition from American traders. The HBC fur returns which are available for the Lake Superior district between 1825 and 1863 show an increase in the number of beaver pelts traded near the end of that period (see Table 1). Other kinds of fur-bearing animals such as lynx were subject to cyclical fluctuations, but on average these populations appear to have remained relatively stable.

The Impact of the Robinson-Superior Treaty of 1850

The colonial government in Canada had little to do with the upper Great Lakes region before the mid-nineteenth century. Although technically the drainage basin of Lake Superior north of the Pigeon River was within the domain of the government of Canada West, officials from the British colony were uninterested in exercising control in the region until minerals were discovered in the 1840s. Sparked by significant discoveries in the United States portion of the watershed, Canadian miners were eager to exploit the mineral riches on the Canadian side. Geological surveyors were sent to examine the northern and western shores of Lake Superior in the summer of 1846, and they provided optimistic reports to the government.[63] Although the government encouraged mining companies and issued mining licenses, the land was still held by Anishinabeg Nations who rebelled against these intrusions into their territory. In 1849, armed conflict between miners and Anishinabeg and Métis erupted at the Quebec and Lake Superior Mining Company operation at Mica Bay. Within weeks troops were dispatched to restore order, and government officials quickly followed to ask the Anishinabeg to make a treaty with the British Crown.

Two commissioners, Thomas G. Anderson and Alexander Vidal, were sent to investigate and report back to the government regarding the possibility of reaching a treaty with the Lake Huron and Lake Superior Anishinabeg. Anderson and Vidal made a quick tour of the lakes and spoke with some of the Anishinabeg leaders, including a small delegation at Fort William in the fall of 1849. The commissioners provided an optimistic report and indicated that the Anishinabeg nations were agreeable to enter into treaties to surrender their territory to the Crown. Other accounts of these meetings were less sanguine about any tentative agreements that may have been reached. For example, Father Nicolas Fremiot, a Jesuit missionary who attended the meeting at Fort William reported that the discussions had not been decisive about the specifics of entering into a treaty.[64] However, the government heard only the commissioners' accounts of these proceedings and prepared to send a treaty delegation to Lake Huron and Lake Superior the following year.

In 1850, William Benjamin Robinson was appointed to make the treaty with the Lake Huron and Lake Superior Anishinabeg Nations. In the end, because of logistical problems, he made two separate treaties with

The Mission of the Immaculate Conception at Fort William, circa 1800. Founded in 1848 by two Jesuit missionaries, Fremiot and Choné, the Fort William Mission offered religious instruction and material comforts to its adherents. The Anishinabeg who converted to Catholicism blended traditional spiritual beliefs with the new religion. The missionaries opposed the Superior-Robinson Treaty of 1850 in which millions of acres of land were surrendered to the British Crown and petitioned on behalf of the Fort William Anishinabeg for better terms under the treaty. TBHMS, 981.39.154.

the Nations on each of the lakes. Robinson had been instructed to obtain as much as he could for the least possible price.[65] The Lake Superior Treaty was signed at Sault Ste. Marie on September 7, 1850. Chief Joseph Peau de Chat claimed to represent all the Lake Superior Anishinabeg and signed on behalf of the Fort William Anishinabeg. Altogether the Treaties covered over nineteen million acres of land. Robinson believed that he had negotiated for the complete extinguishment of Aboriginal title to these lands, except for small reserves near existing villages. The Anishinabeg Chiefs in later petitions claimed that they understood the treaties to be agreements to share their resources with others, and not unconditional sales of their inherited territories.

The impact on the fur trade economy was initially minimal. The government was not interested in administering or possessing the animal or fisheries resources. In fact, Robinson had agreed to a clause in the treaties which affirmed continuing Aboriginal rights to their traditional fur trade economy. This clause stated that the Crown promised to allow the said Chiefs and their tribes the full and free privilege to hunt over the territory now ceded by them and to fish in the waters thereof as they have heretofore been in the habit of doing.[66]

However, the Anishinabeg soon found out that this Treaty promise was ineffective as greater numbers of non-Aboriginal miners, lumbermen, commercial fishermen, trappers, hunters and settlers moved into the region. The colonial British and later Canadian governments permitted (and even licensed) non-Aboriginal people to over-harvest the resources that were critical to their economy and livelihood. Increasingly, the Anishinabeg were prevented from accessing traditional resources by restrictive game and fish laws. Criminal charges, fines and jail terms were levied against many Anishinabeg who attempted to exercise their treaty rights.

While many Anishinabeg suffered during the aftermath of the Robinson Treaty, some of the treaty provisions were taken advantage of by the non-Aboriginal fur traders. Such was the case with the annual payment of treaty money by the Canadian government. Although the per capita amounts were small, fur traders were quick to claim these cash payments in lieu of debts that had accrued from selling trade goods. For example, on September 26, 1882, HBC trader E. Deacon at Fort William boasted to a colleague that: "I am happy to be able to tell you that we secured $350.00 of the Blackstone Band Annuity money this season."[67]

The construction of the transcontinental railway also caused significant disruptions to the fur trade. Many Anishinabeg sought employment on the railroad instead of devoting time to the fur hunt. For example, on March 14, 1883, Thomas Richards, Chief Factor at Fort William, wrote to his colleague P.W. Bell, who was stationed at Michipicoten, and complained that: "the fur trade is a failure, as the Fort William Indians are not hunting fur this year, they are for the most part employed in the shanties and Railroads."[68]

In 1878, the HBC moved its retail store to a new location on Simpson Street in the future town of Fort William.[69] In 1883, the Canadian Pacific Railway (hereinafter CPR) purchased the HBC property at Fort William. That transaction was facilitated by a prior purchase of one-half interest in the HBC property by the CPR, and the fact that the principal shareholder in both firms was Donald Smith.[70] A new era of railway travel and other economic developments in the region had by-passed the old fur trade order, and the new communities of Fort William and Port Arthur, based on other activities such as lumbering, mining and shipping, had supplanted the fur trade society. As the end of the nineteenth century approached the once busy and prosperous grounds of Fort William crumbled and lay in ruins. In 1902 the last standing structure of the old fort was demolished to make room for the expansion of the railway terminal.[71]

The fur trade did not end with the closure of the HBC post at Fort William. Furs continued to be hunted and trapped in the area around the towns of Fort William and Port Arthur by Anishinabeg and other trappers, and sales were made to other fur buyers. However, the fur trade was quickly eclipsed in the economy of the region as new developments overshadowed the once dominant fur post in the Canada.

Conclusion

The fur trade in the Thunder Bay area can be traced to pre-European contact times and it was the foundation for the economic development of the region. The fur trade economy was initially controlled by the Anishinabeg Nation who allowed French traders to settle and trade in their territory. As time passed, the Anishinabeg assisted the French in their expansion into the northwestern interior. The Anishinabeg and French fur traders developed a reciprocal relationship that had its roots in the fur trade economy but also transcended into social and cultural aspects of the respective communities. The British traders in Canada who supplanted the French after 1760 initially operated in much the same way as their predecessors. By the end of the eighteenth century, however, the relationship between the Anishinabeg and the newcomers had changed, and the balance of power tipped toward the British. Contributing to this shift was the virulent smallpox epidemic in 1782-83 which caused a significant reduction in the Anishinabeg population. The heavy use of alcohol in the fur trade also contributed to the weakening of the Anishinabeg nation. After the major re-organization of the fur trade in 1821, the activity in and around Fort William declined as other transportation routes by-passed the once busy *entrepôt*. The Lake Superior Treaty of 1850 between the Anishinabeg Nation and the British Crown led to the takeover of traditional lands and resources by the colonial and (after 1867) Canadian government. The traditional fur trade economy was quick to follow as the Canadian government sponsored other developments that effectively squeezed the fur business into the shadows of the developing towns of Fort William and Port Arthur.

NOTES

[1] Jean Morrison, *Superior Rendezvous-Place: Fort William in the Canadian Fur Trade* (Toronto: Natural Heritage Books, 2001), and Carolyn Gilman, *The Grand Portage Story* (St. Paul: Minnesota Historical Society Press and Borealis Books, 1992).

[2] William W. Warren explained that "An-ish-in-aub-ag" meant "original people;" William Warren, *History of the Ojibway People* (reprint of 1885 ed.; St. Paul: Minnesota Historical Society and Borealis Books, 1984), p. 56. Warren, who was an Anishinabe, also used the term, "Ojibway" to describe his people. Today, the terms Anishinabeg and Ojibwa (or Chippewa in the United States) are both commonly used.

[3] Warren, *History of the Ojibway People*, p. 100.

[4] James V. Wright and Roy L. Carlson, "Prehistoric Trade," plate 14, in R. Cole Harris, ed., *Historical Atlas of Canada, Vol. 1: From the Beginning to 1800* (Toronto: University of Toronto Press, 1987), p. 14.

[5] Bruce G. Trigger, *Natives and Newcomers: Canada's 'Heroic Age' Reconsidered* (Montreal and Kingston: McGill-Queen's University Press, 1985), p. 124.

[6] Ibid., p. 128.

[7] Jacques Cartier, *The Voyages of Jacques Cartier*, ed. And trans. H.P. Biggar (Ottawa: Publications of the Public Archives of Canada, No. 11, 1924), pp. 49-57.

[8] For more information on the role of Aboriginal middleman traders, see Arthur J. Ray, *Indians in the Fur Trade: Their Role as Hunters, Trappers and Middlemen in the Lands Southwest of Hudson Bay, 1660-1870* (Toronto: University of Toronto Press, 1974).

[9] These names were used by Europeans to describe the different groups of people they encountered in Great Lakes region. The name "Ojibway," or variations such as Ojibwa or Chippewa, was used to describe the Anishinabeg.

[10] Reuben G. Thwaites, ed., *The Jesuit Relations and Allied Documents*, 71 vols. (Cleveland: Burrows Brothers, 1896-1901), vol. 45, p. 217.

[11] Victor P. Lytwyn, *Muskekowock Athinuwick: Original People of the Great Swampy Land* (Winnipeg: University of Manitoba Press, 2002), pp. 74-79.

[12] Gilles Havard, *The Great Peace of Montreal of 1701: French-Native Diplomacy in the Seventeenth Century,* trans. Phillis Aronoff and Howard Scott (Montreal and Kingston: McGill-Queen's University Press, 2001).

[13] Victor P. Lytwyn, "A Dish with One Spoon: The Shared Hunting Ground Agreement in the Great Lakes and St. Lawrence Valley Region," *Papers of the Twenty-Eighth Algonquian Conference*, ed. David H. Pentland (Winnipeg: University of Manitoba Press, 1997).

[14] *The Works of Samuel de Champlain*, ed. H.P. Biggar, 6 vols. (Toronto: Champlain Society, 1922-1936), vol. 2, p. 19; vol. 3, p. 105.

[15] Conrad E. Heidenreich, "The Great Lakes Basin," plate 35, in Harris, ed., *Historical Atlas of Canada, Vol. 1: From the Beginning to 1800*, p. 35.

[16] Thwaites, ed., *The Jesuit Relations and Allied Documents*, vol. 33, p. 149.

[17] Pierre Esprit Radisson, *The Explorations of Pierre Esprit Radisson, from the Original Manuscript in the Bodleian Library*

and the British Museum, ed. Arthur Adams (Minneapolis: Ross and Haines, 1961) [originally published in 1885], pp. 146-147.

[18] Jean Morrison explained that "Kaministiquia is an Algonquian word spelt and defined in many ways. ...It has been translated as 'meandering river' or 'river of three mouths,' although one Ojibwa man said it means 'a river with many islands covered with low bushes'" (*Superior Rendezvous-Place*, p. 14).

[19] Nicolas Perrot, "Memoir on the Manners, Customs, and Religion of the Savages of North America, in Emma H. Blair, ed. And trans., *Indian Tribes of the Upper Mississippi Valley and Region of the Great Lakes*, vol. 1 (Cleveland: Arthur H. Clark Co., 1911), p. 230.

[20] Frederic Baraga noted that the Ojibway word for marten was wabistan; Baraga, *A Dictionary of the Ojibway Language* (St. Paul: Minnesota Historical Society, 1992) p. 167. Andrew Graham observed that the Hudson Bay Lowland Cree word for marten was "wappestan"; *Andrew Graham's Observations on Hudson's Bay, 1767-1791*, ed. Glyndwr Williams and intro. Richard Glover (London: The Hudson's Bay Record Society, 1969), p. 13.

[21] Pierre Gaultier de Varennes, sieur de La Verendrye, *Journal and Letters of Pierre Gaultier de Varennes de la Verendrye and His Sons*, ed. Lawrence J. Burpee (Toronto: Champlain Society, 1927), p. 101.

[22] Gilman, *The Grand Portage Story*, p. 40.

[23] Ibid., p. 38.

[24] Pontiac did not attend the Niagara Peace Treaty, but he adhered to the treaty in 1766.

[25] Victor P. Lytwyn, *The Fur Trade of the Little North: Indians, Pedlars, and Englishmen East of Lake Winnipeg, 1760-1821* (Winnipeg: Rupert's Land Record Society, 1986), pp. 9-44.

[26] HBCA, B.78/a/7, fol. 24, Gloucester House Journal.

[27] Gilman, *The Grand Portage Story*, p. 64.

[28] Eric W. Morse, *Fur Trade Canoe Routes of Canada: Then and Now* (2nd ed.) (Toronto: University of Toronto Press, 1979), p. 7.

[29] Sir Alexander Mackenzie, *The Journals and Letters of Sir Alexander Mackenzie*, ed. W. Kaye Lamb (Cambridge: Hakluyt Society, 1970), p. 83.

[30] National Archives of Canada (hereafter NAC), "List by Departments of the Proprietors, Clerks, Interpreters, Etc., of the North West Company, 1799," manuscript, MG 19, C 1, vol. 23, p. 5.

[31] HBCA, York Factory Journal, B.239/a/95, fols. 22d and 44d-45.

[32] John Tanner, *A Narrative of the Captivity and Adventures of John Tanner* (reprint of 1830 ed.: Minneapolis: Ross and Haines, 1956), pp. 51-52.

[33] Gilman, *The Grand Portage Story*, p. 89.

[34] Warren, *History of the Ojibway People*, p. 293.

[35] It was estimated that the move from Grand Portage to Kaministiquia cost the NWC 10,000 pounds sterling; Duncan McGillivray, "Some Account of the Trade Carried on by the North West Company," pp. 56-73, in *Report of the Public Archives, Dominion of Canada, for the Year 1928* (Ottawa: King's Printer, 1929), appendix E, p. 70.1929: 70).

[36] Warren, *History of the Ojibway People*, p. 293.

[37] Duncan Cameron, *Les Bourgeois de la Compagnie du Nord-ouest: Recits de voyagers, letters et rapports inedits relatifs au Nord-ouest canadien* (reprint of 1889-1890 ed.: New York: Antiquarian Press, 1960), vol. 2, p. 297.

[38] Frances Simpson, "Journey for Frances," ed. and intro. Grace Lee Nute, *The Beaver* (March, 1954), 15.

[39] Thunder Bay Historical Museum Society Archives (hereafter TBHMS) Fort William HBC Journal, B.4/2/2, p. 60.

[40] John S. Galbraith, "British-American Competition in the Border Fur Trade of the 1820s," *Minnesota History*, 36 (1959), 241-249.

[41] TBHMS, Fort William HBC Journal, B.4/2/2, p. 17.

[42] Jennifer S.H. Brown, *Strangers in Blood: Fur Trade Company Families in Indian Country* (Vancouver: University of British Columbia Press, 1980), p. 51.

[43] Major Joseph Delafield who surveyed the area near Fort William in 1823, noted that "Engagees of the Hudson's Bay Co. when their term of service is expired are called free-men. During their engagements they are slaves in a sense that none but Canadians could endure"; Joseph Delafield, *The Unfortified Boundary*, ed. Robert McElroy and Thomas Riggs (New York: Privately Published, 1943), p. 396.

[44] HBCA, Fort William District Report, B.231/e/3, fol. 4d.

[45] TBHMS, Fort William HBC Journal, B.4/2/2, pp. 17, 31.

⁴⁶Ibid., B.4/2/1, fol. 3.
⁴⁷HBCA, Fort William District Report, B.231/e/1, fol. 2.
⁴⁸Ibid., B.231/e/6, fol. 1.
⁴⁹Ibid., B.231/e/1, fol. 2.
⁵⁰It was customary for Anishinabeg hunting groups to include sons-in-law. A man often hunted to support the parents and family of the wife for some time after marriage.
⁵¹TBHMS, Fort William HBC Journal, B.4/2/1, fol. 17d.
⁵²HBCA, Fort William District Report, B.231/e/6, fol. 1.
⁵³Simpson, "Journey for Frances," p. 15.
⁵⁴TBHMS, Fort William HBC Journal, B.4/2/1, fol. 17.
⁵⁵Ibid., fol. 8d.
⁵⁶Ibid., B.4/2/2, p. 18.
⁵⁷Ibid., p. 23.
⁵⁸John McLoughlin, "The Indians from Fort William to Lake of the Woods," unpublished manuscript in the Masson Papers, Montreal: McGill University, n.d. (typescript copy in the Archives of the Minnesota Historical Society, M1660).
⁵⁹TBHMS, Fort William HBC Journal, B.4/2/2, p. 31
⁶⁰For more details on the role of Aboriginal women in the fur trade economy, see Sylvia Van Kirk, *'Many Tender Ties': Women in Fur-Trade Society, 1670-1870* (Winnipeg: Watson and Dwyer, 1980).
⁶¹TBHMS, Fort William HBC Journal, B.4/2/1, fol. 21d
⁶²Arthur J. Ray, "Some Conservation Schemes of the Hudson's Bay Company, 1821-1850: An Examination of the Problems of Resource Management in the Fur Trade," *Journal of Historical Geography*, no. 1 (1975), 49-68.
⁶³Elizabeth Arthur, ed., *Thunder Bay District, 1821-1892: A Collection of Documents* (Toronto: University of Toronto Press, 1973), pp. 43-52.
⁶⁴Ibid., pp. 13-16.
⁶⁵Olive P. Dickason, *Canada's First Nations: A history of Founding Peoples from Earliest Times* (Toronto: McClelland and Stewart Inc., 1992), p. 253.
⁶⁶"Treaty No. 60 (Robinson-Superior Treaty, 1850)," in *Indian Treaties and Surrenders* (2 vols.; reprint of 1891 ed.; Saskatoon: Fifth House Publishers, 1992), vol. 1, p. 148.
⁶⁷Letter from E. Deacon to P.W. Bell, Michipicoten, dated Fort William, September 26, 1882, unpublished manuscript, Archives of Ontario (hereafter AO), MU 1388, No. 4.
⁶⁸Letter from Thomas Richards to P.W. Bell, Michipicoten, dated Fort William, March 15, 1883, unpublished manuscript, AO, MU 1388, No. 4.
⁶⁹Morrison, *Superior Rendezvous-Place*, p. 130.
⁷⁰Ibid., p. 129.
⁷¹The HBC retail store in the town of Fort William (Thunder Bay in 1970) was sold in 1987 to a new business venture known as The North West Company. That company closed its store in Thunder Bay in 1991 (Jean Morrison, personal communication, 2002).

The Rainy Lake Region in the Fur Trade*
by Theodore Catton with contributions by Marcia Montgomery

Geography of the Fur Trade

Interior waterways formed the highways of commerce throughout the fur trade era and the lay of the land funneled this commerce into a few main channels. As historian Daniel Francis has remarked, the rivalry between the Hudson's Bay Company (HBC) and the North West Company (NWC)

> was not really between two commercial enterprises at all; rather it was a rivalry between two great geographic possibilities. Would the resources of the western hinterland flow southeastward across the Great Lakes and down the Ottawa River to Canada? Or would they take the shorter route north and east through the stunted forest of the Shield to the swampy shores of Hudson Bay?[1]

To these two possibilities could be added a third. If the political history of North America had been different, the furs might have moved southward through the Mississippi Valley. The Rainy Lake Region was contested terrain in the fur trade largely because it was a key to all three geographic possibilities.

French Trade and Exploration, 1688-1763

The first French trader to reach the Rainy Lake Region was probably Jacques de Noyon, a native of Three Rivers in the St. Lawrence Valley. An independent trader, Noyon appears to have had no official backing for his exploration. In 1688, he ascended the Kaministiquia River to Dog Lake, then to Lac des Milles Lacs and the maze of lakes and rivers leading to Rainy Lake, where he passed the winter. At Rainy Lake he learned from Indians, probably Assiniboine, of a large lake to the west (Lake of the Woods) and a river that flowed from that lake to the Western Sea (or Pacific Ocean), across which lay the fabled riches of Asia. Although Noyon's account had no immediate effect with French officialdom, it steadily gained force through the subsequent travels of numerous adventurers between Lake Superior and Lake of the Woods. Noyon's account finally surfaced nearly thirty years later in a report by the Governor of New France to Duke Philippe of Orleans, regent of France during the minority of Louis XV. They argued that the route pioneered by Noyon showed promise for discovering the long-sought Northwest Passage to the Western Sea which would provide an assumed easy and short access to the Orient.[2]

Vaudreuil and Bégon's report was timely. By the Treaty of Utrecht of 1713, France acceded to Britain's sovereignty over Hudson Bay and yielded posts it had earlier captured from the Hudson's Bay Company. If France were to gain the upper hand in the fur trade of North America's Northwest (the *pays d'en haut*), it would have to get there by way of the Great Lakes or the Mississippi Valley. Thus, the search for the Western Sea offered the inviting prospect of loosening Britain's ties with the Indians who inhabited the interior and who travelled great distances to trade with the British at their forts on Hudson Bay.[3]

The Council of Marine gave Governor Vaudreuil orders to proceed. A chain of posts would be established to support exploration. About fifty men in seven or eight canoes would proceed to Lake Superior, build a new fort on the Kaministiquia to replace the abandoned fort built by Dulhut in 1783, and perhaps a second one at Rainy Lake. Half of the party would occupy the posts; the other half would search for the route to the Western Sea. The posts themselves would be financed by the fur trade, while the government of France would pay for the actual expedition of discovery. "This arrangement was an important one," writes one historian, "and shows better than anything else how the fur trade and the work of exploration were inextricably interwoven."[4]

The leader of this expedition was an officer named Zacharie Robutel de la Noüe. He set out from Montreal

---

*Extracted from Chapter 1, "Special History: The Environment and the Fur Trade Experience in Voyageurs National Park, 1730-1870". Unpublished special history report prepared for Midwest Region, National Park Service by Historical Research Associates, Missoula, Montana, July 2000. (For complete original text see *www.nps.gov/voya/study1*) Copyright reserved. Published here with permission.

in 1717 and erected a fort near the mouth of the Kaministiquia.[5] Apparently he did not succeed in establishing a post at Rainy Lake owing, it seems, to hostilities in the area between the Sioux (or Dakota) and the Cree.[6] After four years of fruitless efforts at diplomacy, Nouë resigned his post. For the next decade and a half, interest in the *postes du nord* and the search for the Western Sea languished.

The project was renewed due largely to the efforts and enthusiasm of one man, Pierre Gaultier de Varennes, Sieur de la Vérendrye. Driven by a thirst for discovery, and glory, more than a desire to obtain riches in the fur trade, La Vérendrye shrewdly blended the two in order to gain the support of the governor of New France. The two aims were less compatible than La Vérendrye supposed, however, and his explorations would be increasingly subordinated to the demands of returning a profit to his creditors in Montreal.

La Vérendrye left Montreal with his three sons, a nephew, and about fifty soldiers and voyageurs in 1731, arriving at the mouth of the Kaministiquia River later that summer. La Vérendrye stopped there with the bulk of his men, who were bordering on mutiny, and sent his nephew, Sieur de la Jémeraye, with an advance party to Rainy Lake (or Lac La Pluie, as it was known to the French). After passing the winter at Kaministiquia, La Vérendrye joined his nephew in 1732 at their new post near the outlet of Lac La Pluie. La Jémeraye named it Fort St. Pierre in honor of his uncle.[7]

In 1732, La Vérendrye established a strong post on the west shore of Lake of the Woods (or Lac des Bois), called Fort St. Charles. From there he sent one of his sons to choose a site for another fort near where the Red River empties into Lake Winnipeg. In succeeding years, forts were established there and at the confluence of the Assiniboine and Red rivers. As historian E. E. Rich remarks, these posts "clearly marked the fact that La Vérendrye had opened up durable communications between Montreal, Lake Superior and Lake Winnipeg."[8]

Another key to La Vérendrye's position was his desire to stay on friendly terms with the Sioux. This powerful nation occupied the head of the Mississippi Valley and ranged as far north as the Rainy Lake region. Sioux neutrality was critical to the French as the latter struggled to maintain peace with the Fox in present-day Wisconsin. The Sioux, for their part, were anxious that the French traders should not aid their own enemies,

Fort Frances, 1857, by Henry Youles Hind [From his Narrative of the Canadian Red River Exploring Expedition of 1857*] Fort Lac La Pluie (Rainy Lake) was re-named Fort Frances in honour of Lady Frances Simpson, the wife of Sir George Simpaon. The newly weds stopped over at the post in 1830 on their way to Lower Fort Garry. Grace Lee Nute,* Rainy River Country *(St. Paul: 1950), p. 26-27.*

the Cree and Ojibwa.[9]

The French advance into the Rainy Lake region and the country around Lake Winnipeg met with a sad reverse in 1736. It was intended that La Jémeraye lead an expedition southwestward to the territory of the Mandan tribe, but in May he died mysteriously near Lake of the Woods. Soon thereafter, a canoe party of 21 men, led by a priest and La Vérendrye's oldest son, were massacred on an island in Lake of the Woods, probably by Sioux who mistrusted the French traders' friendly relations with the Cree and Ojibwa.

Despite his severe personal loss, La Vérendrye did not give up his search for the Western Sea, but his exploits turned increasingly to improving relations with the Indians in order to keep the men in his forts supplied with food and to satisfy the merchants in Montreal. In 1742, he mounted a final expedition southwestward under the command of his remaining two sons; possibly they reached the foot of the Rockies although it seems more likely that they got only as far as the Black Hills. La Vérendrye retired in 1744 and died in Montreal in December of that year while making plans to explore the upper Saskatchewan River.[10]

With the outbreak of the Seven Years War in 1754, the period of French activity in the Rainy Lake Region came to an end. France abandoned its chain of western forts stretching from Rainy Lake to the Saskatchewan, and by the Treaty of Paris of 1763 surrendered all of its claim in North America. For about thirty years, however, France had challenged England's hold on the fur trade around Hudson Bay with its daring explorer/traders in the interior and its naval forces on the Bay. The western forts, the Hudson's Bay Company historian E. E. Rich has written, "made Rainy Lake and Lake of the Woods into French inland seas and diverted much of the furs of the Assiniboine and the Saskatchewan from Hudson Bay to the St. Lawrence."[11] The French thrust foreshadowed the North West Company's challenge to the Hudson's Bay Company monopoly in the period 1790-1821.

RISE OF THE NORTH WEST COMPANY, 1763-1793

The 1760s and 1770s were a time of transition in the fur trade. The area north of the Ohio River and east of the Mississippi River became part of British America, while the area west of the Mississippi River (Louisiana) passed to Spanish dominion. Nevertheless, traders of French extraction (known as "Canadians") still dominated the fur trade throughout this vast territory. Even after the former French forts were closed, the Canadians continued to winter in the region, returning east to Montreal or south to Louisiana each summer to sell their furs and obtain new provisions.[12]

An increasing number of independent British traders also entered the business. Mostly of Scottish extraction, they were called "pedlars" by officials of the Hudson's Bay Company because they followed the French pattern of taking goods to the Indians rather than making the Indians travel to their trading posts. The competition between Canadian and British traders based in Montreal in this period has been documented through an examination of traders' licenses issued by the governor of Quebec.

While licensed Canadian traders outnumbered British by more than four to one, the British traders generally worked in partnerships or combinations, listed larger numbers of canoes per license, and operated farther west where the fur returns were greatest. "Probably the reason for the success of the British in these far fields," writes one historian, "lay in their ability to command more capital than the French traders."[13] A trip to the Northwest in this period was generally a three-year undertaking. Getting outfitted at Montreal or Michilimackinac, a trader transported goods in the first season by large canoe as far as the western end of Lake Superior, wintering either at Grand Portage or Rainy Lake. During the second summer, he might travel the waterways in the region around Lake Winnipeg or establish a post in some central location. Thus, he would not have furs to transport back to Montreal until his third season in the Northwest. Since the trader obtained his goods on credit, he required business connections with substantial creditors in order to reach so far into the interior. Creditors included people of rank in Montreal and Quebec--mostly British who enjoyed the patronage of British rule.[14]

These conditions laid the foundation for the rise of the North West Company. Perhaps the Company's most important innovation, other than its securing of a near monopoly on trade, was to establish a great supply depot at Grand Portage. By outfitting the trader at the west end of Lake Superior instead of at Michilimackinac or Montreal, the trader could get far up the Saskatchewan or into the Athabaska region by his first winter and return to Grand Portage with his packs of fur in the following summer. Peter Pond first demonstrated the advantage of such a forward supply base when he boldly outfitted from Grand Portage in 1776. Three years later he brought out more than 80,000 fine beaver skins from the Athabaska region, convincing the partners in the newly formed North West Company that opening up the Athabaska region should be their ultimate goal.[15]

After the establishment of a fort at Grand Portage, the next important development in this long-distance supply line was the establishment of an advance depot at Rainy Lake. The North West Company established a fort near the falls below the outlet of Rainy Lake in 1787.[16] The rendezvous at Rainy Lake saved the men who were stationed in the interior three to four weeks of toil across the "height of land" separating the inland waterways of the Northwest from the Great Lakes/St. Lawrence River basin. Since the rivers and lakes in the Athabaska region were only ice-free and navigable from the middle of May to the middle of October, this extra time effectively allowed the North West Company to station its wintering men that much farther north and west. Consequently, two wintering partners, Peter Pond and Alexander Mackenzie, reorganized the Athabaska department in the winter of 1787-88. Henceforth, operations in the Athabaska region centered at Fort Chipewyan on the shore of Lake Athabaska. (From here, Mackenzie departed on his first great voyage of discovery down the Mackenzie River to the Arctic Ocean in 1789. Four years later in 1793, he undertook his second great journey up the Peace River and over the Rockies to the Pacific Ocean.).[17]

As the North West Company consolidated its hold on the Northwest and reaped a huge reward in furs, Hudson's Bay Company men saw their own influence over Ojibwa, Cree, and Chipewyan groups grow increasingly tenuous. Looking for a weakness in their rival's operation, they found it in the North West Company's long supply line. Their point of attack was the country from Rainy Lake to Lake Winnipeg, which the Hudson's Bay Company could reach by way of the Albany and English rivers.

The North West Company and the Hudson's Bay Company, 1793-1821

From 1793 to 1821, the North West Company and the Hudson's Bay Company were locked in a bitter struggle for supremacy. In the course of this struggle, the Rainy Lake Region acquired strategic importance beyond its value for furs. The Hudson's Bay Company sought to replace its rival as the main trading partner with the Indians around Rainy Lake, and thereby render this key post on the voyageur route from Grand Portage to Fort Chipewyan untenable for the North West Company. Sharp competition for the Indian trade affected the fur companies' relations with the Indians, generally making conditions worse for the Indians. It also exacerbated differences between Hudson's Bay Company men and North West Company men, who were already separated by ethnicity and contrasting company cultures.

If the Hudson's Bay Company had the advantage of being able to supply its forts on Hudson Bay by sea, the upstart North West Company made the most of its long, tenuous, river-born transportation network. By 1795, the North West Company controlled an estimated 11/14 of the fur trade in Canada. Independent traders held another 1/14, and the Hudson's Bay Company was reduced to a modest 2/14.[18] As early as 1774, Hudson's Bay Company men realized the need to push inland with their own trading posts. They built Cumberland House on the lower Saskatchewan River and other posts, including Osnaburgh House on Lake St. Joseph in 1786. This latter opened the route from Hudson Bay to Lake of the Woods via the Albany and English rivers. It also gave them a purchase on the Indian trade around Lake Nipigon, north of Lake Superior.[19] This was as far south as the Hudson's Bay Company advanced until 1793, when it dispatched John McKay to the Rainy Lake Region.

During his four years in the Rainy Lake Region, McKay recorded day-to-day events in the post journal.[20] His narrative has been summarized both by Grace Lee Nute in *Rainy River Country* and by A. M. Johnson in "Hudson's Bay Company on Rainy River, 1793-95."[21] McKay and his men struggled through two winters as they learned where to fish, traded with the Indians for moose and deer meat, and made a modest start in cultivating a garden. A friendly but insistent rivalry developed between McKay and the North West Company trader, Charles Boyer, whose Fort Lac La Pluie was located only a short distance away. Their men played football, celebrated

Thomas Selkirk, fifth Earl of Selkirk. From a portrait ascribed to Raeburn. TBHMS 972.2.324 (Original: NAC C-1346)

Christmas and New Years, and occasionally extended a helping hand to each other. Meanwhile, Boyer tried to deceive McKay about where to find Indians, and McKay attempted a ruse to get Boyer to build his new post behind his own on the path most often used by trading Indians, but neither man was able to fool the other. This quaint interaction by two unusually civilized traders belied the vicious competition that would develop over the next two decades.

The North West Company contended with internal division as well as external competition. The most serious internal division among the Nor'Westers involved Sir Alexander Mackenzie, the partner who reached the Arctic Ocean in 1789 and the Pacific in 1793. In 1799, he departed the company acrimoniously and left for Britain where he published his *Voyages from Montreal* and received a knighthood. In 1800 Mackenzie became a shareholder in the New North West Company. Founded by disgruntled Nor'westers in 1798 to oppose the North West Company, the New Company was popularly known as the XY Company for the "XY" brand used on its packs of furs. For over four year years ruthless competition and violence prevailed between the two Montreal-based firms until financial losses on both sides forced the contenders to unite in November 1804.[22]

The competition between the Hudson's Bay Company, the North West Company and the XY Company was demonstrated through the rapid proliferation of trading posts all over the Indian Country in the 1790s and 1800s. Several posts appeared along the eastern end of the Grand Portage-Rainy Lake route, including an XY fort.[23] Although the Hudson's Bay Company abandoned its trading house below the outlet of Rainy Lake about 1797, two rival posts were there in 1804 when the Nor'wester Hugh Faries visited a post owned by the XY Company.[24] The year before the North West Company relocated its great wilderness depot at Grand Portage to Kaministiquia (named Fort William in 1807). About the same time it established a subpost at Little Vermilion or Crane Lake where Dr. John McLoughlin served as trader in 1811. The physician at Fort William each summer, McLoughlin wintered as a clerk in the Rainy Lake District most years from 1805 to 1814 when he assumed charge of the District as its wintering partner.[25]

Historian Daniel Francis has remarked that the Hudson's Bay Company and the North West Company were as different "as two trading companies possibly could be."[26] They were organized differently, their employees were of different ethnic and religious backgrounds, and they took different approaches toward trade with the Indians.

These differences in social patterns played an important role in the conflict between the two companies over the Red River colony deeded by the Hudson's Bay Company to its major shareholder, Lord Selkirk, in 1811. Selkirk's settlers would include destitute Scots and Irishmen as well as retired Hudson's Bay Company servants, of mostly British descent, and their mixed-blood families. Meanwhile, the North West Company also recognized the growing need to provide some form of support for its retired employees, mostly French Canadian, and their native dependents, the *Métis*. A plan to develop a retirement settlement for these mixed-blood families at Rainy Lake failed to materialize, and instead *Métis* settlements arose along the Red River.[27]

Named Assiniboia, Selkirk's Red River Settlement covered 116,000 square miles and stretched from Lake

Winnipeg to the headwaters of the Red River in present-day North Dakota. Never had the North West Company's long supply line through the Rainy Lake Region been so vulnerable. Indeed, so close was the Rainy Lake Region to the colony that people traversed the intervening country by two main routes: by canoe down Rainy River to Lake of the Woods and thence up the Winnipeg River, and overland by way of the Warroad River, then a portage and the Roseau River to the Red River.[28] When Selkirk's settlers began arriving by way of Hudson Bay at the Red River colony in 1811, friction soon developed between the North West Company's buffalo hunters, the *Métis,* and the new colonists.

Tensions mounted following the so-called "Pemmican Proclamation" of 1814 which forbade the export of pemmican from the colony. (Pemmican, or pounded buffalo meat, provisioned the North West Company's western canoe brigades). A period of strife culminated in the "Massacre of Seven Oaks" in which the colony's new governor, Robert Semple and twenty-two settlers died at the hands of the *Métis*. To reassert control in the Red River colony, Lord Selkirk employed demobilized mercenaries of the Swiss De Meuron and the De Watteville regiments which had fought in the War of 1812. While en route to the Red River with his military reinforcements in 1816, Selkirk learned of the massacre and directed his party across Lake Superior to the Kaministiquia River where his forces captured Fort William, the North West Company's inland headquarters.[29]

From Fort William a detachment continued westward to the North West Company post at Rainy Lake. Grace Lee Nute describes what followed:

> Peter Fidler was in charge of the attacking party at Rainy Lake late in 1816. The first attempt was unsuccessful, for when Fidler called upon the clerk in charge, J. W. Dease, to surrender, the latter refused. Fidler, lacking men to enforce his demand, returned to Fort William, secured more soldiers, two fieldpieces, and Captain D'Orsonnens, and returned to invest and blockade the fort. As Dease had only seven men with him, all depending on fishing and gathering wild rice for subsistence, he was forced to yield.[30]

Thanks to intervention by the British Government, Selkirk gave up Fort William in 1817 and moved on to the Red River where he re-established his colony. The North West Company regained its post at Rainy Lake, but the Hudson's Bay Company established its own post in the region it had abandoned nearly twenty years earlier.[31] In an effort to restore harmony, Selkirk negotiated with the Catholic Church in Québec to send a mission to the Red River settlements by way of Rainy Lake. As his colonists were predominantly Catholic, Selkirk shrewdly calculated that the Catholic priests would reduce friction between them and the Catholic *Métis*.[32] This initiative resulted in brief Catholic missions to Rainy Lake itself in 1816-18.

The points of conflict between the two great fur companies continued from the courts in Montreal along North West Company's supply line as far as the Athabaska country. Charges against Lord Selkirk himself were still pending when Selkirk died of illness in 1820. The Nor'Westers, alarmed and disgusted by all the strife, finally negotiated a merger with the Hudson's Bay Company in 1821.[33]

The Hudson's Bay Company and the American Fur Company, 1821-1842

The union of the Hudson's Bay Company and the North West Company in 1821 brought an end to the competition and strife that had racked the fur trade in Canada for more than two decades. While the merger secured the HBC monopoly from Hudson Bay to Lake Athabaska and the Pacific Ocean, the company still faced competition along the international boundary with the United States. Nowhere was the threat of competition more significant than at Rainy Lake where the old NWC post came under HBC control. Under the aggressive leadership of George Simpson, who joined the company in 1820 and quickly established himself as its guiding force, the Hudson's Bay Company recognized two sources of competition in the Rainy Lake Region: independent traders and the American Fur Company.[34]

The most important independent trader in the area was George Johnston. Based in Sault Saint Marie (U.S.A.), Johnston established two posts in the Rainy Lake Region in 1821. One post was on Little Vermilion Lake (Crane Lake) in American territory and the other on Mille Lacs in British territory. Johnston put in charge of these posts one Joseph Cadotte and two men by the name of Paul and Bazil Beaulieu. The Hudson's Bay

Company took stern measures to eliminate these competitors, first trading with the Indians for such bargain prices that they would not have any dealings with Johnston's men, and then purchasing all the wild rice around Rainy Lake in order to starve them out. Cadotte's force at Mille Lacs was attacked by Indians and driven back to American territory. Beaulieu's force, augmented by Cadotte's when they were already short of provisions, soon began to desert him. By 1823, Beaulieu himself and his handful of followers were starving. By the following year, Johnston's traders appear to have abandoned the Rainy Lake Region.[35]

The Hudson's Bay Company had a more formidable rival in the American Fur Company. Founded by New York financier John Jacob Astor in 1808, the AFC operated under a different system from either the Hudson's Bay Company or the North West Company. Astor acted as the importing and selling agent for the company, which in turn served as liaison to the traders in the field. Each trader was assigned a department, or "outfit." The American Fur Company tried to minimize competition among its own traders, but was never completely successful.[36]

Historian David Lavender argues that the chief difference between the American Fur Company and its northern rivals––its lack of monopoly control––was due primarily to geography. In Canada the few constricted routes of long-distance trade abetted monopoly, whereas in the United States the opposite was true. Three major routes to the interior were available to the Americans: the Hudson and Mohawk valleys (aided by the Erie Canal after its completion in 1825), the Ohio River, and the Mississippi River. Steamboats aided use of the latter. By 1823, steamboats navigated the Mississippi River as far north as present-day Minneapolis. "Only where a single trade artery dominated a large region, as in the case of the Missouri River," Lavender observes, "did any department of the American Fur Company approach economic dominance." Geography was a deterrent to monopoly in the United States for another reason, too. In the warmer latitudes of the United States, white settlement encroached on the fur trade more readily than it did in British North America. Frontier settlement increased the opportunities for independent traders.[37]

The American Fur Company established posts at Grand Portage, Rainy Lake, Vermilion Lake (not to be confused with Little Vermilion or Crane Lake), and Warroad during the winter of 1822-23. These were all in the Fond du Lac Department, which extended west from Lake Superior along the international boundary. By then, traders generally recognized the old voyageur route from Grand Portage via Basswood Lake as the international boundary. However, the route would not be officially surveyed until 1823 nor finally settled until the Webster-Ashburton Treaty of 1842. Although the U.S. Congress passed a law in 1816 prohibiting British trade with Indians on American soil, Hudson's Bay Company men practically ignored the law in the Rainy Lake Region throughout the 1820s.[38]

The American Fur Company's trader was William Morrison, a former clerk of the North West Company and in George Simpson's judgment, "one of the best and most experienced Salteaux traders in the country."[39] After he retired in 1826, the trade was handled by William Aitken, head trader of the Fond du Lac Department. The Hudson's Bay Company's trader in charge of the Rainy Lake District in 1822-23 was Chief Factor Dr. John McLoughlin, a capable administrator with prior experience in that region under the North West Company. "The choice of McLoughlin," writes historian John S. Galbraith, "was in accord with a basic principle of the Hudson's Bay Company's trading policy that the most energetic and effective officers were sent to areas where the opposition was most severe."[40] Further evidence of the importance that the company attached to the Rainy Lake District, Galbraith notes, is the fact that Chief Trader Simon McGillivray, Jr. was appointed as McLoughlin's assistant, putting two commissioned officers in one small district. In 1824, McLoughlin departed for Oregon and Chief Factor John Dugald Cameron took his place at Rainy Lake. Cameron remained at Rainy Lake until 1830. Although Cameron was friendly toward his rival, William Morrison, he continued the Hudson's Bay Company policy of competitive trading in order to drive the American traders out of the area.

The competition was finally too costly for the American Fur Company. In 1833, Simpson entered an agreement with Aitken. In return for a payment of 300 pounds sterling per year, the American Fur Company agreed to abandon its frontier posts from Lake Superior to the Red River. The agreement of 1833 gave the Hudson's Bay Company monopoly control over the Rainy Lake Region for nearly a decade. When the American Fur Company failed in 1842, it brought renewed competition along the international boundary.

Last years of the Fur Trade, 1842-1870

In the period after 1842, the fur trade in the Rainy Lake Region was increasingly shaped by national developments on either side of the international boundary. On the American side, the growth of settlement and transportation gave independent traders greater ability to challenge the dominance of larger trading outfits. Generally this competition from independent traders acted to the detriment of the Indians and the resource because small traders preferred quick gains over steady returns. Moreover, U.S. Indian policy, which forced tribes to cede most of their lands in exchange for reservations and annuity payments, severely compromised the Indians' ability to hunt and trap. Meanwhile, on the Canadian side, the Hudson's Bay Company remained the only governing body for white-Indian relations throughout British America from the prairie to the Rocky Mountains, and it retained a virtual monopoly. It tried to make the most of its monopoly by implementing measures to conserve the fur resources. The growth of settlement and transportation eventually affected the fur trade north of the border, too, however.

Although the Hudson's Bay Company faced little pressure from white settlement in the region after the union of 1821, fur resources were depleted after years of struggle with the North West Company. As early as 1822, George Simpson sought to implement conservation measures to allow fur-bearer populations a chance to recover. These measures included extending the fur trade into new territories, eliminating posts in depleted areas, encouraging Indians to hunt species other than beaver, discouraging Indians from taking "summer" beaver, eliminating the use of steel traps and castoreum, and introducing a quota system for beaver.[41]

These early efforts largely failed in the Rainy Lake Region because of competition with the Americans and the *Métis*. Moreover, Indians in the Rainy Lake Region and elsewhere in Canada tended to resist the company's conservation measures because they did not understand them. The Indians believed the abundance or scarcity of animals depended on various manitos, or spirits, who controlled the success of their hunts. They also lacked a system of land tenure that recognized property rights, and their political organization did not permit effective sanctions against trespass.[42]

The Hudson's Bay Company embarked on another conservation program in 1841. It was based on a strict quota system that set a limit on each post's fur returns. Any post trader who did not respect the quota would be retired from the company. Such a policy demonstrated the advantage of monopoly, and after a three-year trial period the quota system appeared to produce results. Beaver populations recovered in many areas, and the quotas were relaxed.[43]

Despite this success, the Hudson's Bay Company faced new difficulties by the mid-1840s. As the supply of beaver recovered, the price of beaver pelts fell. Silk generally replaced beaver felt as the material of choice for men's quality hats. Moreover, the Hudson's Bay Company was unable to prevent independent traders from making inroads in the Red River area. Improvements in transportation between Minnesota and the Red River settlements assured a vigorous independent trade in skins and furs, particularly buffalo robes. By 1856, shipments of furs from Pembina and Red River through St. Paul included, according to one statement, "64,292 rats; 8,276 minks; 1,428 martens; 876 foxes; 3,600 coons; 1,045 fishers; …7,500 buffalo robes" and other furs, valued at $97,000.[44]

The growing commercial ties between the Red River settlements and American communities south of the border led to a Canadian expedition in 1857 aimed at locating an overland transportation route north of the international boundary from Upper Canada [Ontario] to the West. The expedition's leader was Henry Hind and its surveyor was Simon J. Dawson. The latter recommended a land and water route from a point on the north shore of Lake Superior near Fort William to the south shore of Lake Winnipeg at Fort Garry. Before anything more was done with this plan, the economic "panic" of 1857 temporarily dampened government interest.[45] In 1868, one year after confederation, the Canadian government organized a second expedition to develop a connecting road to the West, based on Dawson's plan. Dawson began work that year with a crew of 800 labourers. The following year, the government purchased Rupert's Land from the Hudson's Bay Company, clearing the way for the creation of the new province of Manitoba.[46]

When the *Métis* of the Red River country rebelled against this annexation, the young Canadian government faced its baptism by fire. In 1870, it sent the Red River Expedition, a mixed force of Canadian and British soldiers and voyageurs, over the uncompleted land and water road to restore order.[47] The movement of so many men and supplies over the voyageur route was unprecedented. The road, as much as the expedition itself, marked a kind of conquest of the wilderness in the Rainy Lake Region. The road was opened to civilian traffic on June 15, 1871 and by October 1873 it had carried some 2,739 people, of whom 805 were settlers. By 1871, a steam-powered tug was hauling passengers between Kettle Falls and Rainy Lake, marking another significant turning point in the Rainy Lake fur trade.[48]

NOTES

Since some passages in Theodore Catton's report have been omitted, the relevant endnotes to these passages are also omitted and in a few cases, the sequence of the paragraphs has been altered. The Hudson's Bay Company Archives references are to research notes taken at the HBCA by Tom Thiessen, Archeologist, National Park Service, Midwest Archeological Center.

[1] Daniel Francis, "Traders and Indians," in *The Prairie West: Historical Readings*, eds., R. Douglas Francis and Howard Palmer (Edmonton: Pica Pica Press, 1985), p. 58.

[2] Nellis M. Crouse, *La Vérendrye, Fur Trader and Explorer* (Ithaca: Cornell University Press, 1956), pp. 6-8.

[3] Crouse, *La Vérendrye*, p. 8.

[4] Crouse, *La Vérendrye*, p. 9.

[5] E. E. Rich, *Hudson's Bay Company, 1670-1870*, vol. 1 (Toronto: McClelland and Stewart Ltd., 1960), p. 515. Rich states that the post existed since 1713, and "transformed into a strong fort" in 1717.

[6] Crouse, *La Vérendrye*, p. 9; David Lavender cites "perennial warfare between the Sioux and Ojibwas" in *Winner Take All: The Trans-Canada Canoe Trail* (New York: McGraw-Hill Book Company, 1977), p. 170.

[7] Grace Lee Nute, *Rainy River Country* (St. Paul: Minnesota Historical Society, 1950), p. 6. Also see, Lawrence J. Burpee, ed., *Pierre Gaultier de Varennes de La Vérendrye, Journals and Letters* (Toronto: The Champlain Society, 1927).

[8] Rich, *Hudson's Bay Company*, vol. 1, p. 518.

[9] Louise Phelps Kellogg, *The French Régime in Wisconsin and the Northwest* (Madison: State Historical Society of Wisconsin, 1925), pp. 336-337. Also see Rhoda R. Gilman, "The Fur Trade in the Upper Mississippi Valley, 1630-1850," *Wisconsin Magazine of History* 58 (Autumn 1974), pp. 3-18.

[10] Rich, *Hudson's Bay Company*, vol. 1, pp. 520-523.

[11] Rich, *Hudson's Bay Company*, vol. 1, p. 524.

[12] Gilman, "The Fur Trade in the Upper Mississippi Valley," pp. 8-9. According to Duncan McGillivray (1807), "Montreal was taken in 1760 and in the Spring of the following year some English & French traders sent goods to Lake Superior, and a few went even as far north as the Rainy Lake where they continued until 1763 when the Post at Michilimackinac was taken by the Indians; who from affection to their ancient allies the French, and instigated by some traders who as well as the savages were unwilling to recognize the Capitulation, made between the French and English commanders, made war on all the posts occupied by the British from Niagara to La Baye—Sir Alexander Mackenzie says the trade did not recommence until 1766." In "Some Account of the Trade Carried on by the North West Company," in *Report of the Public Archives for the year 1928*, Arthur G. Doughty, ed. (Ottawa, 1929), p. 59.

[13] Louise Phelps Kellogg, *The British Régime in Wisconsin and the Northwest* (Madison: State Historical Society of Wisconsin, 1935)., pp. 103.

[14] Kellogg, *The British Régime*, pp. 103-104; Rich, *The History of the Hudson's Bay Company*, vol. 2, (London: The Hud-

[15] Gregg A. Young, "The Organization of the Transfer of Furs at Fort William: A Study of Historical Geography," Thunder Bay Historical Museum Society *Papers and Records* (1974), pp. 30-31.

[14 cont.] son's Bay Record Society, 1959), pp. 28-29. Note that French and British traders working in the Upper Mississippi Valley at this time tended to return east or south each summer to exchange their furs for new supplies. See Gilman, "The Fur Trade in the Upper Mississippi Valley", p. 9.

[16] Lavender, *Winner Take All*, p. 245. It is possible that the post was already eight or nine years old in 1787.

[17] Young, "The Organization of the Transfer of Furs at Fort William," p. 32. Young provides an excellent discussion of the number of days required on each leg of this complicated relay system. Lavender, *Winner Take All*, p. 245; Innis, *The Fur Trade in Canada*, pp. 200-201.

[18] Harold A. Innis, *The Fur Trade in Canada (New Haven: Yale University Press, 1962)* p. 258.

[19] Gordon Charles Davidson, *The North West Company* (Berkeley: University of California Press, 1918), p. 69. On the Hudson's Bay Company's strategy in pushing south, see Harry W. Duckworth, "The Madness of Donald Mackay," *The Beaver* 68, no. 3 (1988), pp. 25-42; and John Jackson, "Inland from the Bay," *The Beaver* 72 no. 1 (1992), pp. 37-42.

[20] John McKay, Lac La Pluie Post Journals for 1793-1794, 1794-1795, 1795-1796, and 1796-1797, Hudson's Bay Company Archives (HBCA), B.105/a/1-4.

[21] Nute, *Rainy River Country*, pp. 15-16; A. M. Johnson, "Hudson's Bay Company on Rainy River, 1793-95," *The Naturalist* (1961), pp. 9-14.

[22] Davidson, *The North West Company*, pp. 76-78, 89. See also W. Kaye Lamb, ed., *The Journals and Letters of Sir Alexander Mackenzie* (Cambridge: Hakluyt Society Extra Series No. 41, 1970).

[23] Grace Lee Nute, "Posts in the Minnesota Fur-Trading Area, 1660-1855," *Minnesota History* (December 1930), p. 357.

[24] Nute, *Rainy River Country*, p. 17.

[25] Nute, "Posts in the Minnesota Fur-Trading Area, 1660-1855," p. 360.

[26] Francis, "Traders and Indians," p. 59.

[27] Sylvia Van Kirk, *Many Tender Ties: Women in Fur-Trade Society, 1670-1870* (Norman: University of Oklahoma Press, 1976), p. 51.

[28] Nute, *Rainy River Country*, p. 20.

[29] E. E. Rich, *The Fur Trade and the North West to 1857* (Toronto: McClelland and Stewart Limited, 1967), pp. 209-235.

[30] Nute, *Rainy River Country*, p. 31.

[31] Robert M. Ballantyne, *Hudson's Bay; or Every-day Life in the Wilds of North America* (Edinburgh: 1848), pp. 239-240.

[32] Grace L. Nute, *The Voyageur* (New York and London: 1931), p. 27.

[33] Garry, "Diary of Nicholas Garry," p. 122.

[34] Donald McKay, Journal kept by Donald McKay on a trip to Rainy Lake in 1792, HBCA, B.3/a/93b, fo. 10-10d.

[35] William Sinclair, Lac La Pluie Post Journal for 1834-1835, HBCA, B.105/a/19, fo.9.

[36] Lavender, "Some American Characteristics of the American Fur Company," pp. 36-37.

[37] John L. Bigsby, *The Shoe and Canoe Canoe, or Pictures of Travel in the Canadas*. 2 vols. (London: 1850), p. 242.

[38] Garry, "Diary of Nicholas Garry," p. 123.

[39] Henry Nash Smith, *Virgin Land: The American West as Symbol and Myth* (Cambridge: Harvard University Press, 1950); Hans Huth, *Nature and the American: Three Centuries of Changing Attitudes* (Berkeley: University of California Press, 1957); Leo Marx, *The Machine in the Garden: Technology and the Pastoral Ideal in America* (New York: Oxford University Press, 1964).

[40] Delafield, *The Unfortified Boundary*, p. 426; Bigsby, *The Shoe and Canoe*, p. 270; Sir George Simpson, *Narrative of a Journey Round the World during the years 1841 and 1842*, 2 vols. (London: 1847), p. 35; Garry, "Diary of Nicholas Garry," p. 124; Ballantyne, *Hudson's Bay; or Every-day Life*, p. 237; cited in *The Journal of Duncan M'Gillivray*, p. 9.

[41] Arthur J. Ray, "Some Conservation Schemes of the Hudson's Bay Company, 1821-1850: An Examination of the Problems of Resource Management in the Fur Trade," *Journal of Historical Geography* 1 (1975), p. 50.

[42] Ray, "Some Conservation Schemes," pp. 57-58. For a recent overview of Indian conservation practices in the fur trade, see Shepard Krech III, *The Ecological Indian: Myth and History* (New York: W. W. Norton, 1999), pp. 173-209.

[43] Ray, "Some Conservation Schemes," pp. 63-65.

[44] Quoted in Innis, *The Fur Trade in Canada*, pp. 330-331.

[45] Jack Manore, "Mr. Dawson's Road," *The Beaver* (February/March 1991), p. 6.

[46] Manore, "Mr. Dawson's Road," p. 6.
[47] Manore, "Mr. Dawson's Road," p. 7.
[48] Tom Thiessen notes of "Journal" of Colonel Thomas Scott, November 23, 1871, Provincial Archives of Manitoba.

Part Three
Transportation and Logistics

Part Three - Transportation and Logistics

Geography played an huge part in determining the fate of the North West Company and its inland headquarters at Fort William. The Nor'westers' costly, over-extended transportation system that stretched from the Gulf of St. Lawrence to the Pacific Ocean laid the foundation for the future Dominion of Canada, proclaimed Harold A. Innis. The Company, however, had no sentimental attachment to its far-flung, interconnecting, trans-continental, fresh water highway. It fought long and hard to gain shipping rights on Hudson Bay, that body of seawater thrust deep into the heart of its inland trading operations. Its only recourse lay in merging with the Hudson's Bay Company in 1821 but in so doing the North West Company lost more than its name.

Today similar problems of distance bedevil the St. Lawrence Seaway and the Port of Thunder Bay on Lake Superior. Competition from Hudson Bay still prevails for the same reasons as in the days of the North West Company. "Using the Port of Churchill eliminates time-consuming navigation, additional handling, and high-cost transportation through the Great Lakes and St. Lawrence Seaway," a Churchill public relations release claimed in 2002. As in the past, however, Churchill has three months only of ice-free water, a limitation to its success. The Montreal route to Athabasca meanwhile had varying periods of frost-free conditions. Even in summer the weather was, and still is, unpredictable. Too hot, too stormy, too much rain, too little rain, these perennial weather conditions affected company profits and employee safety even more in the past than they probably do now.

The articles by Joe Winterburn and David Kemp reveal different aspects of the North West Company's logistical problems posed by distance and weather. Winterburn's analysis of Lac la Pluie's Bills of Lading uncovers many facets of the North West Company's complex transportation system. The Thunder Bay Historical Museum Society is indeed fortunate to have such a rare and valuable document in its possession.

Elsewhere, David Kemp has analysed the effect of weather on morale in the fur trade. His "Attitudes to Winter in the North-West Fur Trade (*The Canadian Geographer*, No. 1 [1987], 49-57) draws these chilling (no pun intended) observations on the adversities posed by climate in the fur trade:

> The influence of climate on the fur trade was basic and strong. The trade could not have developed as it did without the peculiar weather and climatic conditions of the northwest, yet these same conditions provided some of its major constraints. ... Success depended upon challenging the environment and winning, and the trader's attitude toward winter was part of that challenge.

Surviving winter conditions can still be a challenge for those living and working in Canada's far north.

Lac La Pluie Bills Lading, 1806 - 1809*

by Joseph D. Winterburn

During the 1941 Annual Meeting of the Thunder Bay Historical Society, Mr. Carson Piper, the past president of the Society delivered his report. He informed the assembled members that the Fort William Public Library Board had requested that the Society build shelves and cupboards in the Brodie Street Library vault where the Society's records were being stored. While in the process of reorganising these records, Mr. Piper "found" a small bound volume labelled L.L.P. BILLS LADING.[1]

The initials L.L.P. stood for Lac la Pluie, the advance depot for the North West Company. While Fort William supplied the regular brigades that travelled to the upper Saskatchewan and Churchill (known to the Nor'westers as the "English") rivers, Lac la Pluie supplied the special brigades that travelled to the more remote Athabasca region.[2] The Lac la Pluie depot was located half a mile down the Rainy River from Rainy Lake, about two miles east of the present site of Fort Frances.[3] The entries in this book of printed bills of lading forms provide a record of the men, goods and canoes that made up the brigades that departed from Lac la Pluie for the Athabasca country between the 30th of July, 1806 and the 31st of July 1809.

Pages from the *L.L.P. Bills Lading* have been reproduced to illustrate the contents. The volume originally contained 107 pages, each page titled "Bill of Lading of Canoe". Although entries were made on ninety-nine pages, two of these pages have been removed. The last eight pages of the *L.L.P. Bills Lading* were left blank.

Each page is divided into four columns. The first is headed by the words "N.W. mark", standing for North West Company. This mark (an identifying brand, label, seal, or tag showing ownership) was put on each parcel of freight. The second column headed "Quantity" leaves space to record the number of items beside the various categories of freight which are printed in the third column. These include bales, kegs, bags, cases, cassettes and maccarons. Also in the third column, the mark of the department for which the freight is destined is usually written. The fourth column has three headings. Under "Men" the crew's names are written with their positions in the canoe and the names of any passengers; under "Provisions" the staple foods for consumption by the voyageurs en route and under "Agrès complete" the supplies for repairing the canoe.

This article will discuss the Bills of Lading for the following Canoes:

    No. 13, 1st Brigade, 1806
    No. 14 (guide) 2nd Brigade, 1806
    No. 21 (partner's canoe) 2nd Brigade, 1806
    No. 11 (clerks) 1808 Brigade
    No. 26 (express canoe) 1809 Brigade.

In this context, "brigade" means a group of three or more canoes travelling together under the supervision of a guide, the highest ranking voyageur.

The canoe used by the Athabasca brigades was the north canoe *(canots du Nord)*. As will be seen, this canoe was smaller than the typical 36-foot Montreal canoe *(canot du maître)*. The maximum load of a north canoe, including freight and men, was close to two tons. However, since time and distance necessitated a larger crew and more provisions, the Athabasca canoes carried only 20 to 23 pièces, compared to the 28 pieces carried by other brigades. Sir Alexander Mackenzie, John Macdonell and Capt. John Franklin gave the following descriptions of the north canoe:

    Mackenzie: *The trade from Grande Portage, is, in some particulars, carried on in a different manner with that from Montreal. The canoes used in the latter transport are now too large for the former, and some of about half the size are procured from the natives, and are navigated by four, five, or six men, according to the distance which they have to go. They carry a lading of about thirty-five packages, on an average; of these twenty-three*

---

*From: Thunder Bay Historical Museum Society Papers & Records, vol. IX (1981), pp. 7-12. Revised 2002.

are for the purpose of trade, and the rest are employed for provisions, stores and baggage. In each of these canoes are a foreman and steersman; the one to be always on the look out, and direct the passage of the vessel, and the other to attend the helm. They also carry her, whenever that office is necessary. The foreman has the command, and the middle-men obey both; the latter earn only two-thirds of the wages which are paid to the two former. Independent of these a conductor or pilot is appointed to every four or six of these canoes, whom they are all obliged to obey; and is, or at least intended to be, a person of superior experience, for which he is proportionably paid.[4]

Macdonell: *I assisted my Bourgois in sending off fourteen canoes for the Red River. These N.W. Canoes are about half the size of the Montreal or Grand River Canoes and when loaded to the utmost can carry a Tun and a half. The number of men required to navigate them is four to five i.e. the near hand posts have but [?] four men. A head clerk or Bourgeois is allowed by the concern to have an extra man in his canoe to wait upon him.*[5]

Franklin: *Those feeble vessels of bark will carry twenty-five pieces of goods, each weighing ninety pounds, exclusive of the necessary provision and baggage for the crew of five or six men, amounting in the whole to about three thousand three hundred pounds' weight. This great lading they annually carry between the depots and the posts, in the interior; and it rarely happens that any accidents occur, if they be managed by experienced bowsmen and steersmen, on whose skill the safety of the canoe entirely depends in the rapids and difficult places. When a total portage is made, these two men carry the canoe, and they often run with it, though its weight is estimated at about three hundred pounds, exclusive of the poles and oars, which are occasionally left in where the distance is short.*[6]

Approximate North Canoe Loads & Measurements[7]

Length: 24'	
Width: 5'	
Load: 20 – 28 pieces	2100 lbs.
Provisions	600
Baggage	200
Agrèt[8]	100
Total Freight	3000
5 men	750
Total Weight: approx. 2 tons	3750 lbs.

Canoe No. 13

The Bill of Lading of Canoe No. 13 is typical of the entries made for the Athabasca brigades. This was the thirteenth canoe loaded for the 1st brigade of 1806 (the first canoe of the 2nd brigade commenced with Canoe No. 14).

The term brigade should not to be confused with military usage. The North West Company definition refers to "a group of people organised to function as a unit in some work". The rough terrain demanded that these brigades remain small, and spaced apart, otherwise a bottleneck would create confusion as men, equipment, supplies and trade goods piled up at a portage. This would lead to delays and the possible misdirection of goods if during the confusion packs from different brigades were intermixed. John Macdonell records an occasion when a canoe was sent back to a portage to recover seven pieces that were left behind 'caused by a throng of canoes crossing together'.[9]

The column captioned NW Mark (North West Mark) was left blank on all the entries in the *L.L.P. Bills Lading*. These marks were used to identify the destination of each piece for the different Departments in the North West Company had their own identifying initials. With few exceptions, these North West Department initials were entered in the third column beside "Bales Goods".

Lac La Pluie Bills Lading

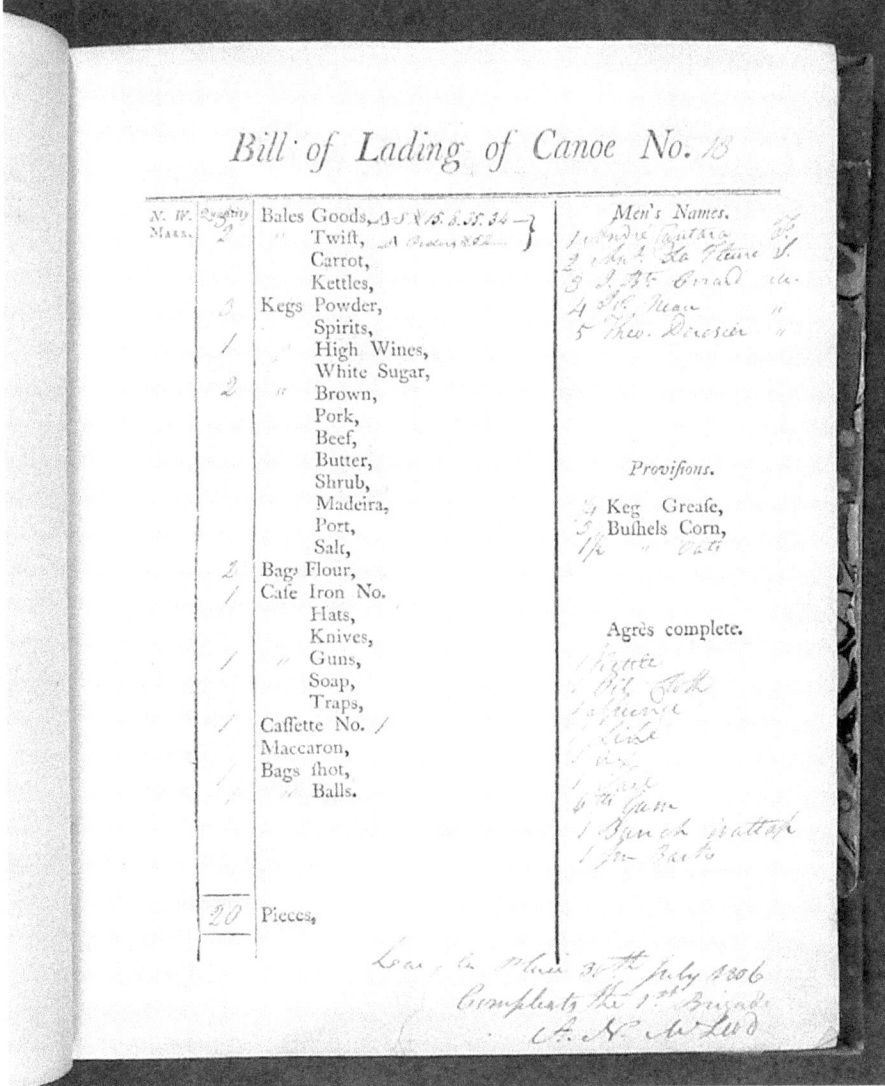

Lac La Pluie Bills of Lading book open at form for Canoe No. 18. The letter "A" for Bales Goods and for Twist reveal that the canoe's destination was the Athabasca Department. TBHMS B 6/1/1.

The second column, "Quantity", lists the number of pieces carried by the canoe. A piece was a package, weighing about ninety pounds that was designed for portaging and proper storage in the canoe. Great care had to be taken to balance the size of each piece by distributing heavier goods among the lighter. This prevented the pieces (in the form of bales, kegs, bags, or cassettes) from becoming too bulky.

Literally, cassette translates as 'small case'. In the North American fur trade this term referred to a small trunk made of well seasoned pine, made strong and light by dovetailing, grooving and binding with sheet iron. The cassette had a hinged lid, held closed by an inlet chest lock. These cassettes were of a standard dimension, typically 2' 4" x 1' 4" x 1' 4". Cassettes were usually painted Spanish brown.

The total number of pieces carried in this canoe was twenty, an average load for a canoe bound for the Athabasca Department. These pieces made up the "outfit"; that is, all the supplies needed to equip a post for an entire season. This included trade goods as well as supplies needed to maintain the post. The Athabasca Department wintering partners assembled their outfits at Lac la Pluie from the supplies shipped up to the depot by the Montreal agents. The Montreal agents were in effect "wholesalers" supplying goods to the "retailers", the wintering partners that carried out the actual trade. An outfit for the Athabasca country for 1818 included 190 pieces of baled goods, 134 pieces of high wines and spirits, 102 bales of tobacco, 164 pieces of guns and ammunition, 24 pieces of hardware and 200 pieces of provisions for a grand total of 848 pieces.[10]

The third column of the *L.L.P. Bills Lading* provides a list of standardised pieces, leaving room at the bottom for hand-written additions. In addition, each bale and each cassette, bales goods and bales twist is identified by department initials and/or a number. Reference to this number would direct a company officer to a ledger where the contents of the pièce were listed. The North West Department initials that most frequently appear are:

Initials	Department
A	Athabasca
Ā	Athabasca-Peace River
Æ	Athabasca-English {Churchill] River
AS	Athabasca-Slave River
B	Bas de la Rivière Ounipique [mouth of Winnipeg River]
D, R	Red River
K	Fort William (Kaministiquia) [until 1807]
NW	North West Company (Fort William) [after 1807]

Canoe No. 13 carried five bales. For the Athabasca-Slave River region, bales No. 15, 8, 35, and 34. For Athabasca, bale No. 52 and Athabasca cassette No. 1. The bill of lading also includes 2 bales of Twist Tobacco, 3 kegs of gunpowder, 1 keg of high wines ('High Wines' is raw whiskey. The North West Company shipped it high in proof. The intent was to water it down before consumption. Why entail the added expense of shipping water all the way west when the high wine can be diluted at its destination point?), 2 kegs of brown sugar, 2 bags of flour, 1 case of iron, 1 case guns, 1 bag of shot and one bag of musket balls for a total of 20 pièces. The clerks at Lac la Pluie would have made an inventory of each bale and cassette before it was sealed and labelled.

While no list of the contents of these bales has survived, we do have detailed lists of bales and cassettes being forwarded to Lac La Pluie in 1816. The following inventoried lists are but a small example of the wide range of goods shipped inland for the use of Natives, traders and their families.

LLP No. 5 Bale[11]

    1 piece Common Blue Strouds
    1 " Molton
    1 plain Blanket 3 points
    2 " " 21/2 "
    2 " " 2 "
    2 " " 11/2 "
    2 " " 1 "
    1 Molton Cappot 4 ells
    1 " " 31/2 "
    1 " " 3 "
    1 " " 21/2 "
    1 " " 2 "
    1 " " 11/2 "
    1 " " 1 "
    4 lbs. Net Thread
    4 " Sturgeon Twine
    2 mens Cotton Shirts
    2 " flannel "

L.L.P. No. 13 Cassette[12]

    26 Rolls 4 doz. Ferretting Silk
    23 " hair ribbon "
    2 " 9 doz. Black "
    2 Pieces 6 doz. Coloured Ribbon
    5 " 4 doz. " "

2	"		Galloon
3	Dozen		Papers of Pins
1	"		playing cards
1	1/6	"	Shaving Boxes
7	5/12	"	Common Razors
7	1/2	lbs.	smallest white beads
3	1/2	doz.	Brass Jews-harps
2	1/4	lbs.	Allspice
21	cases		Razors 1 ea.
26	Setts		Violin Strings
15	1 sts.	"	"
60			lengths basses, same as Spring Inventory
	1/3	doz.	fine Scissors
5		"	Silk Hat Covers
2		"	Tooth Brushes
6	1/4	doz.	Cakes of Windsor Soap
	11/12	"	rolls Blacking
30			Nutmegs
25	Small		Jockey Caps
22	lb.		Colored Thread

In the fourth column of the *L.L.P. Bills Lading*, under the heading "Men's Names" is listed the complement of the canoe. In the L.L.P. Bills Lading, a number of interchangeable names have been entered for the various positions of the canoe crew. The man in the bow of the canoe could be listed as a foreman or *devant*. The man in the back of the canoe has been listed as the steersman or *gouvernail*. The middlemen as *milieux*.[13] Andre Cantara (foreman), Ant. La Fleure (steersman), and J. Bt. Gerard, J.P. Neau and Theo. Derosier (*milieux*). The foreman was charged with the safety of the canoe, and was the senior man on board. He stood in the bow of the canoe directing its course. The steersman stood at the back of the canoe changing its course at the order of the foreman. The Foreman and Steersman were known collectively as *Bouts* (the ends). The *milieux*, the middlemen in a canoe, were the least experienced of the voyageurs. To be chosen for the Athabasca brigades, all of the voyageurs had to be tough, enterprising men. This was reflected in the premium wages they were paid.

The following list dated 15 July 1806 shows the rate of pay in yearly wages and equipments supplied to the *engagés* of the North West Company's Athabasca Department. The currency used for bookkeeping purposes was a money of account known as the *livre* (*l*). There were 6 *livre* to the dollar (the Spanish piastre). In 1806 the bowmen were paid 600 *livres*; steersmen, 600 *livres* and middlemen, 400 *livres*. The equipments are supplies given to the *engagés* over and above their wages. This is mainly in the form of clothing, but could also include personal items and provisions.

ATHABASCA DEPARTMENT[14]

Wages of Devants 600 *l.*, Do. Of Gouvernails 600 *l.* and Milieux 400 *l.*
(By comparison, the average wage of a Montreal voyageur was 250 *l.*, with an additional 150 *l.* if he continued west to Lac la Pluie.)

Equipments
Of Bouts   *of Milieux*
1 Blanket   3 points   1 Blanket   3 points
1 Blanket   2 1/2 points   1 "   2 1/2 points
2 pair Leggings   2 pair Leggings

2 Bracelets   2 Bracelets
2 Shirts   2 Shirts
2 Handkerchiefs   2 Handkerchiefs
4 Carrots Tobacco   3 Carrots Tobacco
3 Large Knives   2 Large Knives
3 Small Knives   2 Small Knives
1/2   pound   beads
1/4   pound   Vermillion

Following the entry for the canoe's complement is the entry for "Provisions". No stops were made to gather or hunt for food along the canoe route. Therefore, all provisions for the journey from Lac la Pluie to Bas de la Rivière Ouinipique (the provision depot for the Athabasca country), was 1/4 of a keg of grease (fat), 3 bushels of corn and 1 1/2 bushels of oats (wild rice). At Bas de la Rivière Ouinipique, located at the mouth of the Winnipeg River, *tauraux* (buffalo hide sacks containing ninety pounds of pemmican) would re-provision the canoes. The provisions for one canoe weighed approximately 600 pounds. In his journal, Alexander Henry the younger listed food required to provision his brigade from Fort William to Fort Vermilion in 1809:

> "Our expenditure of provisions for each canoe during this voyage was: two bags of corn, 1 1/2 bushel each, and 15 lbs. of grease, to Lac la Pluie; two bags of wild rice, 1 1/2 bushel each, and 10 lbs. of grease, to Bas de la Rivière Winipic; four bags of pemmican, 90 lbs. each, to serve until we came among the buffalo — generally near the Montée or at farthest the Elbow of the Saskatchewan." — Journal, p. 539.[15]

The "*agrès*" refers to the equipment with which each canoe was outfitted. It included repair supplies, sails, oilcloths and cooking utensils. For the *L.L.P. Bills Lading* entries for 1806, the contents of the canoe *agrès* has been listed, but as the *agrès* for each canoe appears to have been standardised later entries list only missing or non-standard equipment. The items listed in the *Agrès for Canoe No. 13* include:

1 kettle (the "canoe kettle", a small iron cooking kettle)
1 oilcloth (used to protect the cargo from water damage)
1 sponge (to soak up water that leaked into the canoe)
1 codline (used to track the canoe up rapids)

1 axe
1 sail (under favourable if rare circumstances [a following wind] it is possible to sail a canoe)
6 pounds of gum (refined spruce gum mixed with bear fat and charcoal used to seal the seams in the canoe)
1 bunch of wattap (spruce root used to sew the seams in canoes)
1 fathom (6 feet) of birch bark (for canoe repairs)

The total weight of the "Agrès complete" was approximately 100 pounds.

The final entry on the *L.L.P. Bills Lading* is "Lac la Pluie 30th July 1806 completes the 1st Brigade A.N. McLeod". Archibald Norman McLeod was made a partner of the North West Company before 1799, and was a proprietor in the Athabasca country from 1802 to 1808[16]. The clerk in charge of the Lac la Pluie depot in 1806 was Archibald McLellan[17], who was stationed there from 1799 to 1810 (he became a partner of the company with the outfit

Voyageur re-enactor carrying bales of marked trade goods. Photograph courtesy Fort William Historical Park.

of 1808). McLellan's name does not appear on the bills of lading, as the proprietors in charge of the departments supervised the loading of their canoes, and made the entries on the bill of lading.

The Guide of the Canoe Brigade

Canoe No. 14 differs from Canoe No. 13 in the size of the crew. In addition to the Foreman, Steersman and *Milieux*, this canoe carried a guide, Pierre Blondin. The guide was the leader of a canoe brigade. He navigated the course the canoes took and determined whether to shoot rapids or portage them. With the addition of the guide and another milieux, the number of pièces carried was reduced to 17.

Canoe Passengers: The Wintering Partner

At one time the Wintering partners travelled light with picked crews and only baggage and provisions in their canoes. "A head clerk or Bourgeouis is allowed by the concern to have an extra man in his canoe to wait upon him. There has been great abuse in these things formerly certain gentlemen who were fond of Dashing taking an unnecessary number of chosen men into their canoes from motives of vanity".[18] This practice was abolished in 1804[19], and new regulations were introduced by the North West Company concerning the establishment of Wintering Partners' canoes. The exception to this regulation was the Athabasca Department, which was allowed a light canoe to transport one of its proprietors to Fort William.[20] The Bill of Lading of Canoe No. 21 for the 2nd Brigade, 1806 reflects these changes.[21] The letter "P" following Mr. D. (Daniel) McKenzie's name signifies that he is a proprietor or Wintering Partner of the North West Company (in 1806 he was in charge of the Athabasca district), the "D" following Jos. La Ramme, and "G" following Jos. St. Andre stands for *Devant* and *Gouvernail* respectively. One awl (a canoe awl used to punch holes in birch bark for threading wattap), and an extra 8 fathoms of codline have been added to the Agrès complete.

Canoe Passengers: Clerks

As well as transporting the Wintering partners, room had to be made for the Company's clerks who manned the wintering posts and kept the records. Travelling in Canoe No. 11 of the 1808 Brigade were clerks D.W. (Daniel) Harmon and A. (Archibald) McGillivray. The following is Harmon's account of his journey from Fort William to Lac la Pluie (Rainy Lake) and to Bas de la Rivière Ouinipique:

> Thursday, July 7. Yesterday morning, I arrived at Fort William, where I had only time to read my letters from my friends below, and answer them, and prepare myself for a long journey. This afternoon I embarked for Athabasca, in company with Mr. J.G. McTavish; and both of us are to remain at the place of our destination, for three years, at least.
>
> Wednesday, 20. Rainy Lake. We here find all the Athabasca people, excepting one brigade, which is expected daily.
>
> Saturday, 22. Ever since my arrival here, we have been busily employed in preparing to leave this place, for our winter quarters.
>
> Tuesday, 26. Rainy Lake River. In the morning, I left the fort in company with Mr. Archibald McGillivray. Our brigade consists of ten canoes.
>
> Friday, 29. Portage de L'Isle, in Winnipick River. In the morning, we met Mr. David Thomson and company from the Columbia River.
>
> Monday, August 1. Lake Winnipick. This morning we arrived at the fort on this lake, where we remained until noon.[22]

The trip from Fort William to Lac la Pluie took Harmon approximately 13 days, from Lac la Pluie to Bas de la Rivière (at the mouth of the Winnipeg River) took 5 days, an indication of the difficulties encountered on

Grant of Arms to William and Simon McGillivray, 1823. These Armorial Bearings combine elements of McGillivray clan and North West Company arms. The birchbark canoe with flag bearing the symbol "NW" was incorporated in the City of Fort William arms in 1967 and in the new City of Thunder Bay arms created in 1970. TBHMS 977.113.461. See History of the Clan MacGillivray *by George Macgillivray and Robert McGillivray in Thunder Bay Public Library (Brodie St. Special Collection).*

the route between Fort William and Lac la Pluie, and illustrating the necessity of establishing a depot there. The distance travelled between Fort William and Lac La Pluie is 303 miles (488 kilometres), with 34 portages with an average length of 652 yds. (596m). The distance travelled between Lac La Pluie and Bas de la Rivière is 311 miles (500 kilometres), with 28 portages with an average length of 222 yds.[23] Daniel Harmon finally arrived at Fort Chipewyan, the headquarters of the Athabasca Department on September 7th.

The Light Canoe

The North West Company maintained a regular system of light canoes that carried dispatches to and from the wintering posts in the *pays d'en haut* (translates as *up country*). This area of land beyond the upper reaches of the Grande (Ottawa) River also included the Great Lakes basin, the Upper Mississippi and the broader Hudson Bay watershed). As speed was essential to the operation of these express canoes, only necessary provisions were taken. Canoe No. 26 of the 1809 brigade is listed as a "Light Canoe". No pièces are listed for this canoe, but a complement of 9 voyageurs makes up the crew. With a large crew and a small load, a minimum of time would be spent on portaging, allowing a very fast passage. A light canoe from the mouth of the Columbia River could reach Montreal in one hundred days[24]. There were 26 canoes in the 1809 brigade for the Athabasca department.[25] This, the final entry for the brigade was made by Donald McTavish, a proprietor in the Athabasca Department. This entry also completed the *L.L.P. Bills Lading*.

It is the existence of primary source documents like the *Lac la Pluie Bills Lading* that promote further research into our past. History is not written with an indelible pen; as our society changes its point of view and requirements transform and we must continually 'go back to the well' to decipher these documents from a 'new' perspective. An interpretation of this seemingly dry piece of 19th century bookkeeping gives a fascinating and informative glimpse into the operation of the company that opened up Canada's western frontier. Northwestern

Ontario is fortunate that such a rare document from its fur trade past somehow found its way into the Thunder Bay Historical Museum's archives, and that it remains in our possession.

NOTES

[1] Thunder Bay Historical Society. Minutes of the Annual Meeting, 1941.
[2] Marjorie Wilkins Campbell, *McGillivray: Lord of the Northwest* (Toronto, 1962), p. 53.
[3] Ernest Voorhis, *Historic Forts and Trading Posts of the French Regime and of the English Fur Trading Companies*, (Ottawa: Dept. of the Interior, 1930), p. 158.
[4] W. Kaye Lamb, ed., *The Journals and Letters of Sir Alexander Mackenzie*. (Toronto, 1970), p. 99.
[5] Charles M. Gates, ed., *Five Fur Traders of the Northwest*. (St. Paul, 1965), p. 97.
[6] Capt. John Franklin, RN, FRS, *Journey to the Polar Sea, in 1819-20-21-22: with a brief account of the second Journey in 1825-26-27. Vol. II* (London, 1829), p. 65-66. (identified as Capt.)
[7] Old Fort William Building Kit: Dry Goods Stores - Outfits
[8] Erwin N. Thompson, Grand Portage; *A History of the Sites, People, and Fur Trade*, National Park Service, Washington, D.C., 1969)
[9] Gates, *Five Fur Traders of the Northwest*. (St. Paul, 1965), p. 98.
[10] Harold A. Innis, *The Fur Trade in Canada* (Toronto, 1970), p. 229.
[11] National Archives of Canada, MG 19 E1, Selkirk Papers, Inventory of Goods etc. at Fort William as sold by D. McKenzie to the Earl of Selkirk, 18 September 1816. Statement of Packages Intended for Lac la Pluie. P. 9448.
[12] Selkirk Papers, Inventory of Goods etc. .... P. 9397.
[13] W. Kaye Lamb, ed., *The Journals and Letters of Sir Alexander Mackenzie*. (Toronto, 1970), p. 99.
[14] Adapted from W.S. Wallace, ed., *Documents Relating to the North West Company* (Toronto, 1934), p. 213.
[15] Henry, Alexander & David Thompson. *New Light on the Early History of the Greater Northwest:...* Edited by Elliot Coues. (New York:1897; rpt. Minneapolis: Ross & Haines, 1965), p. 539.
[16] Wallace, ed., *Documents* p. 480.
[17] Wallace, ed., *Documents* p. 479.
[18] Gates, ed., *Five Fur Traders of the Northwest*. p. 97.
[19] Wallace, ed., *Documents* p. 194.
[20] Wallace, ed., *Documents* p. 195.
[21] Wallace, ed., *Documents* p. 260.
[22] Daniel Williams Harmon, *Journal of Voyages and Travels in the Interior of North America*. (Andover, 1820), pp. 164-165.
[23] Henry Youle Hind, *Narrative of the Canadian Red River Exploring Expedition of 1857*. (Edmonton, M.G. Hurtig Ltd., c1971) pp. 399-402.
[24] Old Fort William Building Kit: Canoe Shed
[25] Wallace, ed., *Documents* p. 260.

The Impact of Weather and Climate on the Fur Trade in the Canadian Northwest*

by David Kemp

As befits an activity which made a significant contribution to the development of Canada, the fur trade has evoked considerable interest among a variety of writers and researchers. Historians are a majority in such a group, but economists, geographers and anthropologists have also been involved and one of the results has been the accumulation of a major body of literature on many aspects of the trade. In all of this there are numerous references to environmental conditions, including weather and climate, and there can be little doubt that they were basic elements in the development of the trade, yet they have been treated rather superficially.

Being both resource and liability and working either directly or indirectly, the role of weather and climate in any activity is a complex one and this is evident in the fur trade in Canada in the 18th and 19th centuries. The very basis of the trade was the thick pelts produced by the fur-bearing animals in the cold northern winter, yet these same winters, through the freezing of lakes and rivers, curtailed the activities of the enterprise for as many as seven months of the year. Even in the period when the waterways were free of ice, severe seasonal fluctuations were experienced. The melting of the winter's accumulation of snow and ice produced high water levels and turbulent rivers in spring and early summer but by fall the water levels were often sufficiently low to impede the progress of heavily laden canoes. Superimposed on this general pattern and providing additional complexity was the variability in the elements from year to year.

The Hudson's Bay and North West Companies, the main protagonists in the trade, appreciated the importance of such conditions and from an early date their clerks and officers included references to weather conditions and related phenomena in their journals. With their longer trade routes through the St. Lawrence- Great Lakes system and their reliance on the canoe, the Nor'westers were probably more subject to the vagaries of weather and climate than their rivals and this paper is concerned with that particular aspect of the North West Company's trade.

The employees of the North West Company seem to have been less conscientious in their record keeping than their Hudson's Bay counterparts, but a variety of journals, letters and diaries have survived. Collections of such original manuscript material have been compiled and published by a number of archivists and historians,[1] greatly facilitating the search for reports of contemporary weather conditions or comments on weather-related phenomena.

THE WESTWARD EXPANSION OF THE FUR TRADE

Although almost every fur-bearing animal in North America was involved in the fur trade at some time or other, the dominant species by far was the beaver. Present in large numbers over most of the northern half of the continent, it was also much in demand in Europe, where its fur remained the basic raw material in the hat-making industry for some two hundred years. Such a sustained demand led inevitably to overexploitation of the beaver, aggravated by an intense rivalry among the various trading factions, and resulted in a serious depletion of the species. This was particularly so in the more accessible Great Lakes - St. Lawrence basin which encouraged the expansion of the trade westwards and northwards into the interior where beaver remained plentiful. Harold Innis, an eminent economic historian of half a century ago and one of the first to appreciate the importance of the trade to Canada's early development, dealt with these changes in his classic work, *The Fur Trade in Canada*. Concerned mainly with the economics of the situation, he was also aware of the environmental factors involved,

---

*From: Thunder Bay Historical Museum Society *Papers & Records*, vol. VIII (1980), pp. 32-42. Reprinted with permission.

The Impact of Weather and Climate

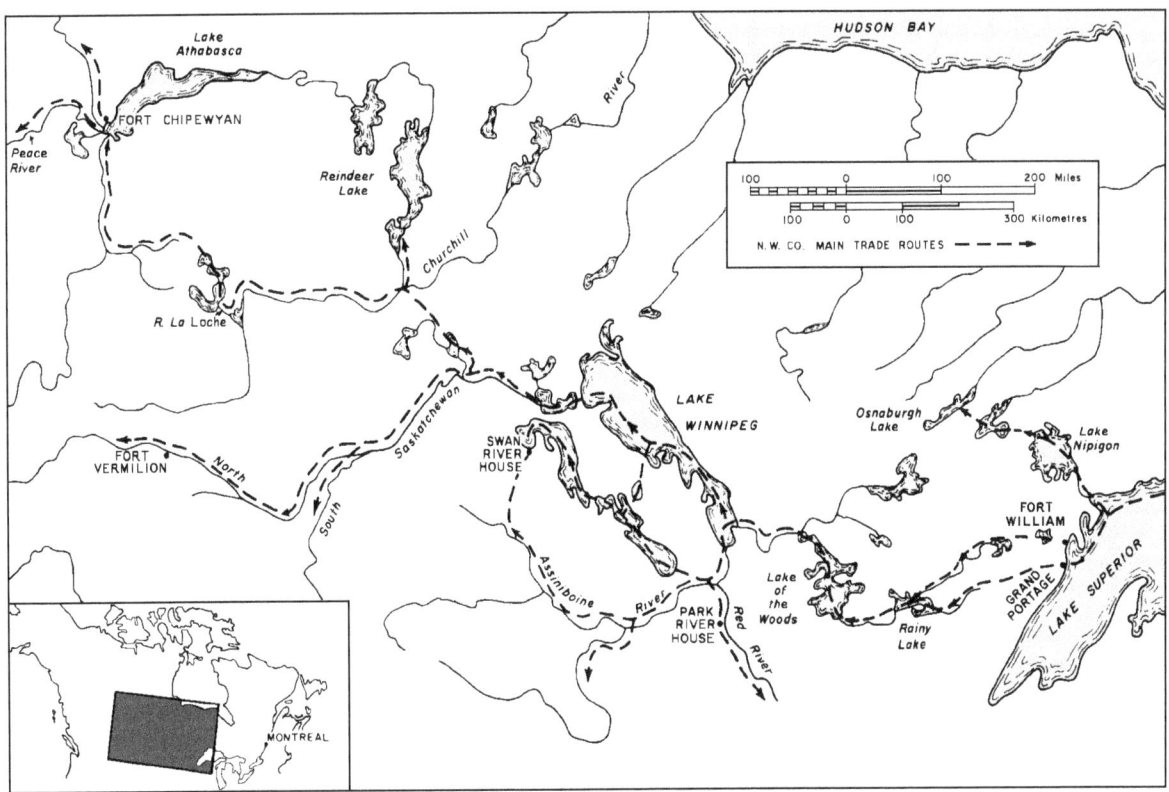

Main trade routes of the North West Company. This map depicts the NWC's major fur-bearing regions whose short summer months compounded the challenges posed by enormous distances throughout the company's fur trade domain. Map by Iain Hastie.

pointing out that, "A vast north temperate land area with a pronounced seasonal climate was a prerequisite to an extensive development of the trade."[2] and the Canadian northwest amply fulfilled these requirements. By the second half of the 18th century, when the North West Company had become established at the head of Lake Superior, the importance of the eastern areas to the trade was very much diminished.

In the northwest, the environmental conditions provided an ideal habitat for the beaver and the long, cold winters caused them to produce a better grade of fur than was common in more southerly areas. In the heyday of the North West Company, this was usually sufficient to ensure the profitability of the enterprise, despite the increased expenditure on wages, provisions and transportation which accompanied westward expansion. Alexander Henry, a wintering partner in the Lower Red River District in the early 19th century and keeper of one of the more detailed journals to come out of the Northwest trade, was well aware of this when he noted in 1800: "It is this vast extent of country from which the North West Company may he said to draw their treasures. It is true, profits arise from the trade in other parts eastward; but nothing to what we obtain from the Athabasca country."[3]

The influence of the general climatic conditions in the northwest on such factors as the habitat and pelt quality of the beaver was an underlying element in the trade as a whole. In addition, the more specific daily or seasonal weather events had a direct effect on the everyday running of the company through their impact on a wide variety of activities from transportation to food supply. In fact, the overall pattern of the northwest fur trade evolved around changing seasonal conditions while the logistics of the trade were such that it was particularly sensitive to adverse weather conditions.

ICE ON THE WATERWAYS

As might be expected in an activity largely dependent on water transport, conditions on the rivers and lakes were of major concern. The climate of the northwest was such that for as many as seven months of the year ice on the waterways restricted or completely prevented navigation and it may be argued that this fact more than any other was responsible for the pattern adopted by the trade.

In general the length of the ice-free season decreased towards the northwest. From the journals of Alexander Henry (the Younger) it is evident that in the early 19th century the rivers and lakes of the lower Red River District were free of ice for 215 to 220 days in the year.[4] Farther north in the Saskatchewan District water communications was restricted to some 170 days[5] while around Fort Chipewyan in the Athabasca country the season was reduced to about 150 days[6] Northwards into the Mackenzie basin and westwards into the mountains, these figures were reduced even further.

As the trade developed, the Company adapted to these conditions. Since the distance between Montreal and the rich fur-producing areas of the Athabasca District was some 5000 km and since a freight canoe could average at most only 1600 km a month,[7] there was no possibility of the canoes from Montreal travelling to the far northwest and back in the short five-month, ice-free season. The Company's solution to this problem was to establish a major interior post at Grand Portage, (and after 1803, at Fort William) on the western shores of Lake Superior, which could be reached by both the Montreal traders and the wintering partners from the north by midsummer. Allowing a month for business, repairs to equipment and recuperation, there was still time for each group to reach its destination on the return journey before the fall freeze-up. The only exception to this arrangement was the Athabasca brigade, which as early as 1788 did not complete the journey to the main rendezvous, but was met at Rainy Lake, some 350 km west of Lake Superior, by a special brigade from Grand Portage.[8] This produced a saving of 25 to 30 days for the northmen, but even with that the round trip of close to 135 days from Fort Chipewyan to Rainy Lake and back[9] allowed little leeway in a 150-day ice-free season. Thus, although the need for posts at the head of Lake Superior and at Rainy Lake involved a combination of several economic and environmental factors, it is evident that the climatic conditions in the northwest played a fundamental role in their establishment.

With such a tight schedule, the northern brigades were always under pressure and the return journey to the Athabasca district must often have been an anxious one. In 1791, for example, the Athabasca brigade was still close to Rainy Lake on August 10 and Alexander Mackenzie, the explorer who later reached the Arctic and Pacific Oceans by way of the interior, was expressing the fear that, "many of the people will not reach their winter quarters without much *misère*. Several may be stopped by the ice."[10] With a 60-65 day journey ahead of them they could not hope to reach their destination before mid-October, by which time ice on the waterways was a distinct possibility. There is no evidence that the 1791 brigade was caught in the ice, but Mackenzie's fears were not unfounded, for in 1787 the Athabasca canoes had been stopped by ice at Rivière La Loche on October 9 and were forced to cache most of their goods.[11] Not only did this mean a shortage of supplies at Fort Chipewyan, but also at the posts — such as those on the Peace River — provisioned from there. Although these northern districts were the most likely to be affected by early ice, more southerly areas were not immune. On October 21, 1802, for example, Hugh McGillis was caught by the ice on his way to Swan River Fort in what is now northern Manitoba and had to complete his journey by sledge.[12] The early winter of that year was also noted by Alexander Henry some 500 km to the south in the Red River district,[13] but there it was less serious than in the north, for the canoe brigades had returned from Lake Superior more than a month before the ice set in.

The outward journeys from the interior posts in the spring were sometimes delayed or disrupted by the late break-up of the winter's ice, but this seems to have been less serious for the trade than early freeze-up. Delays were generally of limited duration because of the advancing season, while the high water levels in the rivers and lakes allowed good time to be made on the downward journeys. Together with the two- to four-week cushion provided by the rendezvous, this allowed most of the lost time to be made up.

In the south, a late spring generally had even less affect on the trade. The Red River brigade seldom set out for Lake Superior before the last week in May, by which time the waterways had been ice-free for about a month. In 1804, for example, the Red River was completely free of ice by April 6, but the canoes did not leave until May 30 which allowed sufficient time to reach Fort William by the end of June.[14] In such circumstances, even a late opening of navigation as was the case in 1802 and 1806, when the Red River was not completely free of ice until April 23,[15] had little effect on the brigade's timetable.

There were years, however, when spring was sufficiently late to cause disruption even in the south. This was certainly so in 1797 when the traders in the Nipigon District had to use snowshoes as late as May 29 and the ice remained on at least some of the lakes until June 24.[16] Such common weather seems to have affected that season's activities, for according to Alexander Mackenzie the brigades were later than usual in returning to Montreal from Grand Portage that year.[17] That same year, David Thompson, later renowned for his extensive exploration and survey work on behalf of the Company, reported that on Reindeer Lake, north of the Churchill River, the ice persisted until July 7,[18] suggesting that the late spring was not confined to the south. Two years later a very severe winter was followed by another cold, late spring. The Montreal canoes were unable to leave Lachine before May 13 in 1799 and Lake Huron, which lay across the route to the north, was not free of ice until May 18.[19] Lake Superior remained ice-bound even longer — until early June, at least—causing the company schooner, the *Otter*, to take 18 days for the passage between Grand Portage and Sault Ste. Marie, a journey normally completed in half that time.[20]

In addition to years such as 1797 and 1799 when the effects of the late spring were widely felt, there were individual years when the season was equally as late but only in limited areas. In 1807, for example, Daniel Harmon's Saskatchewan brigade was held up from June 5-8, by ice on Lake Winnipeg[21] and in 1812 Daniel Mackenzie was stranded by ice on Lac La Rouge, in what is now northern Minnesota, until June 14.[22] Such years seem to have been the exception rather than the rule, however, and writing in 1804, Duncan Cameron of the Nipigon District claimed that after the cold winter and late spring of 1797 the spring weather was actually milder than it had been previously.[23]

Changing Water Levels

Even in those years when spring was on time and the winter ice slow to form, the trade was far from unaffected by the weather. Seasonal changes in the regime of the northern rivers produced high, fast water in the spring as the winter's accumulation of snow melted, but low and sluggish water in the fall, as the high summer temperatures and limited precipitation of the interior reduced the amount of water available for run-off. In the northwest this meant that the outward journey to the rendezvous was often fast and relatively easy compared with the return trip, but such a pattern could be enhanced or weakened in any given year by variations in the seasonal weather conditions.

The effects were greatest on those routes with many portages. High water allowed stretches of river normally by-passed by portaging to be run or tracked, as Alexander Henry noted in his journal entries for the late summer 1800. That year the water level in the Lake of the Woods was so high that no portage was required at Portage du Lac des Bois,[24] commonly half a mile to a mile long, depending upon the state of the water, while the high fast water in the Winnipeg River allowed his brigade to run several rapids normally requiring portages.[25] In contrast to this, low water increased the length and frequency of the carrying places resulting in loss of time plus increased strain on men and equipment. The fur trade journals for 1804, a particularly dry year in central and western Canada, have frequent references to the problems of low water. The Red River brigade encountered such low water levels on the Shield between Lake Superior and Lake Winnipeg that it fell well behind schedule; the provisions ran out and the voyageurs were without food for the last three days of the trip.[26] Duncan Cameron's brigade experienced similar difficulties on its way to winter quarters at Osnaburgh Lake from Lake Nipigon.[27] That journey doubled because of water levels that were lower than the oldest inhabitants of the district had ever known.[28] The time taken for the journey was also doubled and by the end of September three of the canoes that had been brought from Lake Superior were beyond repair,[29] presumably because of the strain imposed by the extra portaging or because of encounters with underwater objects brought closer to the surface by the low water levels.

The Influence of Wind on Lake Travel

The effects of changing water levels were greatest along the rivers. Occasionally, very low water hampered progress on the lakes also, as in the Nipigon District in 1804 when Duncan Cameron complained about, "these muddy lakes in which even the smallest dog cannot swim"[30] but most lakes, particularly the larger ones, could be traversed with little variation in route or timing whether the water was high or low. The major climatic element influencing lake travel was the wind. A following wind would be used to advantage by hoisting a sail and under favourable conditions a canoe might be driven along at eight or nine miles per hour.[31] For the most part, however, heavily laden freight canoes with no keel and limited free-board were always vulnerable to the wind and the waves it produced, especially on larger lakes such as Superior and Winnipeg. Because of local climatic conditions, which caused turbulence from mid-day onwards in the summer, these lakes were often navigable only in the early morning or evening at the best of times. Eric Morse,[32] an acknowledged expert on this mode of transport, has estimated that during July and August unmanageable winds commonly limited canoe travel to one day in three on Lake Superior and continued contrary winds could hold up the brigades for several days in succession. In September 1803, for example, the Red River brigade took ten days to pass through the lower end of Lake Winnipeg, a distance of only 60 km. because of gales.[33] As a result the stock of corn ran out and the starving men were left with nothing to eat but flour.[34] In contrast in 1805 the brigade had favourable winds much of the way and took only 22 days for the complete journey from Fort William.[35] Davidson,[36] in an early history of the North West Company, has suggested that the Fort William route to the interior was climatically superior to that via Grand Portage since there were fewer lakes on the former route and therefore less detention of the canoes by high winds.

Perhaps the most hazardous conditions experienced by the canoe brigades were those associated with the intense localised thunder storms which are characteristic of the summer weather in central Canada. These storms, accompanied by squally winds which can alter the nature of a lake in a very short time, build up rapidly and the evidence from the journals is that the fur-traders often had to suffer the consequences of being caught by rapidly deteriorating conditions and unable to put ashore. In early August, 1800, the Red River brigade was caught by such a storm on Rainy Lake and Alexander Henry has recorded the following evocative description of the event.

> Just at this moment a black thunderstorm was collecting: we could not land, as a reef of rocks prevented approach to the shore; and before we could reach a proper landing, the storm burst upon us with thunder, lightning, rain and a terrible squall from the W. We got under the lee of a large stone, where, all hands clinging to it, with much trouble we kept our canoes from being blown out upon the lake, where we must inevitably have perished.[37]

Two weeks later, on Lake Winnipeg, the brigade survived three similar squalls in one day.[38]

Such events were not uncommon, particularly on the larger lakes, where the temptation to save time and energy by cutting across the mouth of a bay rather than following the coast must have been great, despite the risk of being overtaken by a squall on the open lake. That the traders frequently took the risk is perhaps not surprising, since it was only one of many that had to be faced in an enterprise that was often hazardous. Together, ice, wind, squalls and fluctuating water levels presented significant threats to navigation in a relatively fragile, heavily laden vessel, but they were hazards regularly overcome, for the canoe brigades made their annual journey hauling furs and trade goods across the continent with considerable success.

Weather, Climate and the Fur Trade

Although it is apparent that weather and climate had a definite influence on the fur trade, the overall impact is difficult to assess. Adverse weather conditions and such climatically induced hazards as frostbite, drowning

Charles Graham, "An Early Nip", from his collage of paintings entitled "Winter Scenes in the Northwest - Northern Shore of Lake Superior" (1883). This snow scene at a Northwestern Ontario post tell the story of early winter's impact on a transportation system dependent on the birchbark canoe.TBHMS 972.2.470

or starvation seem to have been accepted as an unavoidable part of the trade. This is well illustrated by the attitude of the traders towards winter. Winter in the Canadian northwest is severe by any standards and while it curtailed certain activities, local trade continued with some vigour; hunting and fishing took men away from the posts for days at a time and even in mid-winter the wintering partners or clerks travelled from post to post to keep abreast of the season's trade. Sometimes the latter trips became tests of endurance if the weather conditions deteriorated. In November 1800, for example, Alexander Henry spent three days in a storm of snow and wind returning to Park River from one of the outlying posts in the Red River District. In his journal he notes that his men were surprised by his arrival because they had supposed it impossible to march in such weather."[39] During a similar trip from New Caledonia to the Peace River in February 1813, Daniel Harmon, an American who spent sixteen years in the interior for the Company, had his upper lip badly frost bitten as a result of low temperatures and strong winds. In great pain and discomfort he continued his journey although he admitted that "was it not absolutely necessary that I should proceed farther down the River, I most assuredly should not leave my bed."[40]

Despite such hazards these trips were necessary in planning the best use of men and materials in a trade where conditions were seldom static. Furthermore, information on the progress of the winter's trade and that of the previous summer had to be sent eastwards so that the Company agents could make a preliminary estimate of the requirements for the following year's enterprise. This was accomplished by the development of the "winter express" which left Athabasca late in the year, collected reports and correspondence throughout the northwest, and reached Sault Ste. Marie in May.[41] The express system generally measured up to Company expectations and, considering the harshness and unpredictability of winter weather in the interior, these were high. At the 1806 rendezvous, for example, the partners agreed on a "Memo to regulate the Winter Express", which gave specific dates for the arrival and departure of the express.[42] That they were able to do so may be seen in part as a tribute to the tenacity and dedication of a group of men, such as Henry and Harmon, whose strong sense of duty allowed them to relegate their personal needs to a secondary position behind those of the Company.

In human terms, then, the impact of weather and climate on the fur trade was strong, although difficult to measure exactly. Part of the difficulty may arise from the attitude of the traders. From their journals it is evident that they were aware of the influence of weather and climate on the trade and the hazards that might ensue, but were quite ready to take the risks involved. Life in general in the late 18th and early 19th centuries was not without its hazards and in an enterprise such as the fur trade, which was already very demanding physically, such conditions seem to have been accepted as an unavoidable part of employment.

With the abundant evidence of the impact of weather and climate on almost all aspects of the fur trade it is perhaps surprising that there is little indication of this in the economics of the trade. At the local level it might be possible to assess climate-related costs for such events as the destruction of Company property, increased food consumption on a journey extended by low water. unfavourable winds or ice, or the shortage of trade goods because of similar delays, but these are lost in the overall trade figures. To a large extent this is due to the nature of the trade with its extensive use of credit and the extended timetables associated with 18th and 19th century travel and transportation. Normally some 42 months passed between the ordering the goods by traders in the interior and the arrival of the furs in London to pay for them.[43] With such a time lag and given the politically and economically volatile conditions of that period it is perhaps not surprising that it is difficult, if not impossible, to isolate the effects of weather and climate from trade figures representing the interplay of the many elements that influenced the enterprise. Despite such difficulties, the available evidence suggests that the relationship between weather and climate and the Canadian fur trade was basic and strong, with its importance generally underestimated. The trade could not have developed as it did without the peculiar weather and climatic conditions of the north yet these same conditions provided some of its major constraints.

NOTES

[1] See E. Coues, ed., *New Light on the Early History of the Greater Northwest. The Manuscript Journals of Alexander Henry and of David Thompson*, 1799-1814 (Minneapolis: 1897; reprinted 1965). W.K. Lamb, ed., *The Journals and Letters of Sir Alexander Mackenzie* (Cambridge: 1970). W.S. Wallace, ed., *Documents Relating to the North West Company* (Toronto: 1934).

[2] H.A. lnnis, *The Fur Trade in Canada* (Toronto: 1970), p. 387.

[3] E. Coues, *The Saskatchewan and Columbia Rivers*, II, p. 474.

[4] Ibid., I, *The Red River of the North*.

[5] E. Ross. *Beyond the River and the Bay* (Toronto: 1970), p. 124.

[6] GA. Young. "The Organization of the Transfer of Furs at Fort William: A Study in Historical Geography", in Thunder Bay Historical Museum Society *Papers & Records*, II, (1974), pp. 29-36. 32.

[7] E.W. Morse. *Fur Trade Canoe Routes of Canada: Then and Now* (Ottawa: 1968), p. 18.

[8] W.K. Lamb, *Journals and Letters*, pp. 97-98.

[9] Ibid., p. 129.

[10] Ibid., p. 448. Letter to Roderic McKenzie.

[11] Ibid,, p. 429. Letter to Roderic McKenzie.

[12] W.K. Lamb, ed., *Sixteen Years in the Indian Country. The Journal of Daniel Williams Harmon, 1800-1816* (Toronto: 1957), p. 63.

[13] E. Coues, *New Light,* I, p. 206.

[14] Ibid., I, pp. 245-246.

[15] Ibid., I, pp. 195, 275.

[16] L.R. Masson, ed., *Les Bourgeois de la Compagnie du Nord-Ouest* (Quebec. 1889-1890; reprinted 1960), p. 240. Mr. Duncan Cameron: *The Nipigon Country*, I, p. 804.

[17] W.K. Lamb, ed., *Letters of Alexander Mackenzie*, p. 461.

[18] J.B. Tyrrell, ed., *David Thompson's Narrative of his Explorations in Western, America, 1784-1812* (Toronto: 1916; reprinted 1968), p. 155.

[19] W.K. Lamb, ed., *Letters of Alexander Mackenzie*, p. 475.

[20] Ibid., p. 475.

[21] W.K. Lamb, ed., *Journal of Daniel Harmon*, p. 103.

[22] E. Coues, *New Light,* I, p. 216.

[23] L.R. Masson, *Les Bourgeois,* p. 299.

[24] E. Coues, *New Light,* I, pp. 25-26.

[25] Ibid., pp. 30-34.

[26] Ibid., p. 249.

[27] L.R. Masson, *Les Bourgeois,* pp. 267-272.
[28] Ibid., p. 276.
[29] Ibid., p. 286.
[30] Ibid., p. 269.
[31] Ibid., p. 314. Mr. Peter Grant: The Sauteux Indians about 1804.
[32] E.W. Morse, *Fur Trade Canoe Routes,* p. 68.
[33] E. Coues, *New Light,* I, p. 224.
[34] Ibid., p. 224.
[35] Ibid., p. 260.
[36] G.C. Davidson, *The North West Company* (New York. 1918; reprinted 1967), p. 232.
[37] E. Coues, *New Light,* I, p. 19.
[38] Ibid., p. 37.
[39] Ibid., p. 155.
[40] W.K. Lamb, ed., *Journal of Daniel Harmon,* p. 156.
[41] H.A. lnnis, *The Fur Trade,* p. 245.
[42] W.S. Wallace, *Documents,* p. 218.
[43] W.K. Lamb, ed., *Letters of Alexander Mackenzie,* p. 81.

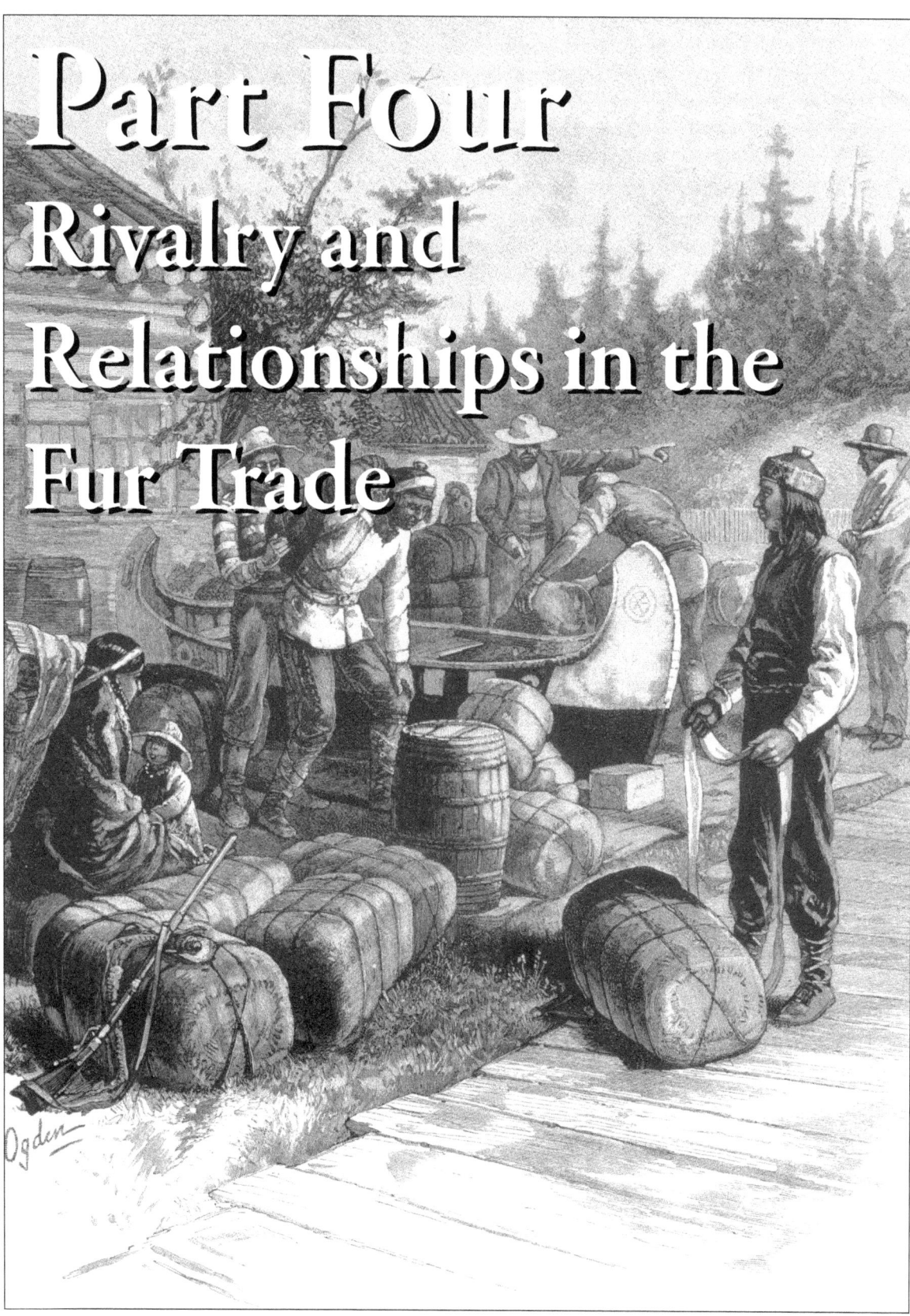

Part Four
Rivalry and Relationships in the Fur Trade

Part Four: Rivalry and Relationships in the Fur Trade

In "The Fur Trade Experience in the Rainy Lake Region", Theodore Catton uses the word "experience" to convey a holistic approach to the fur trade. Here the author explores the exchange between trader and Indian not only in furs but also in provisions and forest products. Material culture is important to any comprehensive study of the fur trade; in the Rainy Lake Region it includes the manufacture of birchbark canoes and the gathering of wild rice. Catton also touches on the social culture of fur trade relationships, including fur trade marriages, a topic examined more closely later in this book.

Until 1821, rivalry between the Hudson's Bay Company and Montreal traders flared sporadically along the Height of Land and in the contested Rainy Lake region. After 1821, it continued between the Hudson's Bay Company and independent American and Canadian traders along the corridor's southern margins. Catton and Stuart look at the effect of rivalry on the Native population. Both come to conclusions that may not be entirely politically correct.

In Part 2 of "Fur Trading at St. Joseph Island and Beyond", Stuart analyses the state of research into the role of Natives in the fur trade as of 1986. By then, the dearth of such studies prevailing twenty years earlier had been largely overcome. Now in 2003, almost twenty years later, a profusion of writings, audio-visual productions and educational courses on Native Studies proves the wide popularity of this topic at many levels of society, Native and non-Native alike.

Back in 1986, Stuart pointed to differing views on Indian participation in the fur trade. Some scholars viewed "any form of contact between Indian and European as inherently destructive." Others, however, saw "native society as adaptive and dynamic, able to adjust to changing circumstances brought about by cross-cultural contact." (Stuart, pp. 242-3) The debate continues. In her *The Ojibway of Western Canada, 1780 to 1870* (St. Paul: 1994), Laura Peers's subjects are the Anishinabeg who migrated westward from Sault Ste. Marie over many decades but whether this includes those who dropped off the way and remained at spots on Lake Superior or the waterways leading to Lake Winnipeg is not clear.

The Natives participated in the fur trade through choice, Peers insists. But while she acknowledges the devastating effects of alcohol, food shortages and depletion of resources on the Indians, she denies that they were "pawns in the trade, exploited, despoiled, and finally extinguished. " (Peers, p. 211) Stuart, on the other hand, reveals some of the more unsavory effects of the trade on the Michipicoten Ojibwa and draws some pessimistic conclusions about their fate. Catton has a similar view about the Rainy Lake Indians whose "relatively primitive political and material culture placed them at a disadvantage with the Europeans and the system tended to reward those traders who were most adept at manipulating the Indians according to their vulnerabilities."

Evidence for both sides of the debate may be found in the abundant store of primary sources on Canada's fur trade. By touching on this important issue, *From Lake Superior to Rainy Lake* hopefully will stimulate much more investigation into the impact of the fur trade on the Aboriginal peoples of Northwestern Ontario.

The Fur Trade Experience in the Rainy Lake Region*

By Theodore Catton with contributions by Marcia Montgomery

Trade was at the heart of fur trade society. It brought together Indians and non-Indians and encouraged them to bridge an enormous cultural divide. It also entailed competition between rival companies and highlighted significant differences between company cultures. While exchanges of goods and furs sometimes occurred when Europeans and Natives encountered one another on the move, most of the trade took place when the Natives brought their furs and other products to the post or when traders visited the Natives at their encampments. Reminiscences and travel diaries provide considerable information on the trade, but post journals are the best source for details about its conduct.

From a strictly economic standpoint, the fur trade consisted of two kinds of staple products exchanged for trade goods: a primary concern with furs, skins, and other animal products that had value in distant markets, and a secondary concern with other natural resources. As will be seen, the so-called "provisioning trade" encompassed foodstuffs such as wild rice, fish, berries, maple syrup and game. Also important were forest materials used in birchbark canoes, snowshoes, buildings and containers such as kegs and crates. The fur companies in the Rainy Lake Region acquired native-built canoes as trade items, but they also hired their own canoe builders to help meet their transportation needs. Company officers might differentiate between fur and non-fur trade items in their account books and year-end reports, but in other respects the two kinds of exchange overlapped. Trade was as much a basis of social relations as a system for economic gain.

The Ojibwa supplied the vast majority of furs and hides that were shipped out of the Rainy Lake Region. They hunted animals for their furs and hides at all times of year, although most often in the winter when the animals' fur coats were at their "prime" and would fetch a better price. Beaver pelts were the most common product in the early years, while muskrat skins became more common (though not the most valuable) in the later years of the fur trade. Other kinds of furs harvested by the Ojibwa of the Rainy Lake Region included bear, "cat" (lynx), fisher, marten, mink, moose, and otter. Rare but present in the Rainy Lake trade were caribou, porcupine, fox, and weasel. Seemingly no fur-bearing animal was too small to be harvested: ground squirrels and skunks were traded as well.

One of the earliest accounts of trade in the Rainy Lake Region is that of Alexander Henry (the Elder) in his *Travels and Adventures*, in which he describes an encounter with Ojibwa during his journey westward in 1775.

> We encamped at Les Fourches, on the River a la Pluie, where there was a village of Chipeways [the Ojibwa], of fifty lodges, of whom I bought new canoes. They insisted further on having goods given to them on credit, as well as on receiving some presents. The latter they regarded as an established tribute, paid them on account of the ability which they possessed, to put a stop to all trade with the interior. I gave them rum, with which they became drunk and troublesome; and in the night I left them.[1]

Typical of so many descriptions of trade, Henry's succinct account is deceptively simple. It touches on no less than four significant features of trading. First, his party traded for canoes rather than pelts—an example of the trade in non-fur items. Second, he mentions the Indians' desire for credit, a feature that became more common as time passed. Third, he notes that the Indians demanded presents, an important part of the ritual that surrounded trade. Fourth, he alludes to the role of liquor and its effect on how the encounter ended. Trad-

---

*Extracted with slight revisions from Chapters 2 and 3, "Special History: The Environment and the Fur Trade Experience in Voyageurs National Park, 1730-1870". Unpublished special history report prepared for Midwest Region, National Park Service by Historical Research Associates, Missoula, Montana, July 2000. Copyright reserved. Published here with permission.

ing involved much more than an exchange of goods; economic interests were tightly bundled with social and cultural meanings that formed the foundation of fur trade society.

Traders often recorded specific types and quantities of goods they exchanged. In 1793, John McKay of the Hudson's Bay Company traded an unidentified Indian chief two gallons of spirits and two pounds of tobacco for sixteen gallons of [wild] rice.[2] In 1819, an Ojibwa named The Little Rat brought twenty muskrat skins and a half beaver pelt to the Rainy Lake Fort, for which he received one gallon of "Leeward Island Rum." A few days later, another Ojibwa named The Little Deer obtained a credit of fifty Made Beaver at the post. For this quantity of furs, the Little Deer received "a Complete Chief Clothing with a Flag," plus two and a half gallons of rum, one and a half pounds of powder, three pounds of BB shot, one and a half pounds of "low India," one comb, three knives, one fire steel, one pound of tobacco, eight flints, and one fourth pound vermillion-–all taken from the store.[3]

The Little Deer's purchase of "a Complete Chief Clothing with a Flag" on credit illustrates an important strategy that traders employed to secure trading relationships with more Indians. By giving certain Indians extra presents and outfitting them in scarlet coats and pants, traders hoped to influence these "chiefs" to encourage other Indians to trade with them as well. Honouring such men as "chiefs" benefited both parties: The Little Deer gained prestige among his own people, and the trader gained new trading partners.

Roderick McKenzie, master of the HBC fort, alluded to this practice when he recorded, on September 29, 1819, that The Little Deer and The Little Rat had both been promised "chief's clothing" by his predecessor, Robert Logan. The two Indians, he wrote, "expect those articles & likewise better treatment than the rest of there [sic] tribe." A shrewd trader such as McKenzie tried to be sensitive to such relationships when he started at a new post. "The rat again made a Second demand for Rum," McKenzie noted in the post journal on the following day, "which I was obliged to give him it would appear that this Indian has been indulged a good deal by the deceased Mr. Don[al]d McPherson & afterwards by Mr. Logan...."[4]

Little Deer's credit was measured in 50 "Made Beaver." Made Beaver was the term HBC traders used to describe a certain quantity and value of furs. A Made Beaver was the equivalent of a single prime beaver pelt. It took a number of lowly muskrat skins to equal one Made Beaver, while a single good bearskin was typically worth three Made Beaver. The fur trade was based on the barter system, yet the Made Beaver increasingly served as a kind of "currency" that standardized the value of pelts. European trade goods could also be measured in terms of Made Beaver. For instance, a gun could be priced at fourteen Made Beaver, a blanket valued at seven Made Beaver, and a hatchet exchanged for one Made Beaver.

Credit, or "debt" as the traders called it, defined the "mode" of trade. The credit system developed early in the Rainy Lake Region where competition between companies was particularly keen. Traders offered credit as a means of securing trade, often at the expense of their rivals. The Hudson's Bay trader John McKay alluded to "giving debt" in 1793.[5] He complained three years later of the amount of credit being extended by North West Company traders in the region. "The more outfits in such a small area the more dearer they must buy their trade," he observed, "for an Indian will take debt from one and trade his furs to another of the same concern." McKay accused his Canadian competitors of encouraging the Indians to cheat on their debts.[6]

The overuse of credit became prominent again in the years 1816-1817 when the Hudson's Bay Company and the North West Company actually came to armed conflict in the Rainy Lake Region.[7] It was frequently mentioned again in the early 1820s when the Hudson's Bay Company sought to force the American Fur Company to abandon its tenuous hold in the border lakes country. In 1825, Chief Factor John Dugald Cameron described the credit system as he had applied it over the previous few years. The details he entered in his district report for that year display a remarkable degree of sensitivity and moral ambivalence, as well as self-justification, about his trading practices. [They also reveal much about the material conditions in which the Indians lived and laboured. ed.] Following is a shortened version of his "article" on "mode of trade".

John Dugald Cameron's Mode of Trade [extracts]

This is a difficult article to dwell upon. when people are alone, they may act as they please, but when along side of opposition a trader must be guided by Circumstances which are liable to frequent changes. He must Sometimes act differently with different Indians and at times must vary his Conduct with Some Indian. An Indian is not always the same thing. However the general mode is, to Supply an Indian in the Fall, if not with his wants, at least, with a Sufficiency to enable him to pass the Winter. The Summer is not the Season for hunting. Indians therefore with their families are generally Naked in Autumn, hence the absolute necessity of advancing an Indian Some goods on Debt, without which it would be impossible for him, in this Department, to get through the Winter.

In other parts of the Country where large Animals are numerous, An Indian may Cloath himself with leather: but here it is impossible, he can have no other recourse whatever but to our Goods, Nay, we are obliged to bring in drest leather & parchments, to Supply him with the Means of Making his shoes & Snowshoes. We make a point however, of dealing out his Supplies according to his ability as a hunter. To Some More, others less. It must be observed that there is Some Art in refusing an Indian, as well as in making him a present. A quality too much neglected by Some Traders; and altogether unattainable by others.

My custom when giving out debts is I have a Blotter [record book] made for the purpose before me I call each Indian who is present and desire him to name the Articles he is most in want when he names an Article that I think he can do without, I tell him so, & make him acknowledge his inability from the poverty of his Lands to pay a heavy debt.–

After I have written what he is to get on debt I add the gratuities Such as a Couple of Measures of Ammunition to every Man of family, two Knives, a Steel, an Awl, five Needles five flints–Some Thread, a little Vermillion and half a fathom of Tobacco besides Liquor– To young men who have no families one Knife, a Steel, three flints & Some vermillion besides Liquor. Sometimes a foot of Tobacco. After the wants of all present are are [sic] written down, I give the Blotter to the Clerk, who calls the Indians to the Shop One after the other, and delivers to each the Articles Mentioned to his name– Every one gets their Liquor apart. Once the Blotter is taken to the Shop, it is in vain for any to recall to his Mind Articles that he has forgotten, unless it is a file or an ax I always make it a point to Send off an Indian pleased after he has taken debt, and I Seldom or never fail, but then, I am lavish with the Liquor– In Winter however, I generally make up for my extravagance in the fall. I always give them a Dram on their arrival and on their departure.
…

The Doctor [John McLoughlin] was in the habit of Cloathing a few of the Chiefs, whether they had paid their debts or not. In this I have differed from My Friend as I found the Chiefs did not lay a Sufficient Value on the cloathings consequently had become rather remiss in their exertions. Indeed they Considered the Cloathings as their due providing they had not given a Skin to the O.P. [opposing or rival post]. However I gave them to understand: that I had never despised my Cloathings So far as to put them on Chiefs who were so largely in debt as they were; that any stranger who would look in the Books and see their Balances, would not believe they were Chiefs but consider the word Chief attached to their names as a Mistake, that they appeared to look on a Chiefs Cloathing as a mere common dress to deserve which, they did not deem it worth their while to exert themselves: that they must be more sparing in taking debt, and more diligent in paying: that I did not intend to break them but Still Considered them as Chiefs; and would always feel a pride in cloathing them, providing I would See no Balances against them; with much more to the Same purpose. Their pride was hurt; but no feelings wounded. ....

After my arrival last September I told the Indians that not one was to get a Skins worth of Goods before he had paid the balance due on the Goods he had from me the Autumn before. As for the Balances due the Doctor, I would pass over them for the present. nor had I any intentions of exacting furs for them, but whenever they would be Successful in gathering a good Crop of rice I would then insist on the Doctors debts being paid. Though they did not all pay their Balances, yet, I was well pleased with their exertions, for generally speaking, their Fall Hunts were good. In all my discourses with them Since My arrival last– I never gave them the least hint that I thought there was an Opposition on the opposite Side– no more, than if there never had been an American in the Country.

> My first year here, I made no presents of goods to any Indians whatever, except two, Horse Lake Rat and little Deer of War-road. To the first, I gave a laced Capot & pair Leggens– and Some Silver works to his Wife. To the latter I gave a pr: Leggens, a Breech-Cloth, and a new net. The former was an American Indian, who had given me all his Hunt which was mostly Beaver. The little Deer had made a very good hunt and was almost uncommonly honest.
>
> Last fall I was more generous– I gave four Capots, with as many pairs leggens and as Many Sleeves to Indians good hunters who have large families and who were going to a great distance to hunt. This Spring after they had finished their winter Hunts and returned from their ineffectual efforts; I treated them as if they had made good spring hunts since their want of Success Was by no means owing to a want of exertion as I never Saw Indians got to work more heartily. But from the amazing height of the water it was impossible for them to make rat Hunt[s]. ... In My speeches to them I condoled with them on the Starving State that the Major part of them had past the winter, in the mean time pointed out the necessity, as well as Suggested the Means, to the best of my judgement, of Collecting as much Provisions during Summer as possible. I lamented the cause which led to the failure of their Spring hunts which desabled them from clearing off their debts. I should have been happy, for their own Sakes, as well as mine that they had been Successful; but Still, I was Satisfied with their exertions therefore exonerated them from all Blame. To two or three with whom I was not pleased for want of exertion in winter because the[y] had not Starvation for an excuse, I gave proper repremands. I encouraged the whole to bring good bark in Summer in order to Score off their debts. They all went off highly pleased after repeatedly observing that they were much better treated than they expected or deserved.[8]

Was the relationship between trader and Indian exploitative? Certainly it contained many harsh features and probably most traders and Indians wrestled with the issue to one degree or another. Compared to the harsh conditions surrounding the terms of employment of *engagés*, Indians had considerable freedom to come and go, work when they pleased, and negotiate the price of their labour. Yet the Indians' relatively primitive political and material culture placed them at a disadvantage with the Europeans and the system tended to reward those traders who were most adept at manipulating the Indians according to their vulnerabilities. Traders tacitly acknowledged the Indians' growing dependency in the way they identified them. In the early years, traders referred to the Indians in the Rainy Lake Region by their tribe or clan name. As time passed, they increasingly identified them by company affiliation. Dr. John McLoughlin, in particular, wrote frequently of "our Indians" when he was in competition with the Americans.[9]

As Cameron's article attests, the credit system involved traders and Indians in highly personalized relationships. Traders came to know much more about their trading partners than simply their trustworthiness and hunting ability. They were aware of feuds between Ojibwa bands. They knew the number of wives and children who were dependent on each Indian hunter. In 1817, the HBC trader Donald McPherson noted the deaths of two Indians, remarking that he had had to cancel their combined debt of 80 Made Beaver and that they had both left "numerous family to deplore their loss."[10] In 1830, Cameron had been in the Rainy Lake Region for six years and knew hundreds of Indians by name. He listed all 629 Indians–men, women, and children–in the district report for that year. Allowing for three or four exceptions, he noted that they were "honest enough" and would "give hunts" to pay their debts.[11]

The Rainy Lake post journals are filled with references to the use of liquor in trading and to displays of Indian drunkenness. Indeed, liquor was as much a part of the ritual of trade as an actual commodity of trade. Traders usually dispensed liquor and tobacco to Indians as gifts in order to initiate or conclude a trading session. Often when Indians arrived at the fort there would be a day or two of drunken revelry and only afterward did traders and Indians exchange manufactured goods for furs. Traders found the Indians' desire for liquor and the Indians' drunken behavior rather appalling, even frightening, but the protocols of trade nevertheless demanded the liberal use of liquor. In the Rainy Lake Region, where competition between traders was often intense, liquor probably flowed even more freely than elsewhere.[12]

Hudson's Bay Company Post at Rat Portage, 1857. Grace Lee Nute, Rainy River Country *(St. Paul: MHS, 1950). In 1857 this post was on an island at the outflow from Lake of the Woods into the Winnipeg River on the fur trade route to the west. The Ojibwa called the area* Wauzhushk Onigum, *or portage to the country of the muskrat. After its removal to the mainland in 1861, Rat Portage became the nucleus for a new settlement by that name. In 1905 the town adopted the name KENORA by combining the first two letters of KEewatin, a sister town; NOrman, an adjacent village; and RAt Portage.*

Provisioning trade

Traders' journals also make many references to the provisioning trade. When traders were travelling between posts, they were generally more concerned with obtaining food than furs, and invariably their supplies for the trip included a stock of liquor and tobacco for purposes of trade. Jonathan Carver recalled that his party in 1767 procured "some rice and plenty of fish" from Ojibwa at Grand Portage. "Otherwise we must have starved to death, for hunting had been poor." Alexander Henry the Elder traded with Ojibwa at the Forks on Rainy River in 1775.

On his first trip from Osnaburgh to Rainy Lake in September 1793, John McKay and his party relied on a combination of food traded from the Indians, "European provisions," and fish they caught along the way. On one day, for example, he obtained "3 days fresh venison and twelve gallons of rice" from trade. Shortly after his arrival at Rainy Lake, McKay made a trip to Lake of the Woods for the purpose of obtaining rice for the fort's pantry. He reported in the post journal that one Ojibwa chief traded him 16 gallons of rice for two gallons of liquor and 2 pounds of tobacco. In all he procured only 30 gallons of rice from the Lake of the Woods Ojibwa, and concluded that the men of the North West Company had beat him to the trade.

Another important contribution to the provisioning trade was dried fish. Traders soon learned from the Ojibwa where the best fishing places were located, but they were not as successful at fishing. The traders only employed nets to catch sturgeon, whereas the Ojibwa caught them with nets or spears. The Ojibwa cut the sturgeon into thin flakes, which they dried over a slow fire. They then pounded the dried flakes between stones until they became like a kind of sponge. When eaten, the absorbent pieces of dried fish were dipped in oil (animal fat), making them "a rich and substantial food of which they are fond." The most productive sturgeon fisheries were located along the Rainy River.

Ojibwa also supplied the traders with "grease" or animal fat, venison, fowl, and berries. A list of provisions served to the men over a six-month period at the Hudson's Bay Company's Rainy Lake fort in 1796 gives some indication of the importance of the provisioning trade, as native foods easily overshadow imported foods. John McKay listed: 30 gallons brandy, 234 gallons rice, 7 gallons bear oil, 151 pounds bacon, 40 pounds beef, 3439 pounds fish, 324 pounds pork, 418 pounds venison, 21 geese, and 97 ducks.

FUR TRADE SOCIETY

Besides the system of credit or "debt" and the ritual use of liquor, another crucial aspect of trade involved intermarriage and the resulting ties of kinship between European and Indian. The experience of John McKay shows how marriages *à la façon du pays* benefited the traders. The North West Company had allowed McKay to store some Hudson's Bay Company goods at its Lac La Pluie post.[13] McKay returned to pick up the goods in 1796 hoping to trade with some local Indians whom he had previously befriended with lavish presents. But the fort's proprietor, Peter Grant, had recently married the daughter of the Indians' late chief. The chief's sons now would trade only with Grant, their brother-in-law, and not with the unfortunate McKay. Another instance is that of Donald McPherson, the Hudson's Bay Company trader at Rainy Lake after its seizure by Lord Selkirk's De Meurons from the North West Company in 1817. McPherson had a Canadian wife while his assistant was married to "a small metis." Joining his fellow De Meurons after their seizure of the post later that year, Lieutenant Frederic Graffenried, a German, revealed the outsider's prejudice toward such marriages when he remarked in his diary, "It felt odd that I had to be entertained by two individuals and their wives, one of whom was half savage and the other in no way belonged to the Canadian upper class."[14] These examples show how interracial marriages were important in securing trade with neighboring Indians, but traders also attributed their success or difficulty to other factors such as the supply of rum or the offering of debt by rivals.

Perhaps the two companies' proximity in the Rainy Lake Region made the rival company cultures more alike than in other regions. Certainly the Hudson's Bay Company employed a large number of Canadians with French surnames at its Rainy Lake Fort. Lord Selkirk recognized this element in the population when he worked with the Roman Catholic Church to send missionaries to the area in 1816-1818. When the priest Joseph Norbert Provencher arrived at Rainy Lake in July 1818, he held Mass at the North West Company fort one day and the Hudson's Bay Company fort the next. Significantly, the first Mass included a baptism of nineteen children from both forts, and the families of both companies gathered again for an evening service.[15]

Labour relations were also probably more alike at these two rival forts than was typical for other North West and Hudson's Bay establishments because the employees fraternized and company officers colluded in maintaining discipline. It was not possible for a hired man, or *engagé*, to quit one company and go to work for the other. When a man named Gayou deserted the North West Company and sought a new place at the XY Company fort at Rainy Lake in 1804, the master of the fort co-operated in his arrest and immediate return to his original employer.[16]

"Deserters" of either company were treated harshly. When a man named Roy deserted from the North West Company fort at Rainy Lake in 1806, the master trader "made an example of him by making him stand an Hour naked on the Roof of the A. Store."[17] When several *engagés* conspired to mutiny at Rainy Lake in 1794, the company arrested the ringleaders and sent them "down to Montreal in disgrace."[18]

The traders who served the rival companies at Rainy Lake were nevertheless aware of certain differences between the companies. For example, the Hudson's Bay Company had a more structured hierarchy based on class and kinship; the North West Company was more open to risk-taking and advancement based on merit. A trader like John McKay of the Hudson's Bay Company was probably a little in awe of his counterpart, Peter Grant of the North West Company, who, according to McKay, had "a share of the profits and of course must have a share of the loss."[19] The North West Company's Duncan McDonald, meanwhile, expressed disgust at the way the more class-conscious Hudson's Bay Company promoted "drunkards" as long as they could speak and write well.[20]

Seasonal Routines

Daily life at either fort revolved around physical toil, mostly outdoors. These tasks were designed not only to further the trade but also to ensure the survival of the traders and their employees. John McLoughlin described the array of tasks on May 26, 1823: "The Men Employed making Canoes–planting potatoes–sowing wheat all at once–the Women of the fort drying sturgeon and sowing Indian corn."[21] Work routines followed a seasonal rhythm: fishing, hunting, and harvesting crops in the fall; trading and ice-fishing in the winter; planting crops, building canoes, and storing ice in the spring; transporting goods in and out of the country in the summer. The harvest might be concluded with a celebration. John Cameron wrote in the post journal for October 2, 1824: "On the 28th ulto in the Evening Mr McGillivray gave us a Dance. This was called the Harvest Dance in Consequence of the Men having tyed a dozen Ears of Corn taken from the last Sheave put into the Barn, with a little ribbon and presented to Mr McG. as a *Bousquet*."[22]

Fall fishing centered on the sturgeon migration, and the more sturgeon that could be caught or traded in the fall the better the outlook for getting through the winter without too much hunger. Fall hunts were also common, although this activity could continue into the winter especially when fall fishing was poor. John McKay described his bitter frustration during the winter of 1793-94 when a pack of wolves stole some 200 pounds of venison and he had to send his hunters out to get more meat. Killing some moose that February, the hunters slept by their kills each night till they were able to get the meat back to the fort.[23]

The winter months featured trade, for it was at this time of year that animal furs were at their best. To facilitate trade, men sometimes drew the unwelcome assignment to pass time in "watching tents" and steer Indians toward their fort and away from their competitor's. Sometimes pairs of Hudson's Bay and North West Company men occupied neighboring tents, watching for Indians and hoping to see them and get out to them ahead of their rivals. Sometimes the men traveled to Indian camps to encourage the Indians to bring in their hunts.[24] And on still other occasions the company men went to trade directly in native camps and villages. This form of trade was known as *en dérouine*.[25]

Undoubtedly, winter tested the men's morale more than any other season. Short days and long nights, frightfully cold temperatures, strict rationing of provisions, and stoppage of mail all tended to make the winter months an experience to be endured. Christmas and New Year's celebrations relieved the tedium and hardship somewhat and usually framed a full week of merriment, as the stern John McLoughlin recorded in 1823-24:

> [December 25, 1823.] This being Christmas gave the men twenty five pounds flour and four Sturgeons to feast themselves
> [December 26.] All hands [illegible] gave the men a diner and a Gallon spirits
> [December 29.] The men bought a little liquor and are Keeping up the Holidays
> [December 30.] the men unwell or rather too much [illegible] to work after their frolic.
> [January 1, 1824.] this being the new Year gave the men a treat of twenty five pounds flour and three Sturgeons to feast themselves in the Evening as usual on this day gave them a dance invited Cote the American Clerk with the women of their [illegible]– but told him that none of his men must come—none of the American people are allowed to come except Cote the Master I do this to prevent any misunderstanding arising in consequence of men going with Stories from one house to the other.[26]

Transportation: The Canoe

Transportation was nearly as prominent in the fur trade experience as trade itself. For the semi-nomadic Ojibwa, canoe travel was integral to their aboriginal way of life; the fur trade only encouraged Indians to make longer trips such as that of John Tanner and his family from the Rainy Lake Region to Michilimackinac as described in *A Narrative of Captivity and Adventures of John Tanner* (1830). For European and American traders, however, the adaptation to canoe travel formed one of the most distinctive aspects of their experience. Even those traders

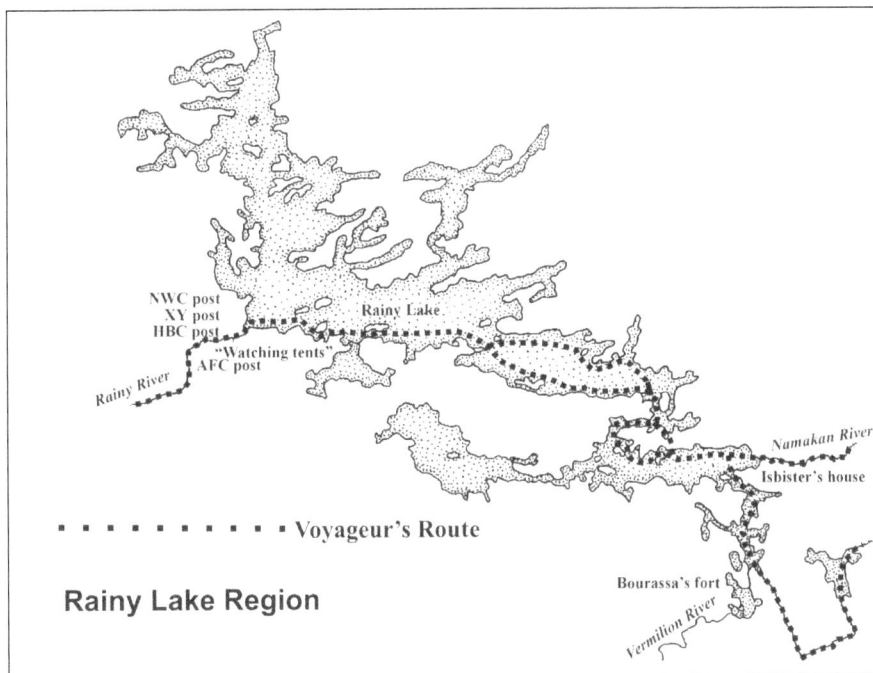

Rainy Lake Region. The NWC's Fort Lac la Pluie was on the Rainy River just west of Chaudiere Falls. In 1817 the HBC opened a new Lac la Pluie post about one mile upstream. This post was renamed Fort Frances in honour of George Simpson's wife. La Verendrye's Fort St. Pierre was nearby as was the XY post. The American Fur Company (AFC) operated in U.S. territory across the river. Bourassa's fort was a French post. Isbister's house was occupied by James Isbister, Hudson's Bay Company post master of the Lac La Pluie District in the mid-nineteenth century. Courtesy: Historical Research Associates, Missoula, Montana

who occupied posts for most of the year traveled locally on a frequent basis and made long journeys once a year or more. Post journals are useful sources of information on transportation, but the many published diaries and reminiscences are the richest source for this theme.

At Rainy Lake, one of the most important tasks each spring was canoe construction. The birch and cedar forests in the region provided essential raw materials for canoes, making Rainy Lake a prime location for canoe manufacture and adding to the area's strategic importance for both the Hudson's Bay and North West companies. Sometimes the men at the post secured the supply of wood for canoes, and on other occasions they traded with Indians for these materials. Two Indians in 1830, for example, brought 59 rolls of bark to the fort "which was taken on their debts." For many years, a man named Augee built all of the canoes at Rainy Lake Fort. He would build as many as eight canoes in a season.[27]

Springtime also saw the return of water transportation, the renewal of long-distance communications with the arrival of mail packets in the light, fast canoes, and preparations for the supply of large brigades moving east or west through the country. Many of the employees of the fort undertook long journeys by canoe during the summer months, mostly to the rendezvous at Fort William, leaving their wives and children behind. Sometimes, on the eve of such a mass departure, the fort would stage an all-night farewell dance.[28]

The speed of travel over the canoe routes in the Rainy Lake Region varied considerably depending on the type of canoe, the experience of the crews, the kind of weather encountered, and the current water levels. To make the trip from Rainy Lake to Lake Superior in ten days was to make good time, although it could be done in half that. Two weeks was perhaps an average time, and if conditions were unfavorable it could take much longer. Experienced crews of voyageurs could propel the canoes at an amazing speed, but travelers had to allow for frequent interruptions. Portages were, of course, the biggest cause of delay along most rivers.[29]

Another source of delay involved the frequent need for gumming the canoes. Crews had to stop often to daub the birchbark canoes with pitch, which acted as a sealant and helped the canoes cut the water more cleanly. Delays also occurred whenever a canoe's lading got wet, for it became necessary to disembark the goods and lay them out on the ground to dry. If it was a cool day and the sun became hidden, or if it began to rain, the whole operation might have to be interrupted and resumed again later.[30]

Bad weather not only caused delays, it could imperil the lives of the travelers. Although crews made better time on the big waters, especially if there was a fair breeze to hoist a sail, they had to put ashore when winds became too strong. Cold temperatures and pan ice were also a threat to the fragile birchbark canoes, rendering canoe travel in late fall or early spring both hazardous and problematic. When the lake surfaces were partially frozen, floating ice could tear a hole in a canoe and sink it. One party arrived at Fort Frances in late November 1834 terrified and exhausted after breaking through new ice the whole length of Rainy Lake. "The only thing that saved them from going to the bottom," the chief trader wrote, "was that their canoe with the cold was cased over both in and out with ice."[31] As well, birchbark canoes were known to crack in the cold air when hauled out of water.[32]

Fur Trade Posts in the Rainy Lake Region

As seen the park's terrain is a representative portion of a much greater historical geography. The voyageurs' travels through what is now Voyageurs National Park were generally part of much larger journeys. Rainy Lake was a transportation hub and a strategic crossroads in the fur trade. All of the major fur trading companies that operated in the area had posts near the outlet of Rainy Lake in the vicinity of what is now Fort Frances, Ontario and International Falls, Minnesota. Historic activities surrounding these posts give the Rainy Lake Region much of its historical significance, but the posts themselves were situated a few miles outside of the park boundary. The origin and present condition of these posts may be briefly described:

Fort St. Pierre. This small wintering post was built by the French in 1731. Currently there is a reconstruction of this post at Pithers Point. Although an archaeological survey was conducted at Pithers Point in the late 1950s, the exact site of the post is not confirmed.

North West Company Post. This post was used as a relay point for cargoes moving between the interior and Montreal. No drawing or plan of the post is known. There is a Heritage Foundation commemorative plaque at the presumed site of the post on private property near the Red Dog Inn Hotel, located on Keating Avenue and River Drive in Fort Frances, Ontario.

Hudson's Bay Company Post. This post was built subsequent to the North West Company post and continued to serve as a store until 1923. Plans, drawings, and photographs of this post have been collected to assist with interpretation of this site, which is similarly marked with a Heritage Foundation commemorative plaque. Some archaeological survey was done at the site in the 1980s. The site is now occupied by offices of the paper mill in Fort Frances, Ontario.

American Fur Company Post. This post was located on the south bank of the Rainy River near the Hudson's Bay Company post. The exact location has not been determined and there is no site interpretation.

Bourassa's Fort. This small outpost was built by the French and later re-established by the British in the early 1800s. Archaeological survey was done in the mid-1990s, establishing its precise location on the west shore of Crane Lake. Nothing remains of the post that is visible to the untrained eye.

Besides occupying these posts, fur traders frequently came to shore on their watery passage through what is now Voyageurs National Park. The water, accompanying scenery, geology and rich cultural and natural resources that give the Park its national significance, merits its protection for the enjoyment of present and future generations.

NOTES

[1] Alexander Henry, *Travels and Adventures in Canada and the Indian Territories* (Toronto: George Dorang, 1901), p. 240.
[2] HBCA, B.105/a/1, fol. 5.
[3] HBCA, B.105/a/7, fol. 37.
[4] Roderick McKenzie, Lac La Pluie Post Journal for 1819-1820, HBCA, B.105/a/7, fol. 36.
[5] HBCA, B. 105/a/1, fol. 5-fol.7.

[6] HBCA, B. 105/a/1, fol. 10d-fol.11.
[7] See, for example, Friedrich Von Graffenried, *Sechs Jahre in Canada, 1813-1819* (Bern: 1891), p. 10. Trans. by Elsbeth Glocker.
[8] HBCA, B. 105/e/6, fol. 4d-fol.6d.
[9] HBCA, B.105/a/9, passim.
[10] HBCA, B.105/e1, fol. l0.17. HBCA, B. 105/e/9, fol.4d-10.
[11] HBCA, B.105/e/9, fol. 4d-10.
[12] For a study of Indian use of liquor during the fur trade, see R.D. Dailey, "The Role of Alcohol among North American Indian Tribes as reported in The Jesuit Relations," *Anthropologica*, vol. 10, no 1 (1968), pp. 45-57. For a focus on liquor in trade ritual, see Bruce M. White, "A Skilled Game of Exchange: Ojibway Fur Trade Protocol," *Minnesota History*, Vol. 50 (Summer 1987), pp. 229-240.
[13] See Part V below for more on fur trade society.
[14] Alma E. Henry, ed. David M. Chapman, "Fur Trade Rivalry on the Rainy River (1793-1797), Thunder Bay Historical Museum Society *Papers & Records,* XXVII (2000), p. 65; [Grant reference added)]. Graffenried, *Sechs Jahre in Canada*, p. l0.
[15] Grace Lee Nute, ed. and trans., *Documents relating to Northwest Missions, 1815-1827* (St. Paul: Minnesota Historical Society, 1942), pp. 123-4.
[16] Charles M. Gates, ed., *Five Fur Traders of the North West* (St. Paul: Minnesota Historical Society, 1965), p. 206
[17] NAC, MG 19 E l (1) Selkirk Papers, p. 9259.
[18] Arthur S. Morton, ed., *The Journal of Duncan M'Gillivray of the North West Company* (Toronto: MacMillan, 1929), p. 8.
[19] HBCA, B.105/a/4, fol. 7.
[20] Selkirk Papers, p. 15.
[21] HBCA, B.105/a/8, fol. 14d.
[22] HBCA, B.105/a/10, fol. 3d.
[23] HBCA, B.105a1, fol. 13-15.
[24] HBCA, B.105a/5, fol. 11-12.
[25] John Francis McDermott, *A Glossary of Mississippi Valley French, 1673-1850* (St. Louis, 1941), p. 66.
[26] HBCA, B. 105/a/9, fol. 39.
[27] HBCA, B.105/a/14-15, passim, quote on fol. 5d.
[28] HBCA, B.105/a/10, fol.19d.
[29] John Emslie, "Journal of Expedition to Fort Garry, 1870," Microfilm Collection, NAC, p. 5.
[30] Gates, ed., *Five Fur Traders*, p. 200.
[31] HBCA, B.105/a/19, fol. 9.
[32] Minnesota History Center (MHS), Manuscript Collection P 489, Box 6, p. 4. James Evans Diary

Indians and the Lake Superior Trade*

By Ian T. Stuart

Numerically the Chippewa or Ojibwa were the strongest nation in the Lake Superior region, numbering about 6000 individuals in 1804. They controlled territory to the south in present day Wisconsin and north as far as the Hudson Bay watershed where they came into contact with Cree. The French named the Chippewa who frequented the St. Mary's River "Saulteurs" [because they lived by the river's "sault" or rapids.] The Saulteurs were a single tribe of the Chippewa nation. The tribe itself was subdivided into individual bands, each led by a chief who had charge over a specified territory. The band was bound together by strong kinship ties.

The Saulteurs were nomadic, travelling to the St. Mary's River in the spring and summer to fish, and then dispersing inland north of Lake Superior over the winter to hunt beaver and moose. The Hudson's Bay Company posts north of the Height of Land were visited by Indians of the Cree nation, which flanked the Chippewa on the north and west.[1]

The fur trade of the Chippewa and Cree of northern Lake Superior provides an interesting case study for testing whether Indians were simply pawns in a European game or if they were able to manipulate the competitive situation which existed between the Hudson's Bay Company and the North West Company to their advantage. Fortunately, post journals for the Hudson's Bay Company post at Michipicoten have survived for the period prior to 1821 and they provide an insight into the role played by the Indians in the fur trade in that vicinity.[2]

Originally a French post, Michipicoten was visited first by Alexander Henry the Elder shortly after the Conquest. In 1778 he sold the operation to Jean Baptiste Nolin and Venant St. Germain. The North West Company took over from Nolin and St. Germain after 1784. The Montreal men were so successful in controlling the trade of the north shore from their lake side posts that the Hudson's Bay Company was forced to move inland in an attempt to recapture their share of the returns. On 15 May 1797 Henry John Moze, along with an Indian guide and three men left Micabanish House on Brunswick Lake and travelled to Michipicoten, there to establish a Hudson's Bay Company post to compete directly with the North West Company. They arrived at the "Canadian" house, which was commanded by Alexander Henry the Younger, on June 8th and immediately set about building their establishment.

Moze had no difficulty attracting Indians to his encampment. Unfortunately for him, they came looking for brandy and tobacco but had no furs to trade, having already given them to Henry. Still, Moze was obliged to provide for the Indians in an attempt to lure them away from the North West Company. Over June, July and August Moze distributed the equivalent of forty-two made beaver in brandy and five made beaver in tobacco to the Indians. A total value of 162½ made beaver of various trade goods were distributed to Indians taking debts in the first year of operation from 1797 to 1798. Returns fell short by over 62 made beaver.[3]

The following season expenses at the post reached $728^{1/6}$ made beaver. Expenses at Michipicoten were much higher than at the Bay posts. The costs associated with transportation and communication were understandably great. Distance added to the cost of provisioning and supplying the post. Even if returns had been higher chances are Michipicoten would have been hard pressed to turn a profit. The value of furs sent from Michipicoten in July equalled only 470 made beaver, or a deficiency of approximately 268. It was obvious that the post was operating at a loss. In response to the competition provided by the Hudson's Bay Company Henry proposed a fair trade agreement which was ratified by both men in June 1797. It stated that neither party would interfere with Indians in the interior and allow them to choose freely between the two houses. This freedom was non-existent.

---

*Extracted from "Fur Trading at St. Joseph Island and Beyond: From the French Regime to 1821". Part 2 of 2, pp. 252-258. Report prepared for Environment Canada, Parks, 1986. Copyright reserved. Permission to publish kindly granted.

In May 1798 an Indian slipped away from the North West Company house with a single damaged cat skin to pay his debt with Moze. He informed Moze that it was the only fur Henry would permit him to take away.

The problem for Moze was breaking the hold of the North West Company men over the Indians. This he was unable to do. In its first year Michipicoten secured 100 made beaver. By 1800 this total had risen to 500 made beaver but thereafter declined. Faced with declining returns Moze took the offensive. In July 1801 he quarrelled with a "gang" of Indians from Sault Ste. Marie who traded all their furs to the "Canadians" and then showed up at his post requesting liquor. He refused. During the following spring Maze ordered his men to seize Indian canoes as they passed the post and forcibly remove furs as payment on outstanding debts. This type of activity was unlikely to endear him to his customers. In fact Moze concluded that the post would be a continual drain on the Company and source of anxiety to present and future residents. The result was that the fur trade at Michipicoten remained firmly within the control of the North West Company. In 1803 the Hudson's Bay Company agreed to remove from Michipicoten if the North West Company removed from Micabanish on Brunswick Lake.[4]

What can this brief episode at one post tell us about the role played by the Indian in the Lake Superior trade? Unfortunately, because the journals were written from the perspective of a European trader, not very much. Conclusions must be necessarily tentative. In the first place it is clear that the Indians benefitted from the competitive situation. Moze was obliged on many occasions to be more generous in granting presents than he would have liked because he wanted to attract more business. Moreover, according to post accounts the value of Indian presents, exclusive of other operating expenses, was consistently higher than fifty percent of the value of returns. These figures are for Indian presents only. If the regular expenses of operating the post were included, Michipicoten consistently lost money during this seven year period. That Moze was forced to seize Indian canoes travelling down to the North West Company fort suggests that natives took advantage of the situation by taking a debt at one post and trading with the other.[5]

It could be argued, however, that rather than being exploited by the market-wise Indian, Moze, by distributing generous amounts of presents, was simply investing in the future well-being of his post. For instance, when Moze ministered to an Indian who had been shot by his son-in-law during a drinking bout he saw only an opportunity to convince the family "to bring a part of [their] Furrs, at least, to us...."[6] Similarly, it is likely that the Hudson's Bay Company established the post at Michipicoten in response to incursions by the North West Company across the Hudson Bay watershed. As such the post served as leverage in the contest to control the fur trade of the interior.

For competition to work in favour of the consumer it required roughly equal combatants. This was not the case at Michipicoten where the North West Company retained a stranglehold on the loyalty of the Indians. In fact, in 1818 Donald McIntosh gave some Indians who had dared to trade with the Hudson's Bay Company "a most severe beating" which had "struck terror into their hearts."[7] From this it appears that competition did little to enhance the situation of the Lake Superior Indians.

Prior to the arrival of Europeans Indians of the Lake Superior region lived at or near a subsistence level, engaging in almost constant hunting, fishing and trapping. It could be argued that they were dependent on the vicissitudes of climate and habitat. Their entrance into the fur economy in essence freed them from the bonds imposed by their stone age existence. In short order tribes became dependent on European trade goods for their survival. As time progressed the Indian's dependence on the trading post increased until they could not return to their old ways of life. Perhaps an outdated opinion, this, nonetheless, was the scenario played out in the northwest during the 18th and early 19th centuries. Despite attempts to portray the Indian as adaptable and dynamic, evidence suggests that the Native economy and social structure was destroyed by the introduction of European manners and material.

Conclusion [extracts]

There is a trend away from the school of thought which argued that any contact with non-native or non-traditional cultures was by definition destructive. Many scholars, rather than seeing Indian society as passive, have found that native groups adapted to European civilization and often manipulated the situation to their advantage. In fact, their entrance into the fur trade economy freed Native groups from living at or near the subsistence level. Despite these findings, evidence taken from the specified region suggests that the Native economy and social structure were obliterated by the introduction of European manners and material. [*It also indicates that in the area now known as Northwestern Ontario, living at or near the subsistence level was not unusual for the Native population during the fur trade era. Ed.*]

The question remains: how important was the fur trade of St. Joseph Island and the Lake Superior north shore? It is a difficult question to answer because evidence suggests that taken as a continental phenomenon it was not very important.... The north shore posts were clearly declining in importance following the British Conquest as beaver were mined out. Trading certainly occurred but costs were high and returns low. Nevertheless, these posts did remain important links on the transportation route west. It is perhaps more accurate to portray these posts in this light than see them as places of active trading.

Notes

[1] W. Vernon Kinietz, *Indians of the Western Great Lakes, 1615-1760* (Ann Arbor: University of Michigan Press, 1940), pp. 317-319; Desmond Jenness, *The Indians of Canada* (Ottawa: National Museum of Canada, Bulletin No. 65, Anthropolicials Series No. 115, 1958).

[2] This section is based on NAC, MG30, Hudson's Bay Company Records B.129/a/1-10, Michipicoten Posts Journals, 1797-1820, and MG 20 B. 129/3/1-4. Michipicoten, Reports on District, 1817-1821.

[3] "Made Beaver (MB)" was a comparative standard used for accounting purposes by the Hudson's Bay Company. European goods and commodities as well as all returns in furs were assigned a value in Made Beaver, the equivalent of one prime beaver skin.

[4] Doug Baldwin, *The Fur Trade in the Moose-Missinabi Valley 1770-1917*, (Toronto: Ministry of Culture and Recreation, Historical Planning and Research Branch, c.1975), p. 32

[5] NAC, MG20. B.129/1/2-7, Post Journals, Michipicoten, 1797-1803.

[6] NAC, MG20 B.129/a/2. Post Journal, Michipicoten, 1797-1798, 17 October 1797.

Part Five
À la façon du pays

Part Five: *À la façon du pays*

À la façon du pays — in the fashion of the country — is the term often used to describe marital liaisons in fur trade society between European men and Native women or those of mixed-blood. *À la façon du nord* implies that these marriages took place without benefit of clergy which was inevitable since no clergy lived in the Indian Country. The progeny of these marriages and the following generations have led very diverse lives in all segments of society mostly in Canada and the United States. The articles below look at some of their stories and into the varieties of the mixed-blood experience.

"Fur Trade Families" evolved out of the author's years as historian at Old Fort William. Some descendants of Nor'westers uncovered during that time had to be omitted from this article, but perhaps it should be noted that besides visitors and family genealogists, a few staff members, besides the fiddler Joe Harrison, had family ties to North West Company personnel. Among them was a university history major with an uncanny knack of drawing accurate maps freehand who no doubt inherited her talent from her great-great-great-grandfather, Canada's most renowned mapmaker, David Thompson. Another was an Ojibwa woman from Fort Alexander whose maiden name, Courchene, came from one of three voyageurs who happened to be in the Winnipeg River area around 1800. No doubt he was one of the three voyageurs named Courchene whose photocopied contracts are in Old Fort William's library.

Ruth Swan and Ed Jerome have written a fascinating study tracing the family of Antoine Collins, Fort William's canoemaker, back to the French fur trade on the Upper Lakes, down to the Fort William First Nation today and to the Métis community at Pembina on the Red River. Ed Jerome himself is evidence of the continuity between past and present as a descendant not only of Antoine Collin but also of the North West Company partner, Alexander Henry the Younger.

The name Roderick MacKenzie appears many times in this book with various spellings but it does not always refer to the same person. Roderick Mackenzie, the cousin of Sir Alexander Mackenzie and father of Louisa MacKenzie Bethune became a North West Company agent in 1800 and retired to Terrebonne in 1805. Appointed to the Legislative Council of Upper Canada in 1817, he is often identified as The Honourable Roderick Mackenzie. Although his name often appears as "McKenzie", he himself signed "Mackenzie". Roderick McKenzie, Senior, was a North West Company clerk at Nipigon who was taken into the Hudson's Bay Company as chief trader in 1821, a position he held at Fort William from 1824 to 1829. Roderick McKenzie, Junior, was his son. Roderic McKenzie, the mixed-blood son of Daniel McKenzie, took part in the Seven Oaks "Massacre" of 1816. Yet another Roderick McKenzie was master of the Hudson's Bay Company post at Rainy Lake in 1819.

Fur Trade Families in the Lake Superior-Rainy Lake Region*

by Jean Morrison

A Genealogical Coincidence: The Lagimodière-Harrison Connection

In 1975, Old Fort William hired a fiddler to add a French Canadian ambience to its interpretive program. Wearing the striped shirt, corduroy trousers, moccasins and colourful sash (*ceinture flechée*) of a typical voyageur, this portly, naturally talented musician, Joe Harrison, had a French Canadian accent despite his English name.[1]

Sitting outside the fort's Common Gaol (pronounced "jail") one summer afternoon in 1975, Joe struck up a Red River jig. Three women began dancing to the obviously familiar tunes and when the music stopped the youngest, Miss Agnes Rose Goulet, asked Joe where he came from. It turned out that his birthplace was Ste. Anne's, Manitoba where the three women, Miss Goulet, her mother and her aunt, had also lived. Not had they known Joe in his childhood but they were his cousins! Miss Goulet then astounded Joe and the many onlookers by announcing that their shared ancestor had been a prisoner in Fort William's original jail back in 1816.

That prisoner was Jean-Baptiste Lagimodière, an independent trapper from the Red River and now legendary in Manitoba for his 1,800-mile journey by snowshoe from Winnipeg's present location to Montreal in the winter of 1815-16. Lagimodière's mission was to warn Lord Selkirk that his Red River Settlement was in danger of being destroyed by the North West Company. On his return from Montreal, the Nor'westers intercepted him near Fond du Lac (present-day Duluth, Minnesota) and brought him to Fort William under arrest.

At Miss Goulet's request, a relative in the State of Washington later sent Joe copies of genealogical records salvaged from the burnt-out cathedral at St. Boniface in 1860 along with a copy of Edward Harrison's will from the Provincial Archives of Manitoba. Lagimodière's family tree not only shows his well-known marriage to Marie-Anne Gaboury of Maskinongé, Quebec, the first non-Indian woman to settle in the west, but the descent of their ten children. Through Julie who was born in 1822 and who married Louis Riel, Sr., they became grandparents of the famed Louis Riel, leader of the 1870 and 1885 rebellions. The family tree also shows the birth in 1813 of another Lagimodière daughter, Apolline, and her marriage in 1835 to Thomas Harrison, the son of Thomas Harrison whose parents were Edward Harrison and a Cree woman identified only as Josephte.

The literature of the fur trade has several scattered references to Edward Harrison, a clerk for the North West Company, some not too flattering. At Pembina in 1804, Alexander Henry the Younger recorded, "My fellow traveller, Mr. Harrison, is one of the most awkward and miserable winter travellers in the North West; he can neither walk, run, nor ride with dogs."[2] Harrison's various postings give some indication of North West Company's operations in the mid-west. In 1797, David Thompson met him at the Height of Land near Grand Portage; in 1799 he was at Fort Dauphin, and in 1804 at Portage la Prairie. In 1806 he is listed as a clerk-interpreter in the Fond du Lac Department where he remained for many years.

Edward Harrison made out his will at Fort William on August 1, 1816. This was a time of great uncertainty for the Nor'westers stemming from the Battle at Seven Oaks on June 19 in which twenty-two Selkirk settlers died at the hands of the North West Company's Métis buffalo hunters. In response to Lagimodière's message, Lord Selkirk and his mercenary De Meuron soldiers had left Montreal for the Red River with as yet uncertain repercussions for Fort William. As will be seen, Kenneth Mackenzie also wrote his will that August while waiting for the worst. The beneficiaries named in Harrison's will are his "natural sons, Joseph and William, now in Canada and my daughters Sarah, Mary, Margaretta, and my son Thomas, now in the North West". For

---

*Based on Jean Morrison, "Fur Trade Families Then and Now: The North West Company Connection", in *Families* (Ontario Genealogical Society), February 1997, pp. 23-30.

Joe Harrison, Old Fort William's fiddler, it was by a happy coincidence that he learned that he was descended from Jean-Baptiste Lagimodière and Edward Harrison both of whom were at Fort William in 1816 although on opposite sides of the North West Company-Red River Settlement conflict.

At Old Fort William the Joe Harrison story would not be that unusual. Many descendants of North West Company personnel later discovered their fur trade lineage through the Fort's library, often in the most unexpected ways. They have also shared family genealogical information for inclusion in its research files. Old Fort William is not alone in uncovering this kind of family data about Nor'westers but since its opening in 1973 many individuals have discovered their links to the fur trade society which emerged around the North West Company.

FUR TRADE SOCIETY

Old Fort William represents the North West Company's inland headquarters with its focus on the years 1815-16. This was the time when the Company's domain stretched from the Gulf of St. Lawrence through Montreal to Fort William, and northwest to the Athabasca Country and the Arctic and Pacific Oceans. Each summer, several hundred voyageurs from the interior and Montreal converged at the Fort, the turn-around or transhipment point for furs and trade goods. Also each summer wintering partners and Montreal agents met at the fort to conduct business and attend the company's annual meeting. Few assembling at Fort William for the annual rendezvous brought their Native wives along but a number of women lived at the fort year-round as part of its small population consisting of the officer in charge, a few clerks, some tradesmen and labourers, and their mixed-blood families.

From its opening as a tourist and educational historical attraction in 1973, Old Fort William had two major thematic mandates: (1) to convey the significance of Fort William and the North West Company in Canadian history and (2) to interpret early 19th century fur trade society.

Fur trade society differs vastly from the colonial society portrayed at "pioneer villages" such as Upper Canada Village or Black Creek Pioneer Village in Southern Ontario. Unlike the rather homogeneous communities found in settled parts of Canada, society under the North West Company was made up of three interacting ethno-cultural groups each with its own economic role in the fur trade. With some exceptions, men within the aegis of the North West Company came from these three distinct ethnic backgrounds:

(1) the original inhabitants of the fur trading country, the Indians who hunted, trapped, gathered, fished and performed many other tasks for the company;

(2) the French Canadians who served as voyageurs, tradesmen and labourers; and

(3) the Anglo-Celts (mostly Highland Scots), the "gentlemen" in charge of the trade and the operations needed to keep the trade functioning.

Under the North West Company, no women of European origin lived in the "Indian county". Women in fur trade society were either Aboriginal or had mixed-blood parentage as daughters of Native women and non-native men. Since the Anglo-Scots and French Canadians who entered the fur trade had not taken a vow of celibacy, they entered into marital relations with the women at hand but without the benefit of clergy. (The clergy, as well as women of French Canadian or British origin, did not belong in fur trade society.) These marriages *à la façon du nord* inevitably produced a mixed-blood progeny, a progeny which may be divided into three broad categories:

(1) Those brought up within native society and had an Indian identity;

(2) Those who acquired a separate identity known variously as mixed-bloods, "half-breeds", *Bois-Brulés* or *Métis*;

(3) Those raised in white society and whose descendants often lost all knowledge of their Native ancestry.

The common strand linking these three groups is the Native or mixed-blood background of the mother. Typically, few records give her name or tribe. At least Joe Harrison learned that his great-great grandmother was "Josephte ... (crise)", a Cree, thanks to his chance encounter with his Red River cousins.

Genealogical information about most Nor'westers is scattered hither and yon. The North West Company kept no vital statistics; its post managers sent no annual reports of occurrences for permanent keeping at company headquarters as did those of the Hudson's Bay Company. Until the late 1840's, Fort William had no permanent clergy to keep birth, marriage and death records. Some information, however, can be gleaned about the careers of those in the company's upper echelons from business records, agreements and personal correspondence. Since the company's "gentlemen" were highly literate, many left behind a considerable body of documentation about their lives. Few French Canadians or Natives, however, could write. Some details about their occupations may be found in official records, accounts and traders' journals, but little else of their personal lives except by happenstance as in the case of Joe Harrison.

The McLoughlin-MacKay-McCargo-Taitt Connection

Among the three witnesses to Edward Harrison's will was Dr. John McLoughlin, physician and in 1816 the North West Company partner in charge of Fort William. Today he is remembered on Pacific coast of the United States as "Father of the Oregon Country". In 1811, Dr. McLoughlin entered into a fur trade marriage with Marguerite Waddens McKay, daughter of the Swiss trader Jean-Etienne Waddens and a Native woman, perhaps a Chipewyan. Earlier Marguerite had been married to Alexander MacKay. MacKay had accompanied Sir Alexander Mackenzie on his journey of discovery to the Pacific Ocean in 1793 but in 1808 he left the North West Company, abandoned Marguerite and their children and joined John Jacob Astor's Pacific Fur Company.[3]

At Fort William, Marguerite and John lived in the building referred to today as "Dr. McLoughlin's House and Apothecary". Located inside the palisade east of the Main Gate, their home was next door to the Wintering House just west of the Main Gate. One of the Wintering House's residents was Robert McCargo, captain of the North West Company's schooner on Lake Superior.

In August, 1816 Lord Selkirk captured Fort William and seized any North West Company documents which the Nor'westers had not committed to flame. Not all the seized documents have survived, but a register of them has. One of the entries, the "Marriage Contract of Robert McCargo to Nancy McKay", has not been located but the listing of the marriage record in itself proved useful for Old Fort William's living history program. Knowing that Marguerite McLoughlin's daughter by Alexander MacKay had married Robert McCargo was like a gold nugget to the fort's animation program in which costumed interpreters take on roles of historic personages. But this was all the information available about Nancy McKay and Robert McCargo. Nothing was known about their children, if indeed they had any.[3]

Another year-round resident at Fort William was the superintendent of tradesmen and labourers, James Taitt, with two "t's" at the end of his surname. All that was known about Taitt's family came from a letter in the Selkirk Papers which refers to Taitt's "little girl" at Qu'Appelle on the Assiniboine River. But did Taitt's wife live at the Fort? And why was his "little girl" out west? When further research revealed that "little girl" was fur trade parlance for Indian wife, the questions became, "Who was Taitt's wife and what was she doing in the west?" Finding the answers seemed very remote, indeed.

In 1988, the Metz family of Wisconsin visited Old Fort William's library. "We picked up one of your brochures in Manitoba and noted a reference to Taitt's House, Taitt with two 't's," Mrs. Metz explained. "My maiden name is Taitt with two 't's' so we changed our plans and came here right away. There probably is no connection but my family tree has names like McKay, McCargo, McLoughlin, McKenzie as well as Taitt." We assured her that a connection was most likely!

Mrs. Metz later forwarded the family tree which her great-grandmother had dictated from memory before her death in 1927. Its tantalizing information does not always jibe with the historical evidence yet it unlocks many mysteries about the Taitt and McCargo families. The document gives the names of eleven children born to Nancy McKay and Robert McCargo and hundreds of their descendants dispersed across Canada and the United States. This progeny is thus descended from such famed personages as Jean-Etienne Waddens, Alexander MacKay and Marguerite Waddens MacKay McLoughlin.

The same document names James Taitt's wife (his "little girl") Susan McKenzie, but whether her father was one of the many McKenzies in the fur trade will probably never be known. It also states that while Taitt and Susan "were on their way from a post on the Assinatoine [sic] River to lower Canada Daniel was born." While this statement hardly lessens speculation about the Assiniboine connection, it does suggest that that some connection did exist.

Of special interest was a previously unknown relationship between the Taitt and McCargo families. Christina and Nancy McCargo, two daughters of Robert and Nancy McCargo married Daniel and Robert Taitt, two sons of James Taitt and Susan McKenzie. From a casual glance at an Old Fort William brochure, Old Fort William learned not only of the children born to Nancy McKay and Robert McCargo but also of a fascinating fur trade genealogy. The Taitt-McCargo family ties also explain why James Taitt and Robert McCargo and their families retired together to Chatham near the Ottawa River in Lower Canada.[4]

ALEXANDER WILLIAM MACKAY

As seen, the father of Nancy McKay McCargo was Alexander MacKay (sometimes spelled McKay). Among those who founded Astoria at the mouth of the Columbia in 1811, MacKay died later that year when the Astorians' ship, the *Tonquin* blew up during an altercation with Indians at Clayoquot Sound, Vancouver Island. MacKay's biography was among those I prepared for the *Dictionary of Canadian Biography*.[5] Soon after its publication I heard from Mrs. Edna McKay who lived near Thunder Bay at Squaw Bay on Lake Superior's Sibley Peninsula. I had it all wrong, she told me. Alexander was too smart to get himself killed by the Indians, she insisted. He escaped and fled all the way from the Pacific coast to Sault Ste. Marie. To prove her point, she produced documents showing her late husband's descent from Alexander William McKay of Sault Ste. Marie.

An excellent source for tracing families of Nor'westers of Scottish origin is the Register of the Montreal St. Gabriel's Presbyterian Church.[6] Among the baptisms are those of many mixed-blood children fathered by fur traders, including Nor'westers. Here is the entry for Alexander William McKay:

> Alexander William McKay aged seven years son of William McKay of Montreal, Esquire by a woman of the Indian Country was baptised this eighteenth day of July one thousand eight hundred and nine in the presence of these witnesses.
>
>   Alexr. MacKay, sponsor the father not present
>   Simon Fraser
>   Catherine Fraser

Alexander William's father thus was William McKay not Alexander who was William's brother and Alexander William's uncle. Alexander witnessed the baptism as did his sister Catherine McKay Fraser (Alexander William's aunt) and her husband Simon Fraser (not the explorer but another trader). Mrs. McKay reluctantly accepted the fact that William, not Alexander, was her children's ancestor after being informed that William had been a hero in the War of 1812 with rank of colonel. One indication that William most likely fathered Alexander William is the King George III medal handed down from Alexander William which is still in the family's possession. The medal could have been a wartime gift of Colonel William McKay to his son. (By the time war was declared, Alexander was dead.)

Alexander William McKay is almost certainly the same person as the "McKay Alexr. Wm.", described by George Simpson as a "half breed of the Chippaway Nation" attached to the Lake Huron District. Simpson had a "poor opinion" of McKay for being "rather scampishly inclined" yet a report from Whitefish Lake for 1834-5 describes him as "... a good Trader, well respected by the Indians and a good economist."[7] According to Edna McKay, Alexander William's son Charles McKay became the lighthouse keeper at Battle Island on Lake Superior in 1877 "having rowed up from Saulte St. Marie in a punt". Mrs. McKay's husband George carried on the family tradition by working as a lighthouse keeper and commercial fisherman at Porphyry Island near Silver Islet.

Alexander William McKay's baptismal record in the St. Gabriel's Church registry gives no name for his mother. She is identified simply as "a woman of the Indian Country". This is how most mothers of mixed-blood children baptised at St. Gabriel's church are identified. Registries of other Protestant churches in Quebec undoubtedly have similar entries for children of traders and women of the Indian country. A study of Catholic records would probably reveal a similar practice and at the same time provide useful insights into the children of Indian women and voyageurs who were raised in French Canada.

MARGARETTE AHDIK SONGAB

Given these cryptic references to unknown women of the Indian Country, discovering the origins of any particular mother can be problematic as in the case of Alexander William McKay. But what about the mother(s) of Peter Grant's mixed-blood children? Some of his boys were baptised at St. Gabriel's Church but so were those of another Peter Grant, a trader at Temiskaming. With both Peter Grants, the entry for the mothers of their children is the same, "a woman of the Indian country". Sorting out which baptised children belonged to which Peter Grant was not easy when preparing an item for the *Dictionary of Canadian Biography* on the Peter Grant associated with the Red River and Rainy Lake districts.[8]

This Peter Grant entered the North West Company in 1784 but in 1792 joined an ill-fated opposition to the Nor'westers. After his opposition collapsed in 1795, he was re-admitted to his old firm and made proprietor of the Rainy Lake Department in 1797. Retiring in 1805, he lived first at Ste. Anne's and later at Lachine with three mixed-blood children, Mary, John and Peter. [8] A reference to their possible mother is in a letter written in 1816 by John Charles Sayer at Rainy Lake to John Sayer at Ste. Anne's: "Mr. Peter Grant's former Girl is here and begs that he may make it convenient to send something to his Daughter who I assure you is a fine Girl and remarkably well behaved."[9]

While it seemed most unlikely that anything more about Grant's "former Girl" could be uncovered, information about her did surface although too late for publication in the *DCB*. One day a Minnesotan came to Old Fort William wanting information about Charles Bottineau, a voyageur in Grant's employ. Nothing about Bottineau could be found but a chance mention of his name to a visiting Minnesota genealogist produced a fascinating document by mail. This was a copy of an application for land and tribal rights in 1932 by Laura Bottineau Grey of the Red Lake Band in Minnesota. Laura Grey identified herself as descended from Margarette Ahdik (Reindeer) Songab, a "full-blood Chippewa Indian" and Charles Bottineau, "a guide and voyageur in the employ of the Northwest Fur Company, and Alexander Henry, a fur trader of said company, until 1805. He came into the Chippewa country with the early French [or Montreal - ed.] fur traders about the year 1787."[10]

Before her marriage to Bottineau, Margarette had two previous husbands. The first was to "a full-blooded Indian named Pewanakum". No reason is given but Pewanakum was replaced by her second husband, none other than Peter Grant, a "white man". The issue of this marriage were "a daughter, Susan Grant, a Son, Saganash Grant; and two sons, according to tradition, kidnapped by their father and whose identity is lost." Margarette's third husband was the voyageur and guide Charles Bottineau who probably worked for Peter Grant as well as for Alexander Henry. The document states that Bottineau left the North West Company in 1805, the same year Grant retired. It is apparent that Grant followed the example of many other retired traders by leaving his Native wife behind in the Indian country with a suitable new husband.

Peter Grant's "former Girl" thus was Margarette Ahdik (Reindeer) Songab and her daughter was Susan, perhaps the daughter needing financial assistance as John Charles Sayer reported. One of the kidnapped sons must have been John who was baptised at St. Gabriel's Church in 1805 and Peter could have been the other son. And was Margarette the mother of the Mary who was baptised in 1798 and who lived with Grant after he retired? Her baptismal record describes her simply as, "daughter to Peter Grant Indian Trader the mother to us unknown aged about nine years."

Margarette Ahdik Songab may also be the woman mentioned by the Hudson's Bay Company trader, John McKay, in a journal entry concerning a trip to Rainy Lake House where some HBC goods were stored. As

McKay and Grant conversed, the late Grand Chief's sons and wives arrived with quantities of rice to trade for rum. In 1793 the Chief and his Band had wintered with Grant, then an independent trader at the mouth of the Souris River. On re-joining the North West Company Grant was first posted to Lake Vermilion in the Rainy Lake region where he married the the Grand Chief's daughter. The Grand Chief's sons thus were Peter Grant's brothers-in-law. Before their sister's marriage they had traded with McKay but now it seemed that they were "inclined to give all their hunt to their brother-in-law".[11]

These references to Margarette Ahdik Songab suggest that more research might well bring forth more information about individual women in the fur trade. Usually, however, when Native wives are mentioned in journals or accounts, they are simply "women of the Fort" working in the fields, the maple sugar bush, and the canoe shed, or trading berries, spruce roots or small game in exchange for ribbons, needles and fabric.[12] Even where "little girls" or "women of the Indian country" had long marital relationships, most trader husbands seldom mention them in their journals. For descendants learning more about them can be daunting.

Archives Nationales du Québec

Anonymity is not the case for the upper strata of the North West Company. These "gentlemen"—the merchants and traders—are for the most part well documented, although locating the evidence often involves following a tortuous paper trail in published and manuscript sources. The family data of partners and clerks can sometimes be as elusive as that of their native wives. Even more challenging, especially for the non-French language reader, is finding family details about French Canadian voyageurs and tradesmen, most of whom were illiterate. Yet, although few wrote letters or kept diaries, their names are often found in account books, bills of lading, gentlemen's diaries and other sources.

For the lower orders, however, an invaluable goldmine of documentation exists in the notarial records of Lower Canada which are deposited at the Archives Nationales du Québec's branches in Montreal and other Quebec cities. This goldmine consists of many thousands of *engagements* (or contracts) entered into between *engagés* (the persons engaged or hired) and the firms or individuals who engaged or hired them. In Lower Canada, these legally binding contracts pertained not only to the fur trade but to all labour arrangements between employees and employers. Three copies of each *engagement* were made out, usually on a printed form, before a notary, one for the employer, one for the employee and one for the notary. While extant copies of the first and second category are scarce, the Archives Nationales du Québec has extensive holdings of notarial papers from both the French and British eras.

Pierre Masta

Old Fort William's library is fortunate to have photocopies of three to four thousand *engagements* from the Archives Nationales du Québec à Montréal. These contracts for Montreal and wintering voyageurs, tradesmen, and clerks record the *engagé's* terms of employment as well as his place of residence. This and other evidence made it possible to trace Pierre Masta, Fort William's teamster.

Masta's name first appears on "A List of the men at Kaministiquia for the Year 1805", an indication that he wintered at Kaministiquia as a labourer.[13] His 1816 contract gives his residence as Montreal or Terrebonne and his occupation as *milieu* (or middleman in the canoe) for the journey to and from Fort William, and *hivernant* (winterer) for three years in the northwest. Masta is identified as a *Chartir* (carter in English) and the occupation of one Joseph Masta as *maçon* (mason) in a list of *engagés* who left Montreal for Fort William in 1816. Documents also show that in 1816 a J.B. Masta gave a deposition related to Lord Selkirk's occupation of Fort William while Pierre and J.B. Masta received a blanket and a clasp knife respectively and, on New Year's Day, 1817, rum. In 1819, Pierre Masta's *engagement* with the North West Company gives his residence as Montreal, his occupations as *milieu* for the voyage and as *charretier* for three years at Fort William.

Masta stayed on at Fort William with the Hudson's Bay Company after the 1821 coalition. His name turns up in Journals of Occurrences and Transactions as a teamster, sometimes working along with Vincent Dauphin on the farm. The 1823-4 Journal, for example, shows him ploughing, taking horses to Point Meuron for the winter, moving casks of fish, taking a horse sled for ice. Dauphin is seen at various jobs such as gardening or placing ice in the ice-house. The Journal entry for February 1824 makes this mention of Masta's wife: "Masta did not Work this Week — his wife being dangerously ill." The final references to Masta and Dauphin at Fort William are in the Journal for 1825-26:

> Friday, 16th June...Dauphin and Masta wrought in the garden.
> Tuesday, 25th July ... In the morning Mallette, Dauphin, Masta and two Pork Eaters left this with a Batteau for Michipicoten loaded with canoe bark and Pieces for the District. ....

After this, no mention of Masta nor Dauphin appears in Fort William's records.

For the benefit of Old Fort William's farm staff, this material was compiled in an information packet. After its completion, a mail query about Masta came from an Anthony Mastaw of Sault Ste. Marie, Michigan. Upon receiving this information, Mr. Mastaw visited the Fort armed with family documents going back to France in the l7th century. These records revealed that Pierre had married Marie Dauphin, the daughter of Vincent Dauphin at Fort William and that their son was Jean-Baptiste, probably the J.B. Dauphin whose name appears in various documents. When Masta and Dauphin went by *batteau* to Michipicoten in 1826, they apparently did not return to Fort William but continued on their east-bound journey with their families to Sault Ste. Marie, Canada. Later some of the family moved to the United States where descendants of Pierre Masta and Vincent Dauphin—and their Native wives—abound on the American side of the St. Mary's River and along the southeastern shores of Lake Superior.[14]

Louisa Mackenzie Bethune

For descendants today, learning about their Aboriginal ancestry is especially difficult if traders took their families back to Upper or Lower Canada on their retirement. Raised in white society, successive generations either had no knowledge of their Native heritage or denied it. A typical example are the descendants of Louisa Mackenzie Bethune, wife of Angus Bethune and daughter of the Honourable Roderick MacKenzie by a Native woman. Angus Bethune's parents were the Rev. John Bethune, founder of St. Gabriel's Presbyterian Church in Montreal and Veronique Wadden, daughter of Jean-Etienne Wadden, the trader slain by Peter Pond in 1782.

In 1814 and 1816, Bethune served as supercargo for the North West Company's trading missions from Fort George (Astoria) to Canton, China and in 1821, he and Dr. John McLoughlin unsuccessfully represented the disgruntled wintering partners in London at the negotiations to unite the North West and Hudson's Bay Companies. As a Hudson's Bay Company Chief Factor after the coalition, he served at Moose Factory, Albany, Sault Ste. Marie and Michipicoten where he had charge of the Lake Superior District from 1832 to 1835.

In an old cemetery at Michipicoten near the Hudson's Bay Company's post on the Magpie River is a carved stone bearing this inscription:

> *Sacred*
> *to the memory*
> *of*
> *LOUISA MACKENZIE*
> *wife of*
> *ANGUS BETHUNE*
> *who departed this life*
> *on the 20th April*
> *1833*
> *Aged 40 years*

As stated above, Louisa's parents were the Honourable Roderick MacKenzie and an unknown Indian woman.

In 1793, MacKenzie and his cousin, (Sir) Alexander Mackenzie, were stationed at Fort Chipewyan on Lake Athabasca. This was the year of Louisa's birth and Alexander's momentous voyage to the Pacific Ocean. Louisa's mother could easily have been of the Chipewyan nation.[15]

It is not known where Louisa and her family lived after 1801 when Roderick became a Montreal agent and represented McTavish, Frobisher & Co. at the annual rendezvous on Lake Superior. It is possible that he gave her into the care of his relative, Kenneth MacKenzie, apprentice clerk at Grand Portage in 1800 and at Fort Kaministiquia in 1803, proprietor of the Fort William Department from 1808 to 1815, and Montreal agent until his death by drowning in 1816. Perhaps it is just a coincidence that Kenneth's will of September 15, 1816 names one Louisa MacKenzie as the mother of his two-year old daughter, Margaret. In any event, Angus Bethune could easily have met his Louisa, Roderick MacKenzie's daughter and possibly Kenneth MacKenzie's widow, at Fort William after returning from the Columbia in 1817 and before going to London in 1821 when their first child was born.

The second son of Louisa and Angus Bethune was Norman, a physician and surgeon whose grandson would not only bear his name but also take up medicine. This was the famed Dr. Norman Bethune who pioneered the use of the mobile blood bank in the Spanish Civil War and organized mobile medical services for the Chinese Liberation Army in North China where he died in 1939 from septicemia. It is unlikely that Norman Bethune ever knew that his great-grandfather, Angus Bethune, had been to China before him or that his great-grandmother, Louisa Mackenzie Bethune, was of mixed blood parentage. All that Norman's cousin, Mary Larratt Smith, could recall about Louisa during her childhood were hushed references to her as "Miss Green Blanket". In respectable society around the time of World War I, having native blood was something of an embarrassment, something to be hidden.[16]

Margarette Graves McKenzie

Thus when Marion Elizabeth Fawkes began investigating her father's lineage she knew that her great-grandfather was Dr. Andrew McKenzie but at first nothing of Andrew's parents. When she did discover them as "Daniel McKenzie of the North-West Fur Company and Margaret Gray", her searches eventually led to Old Fort William's library. By coincidence, the fort had been trying to find Daniel McKenzie's descendants. One of three witnesses to Edward Harrison's will of August l, 1816, Daniel McKenzie entered the fur trade at Fort Chipewyan on Lake Athabasca where he joined his kinsmen (Sir) Alexander and Roderick Mackenzie in 1790. His reputation in North West Company history is controversial. One of its fiercest critics, he sold the company's property at Fort William to Lord Selkirk in a state of duress while under arrest.[17]

The St. Gabriel Presbyterian Church register shows the baptism of Daniel's sons, Roderic and George in 1804 and Edward in 1812, but not of Andrew. Documentary evidence arising from Selkirk's occupation of Fort William revealed that Daniel had a Native wife named Margarette and several children and that after the

Louisa Mackenzie Bethune headstone (right and opposite). Located in old Michipicoten cemetery overlooking the Magpie River. Photos courtesy of the Township of Michipicoten Heritage Committee.

Selkirk affair he retired to North Augusta, north of Brockville in Upper Canada. The Daniel McKenzie family thus made ideal subjects for Old Fort William's living history program. While not vital, knowing something of the family and its future progeny is of much interest to staff and visitors alike.

Gary Somerfield, the interpreter then portraying McKenzie in the fort's living history program, had located his will and received a copy just before Mrs. Fawkes' letter arrived. The will gives Margarette's surname as Graves not Gray and describes her not as Daniel's wife but as the mother of his ten children. Their children's names are also listed along with their places of birth. Mrs. Fawkes had already discovered much about Daniel's fur trade career, but what about his wife? she wondered. "I know absolutely nothing about Margaret Gray other than her name. She may have been born in Scotland but possibly in Canada." How to break the news to Mrs. Fawkes that her great-great-grandmother was not from Scotland or from Upper Canada, as she thought, but was probably the daughter of a Cree woman and an early trader about whom little is known, one Booty Graves? Back came her answer:

I spent the morning calling daughters and grandchildren to tell them that yes they do have some Indian blood. Not that they were surprised. Since I was a youngster I have said there was Indian blood

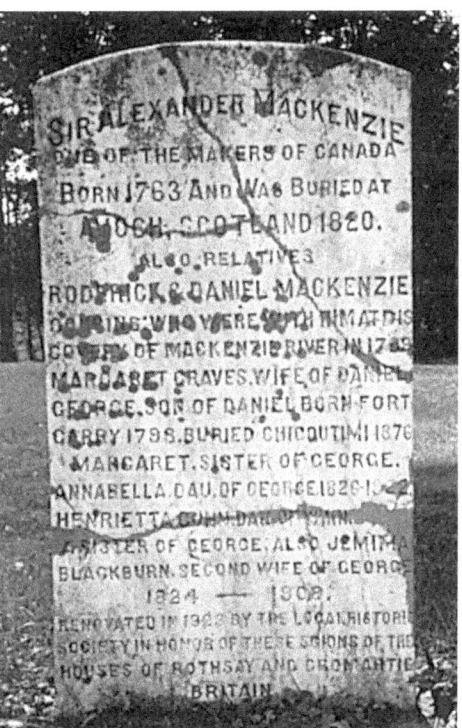

Daniel McKenzie tombstone. Located in the Blue Church Cemetery near Prescott, Ontario. The names of Daniel's family are inscribed on the reverse along with that of his kinsman, Sir Alexander Mackenzie. Photograph by Elizabeth Lemon. Courtesy: Natural Heritage Limited.

in the family but until now had no proof. Kate was particularly interested. She has been with Indian and Northern Affairs and is now working with the off-reserve native people on their special needs. Quite possibly some of the mis-information in various [earlier] biographies was given to cover up the Indian blood factor. They would be surprised to know how happily it was greeted in this generation.

Andrew McKenzie, Mrs. Fawkes' great-grandfather, was born in 1809, possibly at Fond du Lac or Fort William. At the time Daniel McKenzie made out his will in 1830, he was "a Student in Physic & Surgery to Robert Gilmour in Brockville." Thanks to a generous legacy provided by father, Andrew studied medicine in Scotland and then set up a successful practice in London, Ontario.

A nice postscript to this story is the location by Mrs. Fawke's daughter Kate of Daniel McKenzie's grave in the Blue Church Cemetery just east of Prescott, Ontario. One side of the stone gives May 4, 1832 as his date of death at age 63 while the other provides some fascinating family history:

> SIR ALEXANDER MACKENZIE
> One of the makers of Canada
> Born 1763 and was buried at
> Avoch, Scotland 1820
> Also relatives
> Roderick and Daniel Mackenzie
> cousins who were with him at dis
> covery of Mackenzie River in 1789
> Margaret Graves wife of Daniel
> George son of Daniel born Fort
> Garry 1798. Buried Chicoutimi 1876.
> Margaret, sister of George.
> Annabella dau of George 1828-1922
> Henrietta Gunn dau of Winn
> A sister of George, Also Jemima
> Blackburn, second wife of George
> 1824-1908[18]

There is no other evidence that Roderick and Daniel were with their cousin Alexander on his 1789 voyage down the Mackenzie River, but since Alexander embarked from Fort Chipewyan where Roderick and Daniel were then posted, there is no reason to doubt that they helped him prepare for the journey and welcomed him back to Fort Chippewyan on his return from the Arctic Ocean.

Susan McGillivray

Another tombstone of much relevance to Northwestern Ontario's fur trade history is located in Mountainview Cemetery in Thunder Bay not far from Old Fort William. Its inscription reads:

> To the memory of
> SUSAN
> the Mother of
> Simon, Joseph & Peter
> McGillivray
> who died 26th August
> 1819

This is all that is known of Susan, "country" wife of William McGillivray for whom Fort William was named. William began his fur trade career as a clerk, first at the Red River in 1785 and then at Ile à la Crosse on the Upper English (Churchill) River. After becoming a wintering partner in 1790, he had charge of the Athabasca Department but left the Indian country in 1793 on being made a Montreal agent. Susan most likely was a Cree for, given that her son Joseph died at age 42 in 1832, she must have married William *à la façon du pays* during

Memorial stones to Susan McGillivray. Located at Mountainview Cemetery, Thunder Bay. At the left is the original stone (recently repaired) which was moved in 1883 when Fort William's cemetery on the Kaministiquia was razed to make way for Canadian Pacific Railway operations. The newer stone (right) was erected in 1990 by staff and volunteers at Old Fort William. Photos by Glenn Craig. Courtesy: Fort William Historical Park.

his posting to Ile à la Crosse before 1790.[19]

Few mixed-blood sons of traders achieved high rank in their fathers' firms but Simon and Joseph McGillivray became wintering partners in the North West Company where success usually depended on both nepotism and ability. After the 1821 coalition the brothers received the rank of chief trader with the Hudson's Bay Company. Peter, evidently named for Peter Pond, died at birth. Susan and William also had a daughter, Elizabeth, who is not mentioned on Susan's headstone.

What happened to Susan after William no longer wintered in the Indian country is unknown. As with many traders who left their fur trade families behind on leaving the interior, McGillivray undoubtedly provided for Susan's upkeep and that of their children until they could provide for themselves. Did she remain in the Athabasca Department or did William arrange for her to live at Fort William where he could see her during the summer rendezvous? If so, did he continue seeing her annually after 1800 when he married Magdalen, the daughter of Sir John McDonald of Garth in London? In any event William's will bequeathed a considerable legacy to his three surviving mixed-blood children, Simon, Joseph and Elizabeth. Through them, countless hundreds of William and Susan McGillivray's descendants are living today in Canada, the United States and elsewhere.[20]

CONCLUSION

What is the value of all these family histories, and many more, apart from their genealogical or antiquarian interest? Marion Fawkes has given us the answer. For too long, Indians were relegated to the early pages of our history, put out of sight on reserves and forgotten. For many families, having Indian ancestry was a proverbial "skeleton in the closet." This is now changing, thanks, but only in part, to historical agencies like Old Fort William and the many researchers dedicated to uncovering ancestral links between natives and non-natives. This change in attitude must also be credited to the growing power and prestige of the Indian peoples themselves. Fur trade genealogies are more than family history; they are an integral part of Canada's heritage. Much more research into Northwestern Ontario's fur trade families and publication of that research would do much to rescue this heritage for future generations.

[Since completion of this article, Martin Carriere, a descendent of William and Susan McGillivray informed the author that a North West Company ledger at the Hudson's Bay Company Archives shows entries of payments at Fort William to Susan and her daughter Elizabeth for making sashes.]

NOTES

[1] See Jean Morrison, "Old Fort William's Fiddler: Joe Harrison and His Ancestral Links with the Fort William of 1816", Thunder Bay Historical Museum Society *Papers and Records*, Vol. VII (1979), pp. 1-5 for more details about Joe Harrison's lineage.

[2] The authoritative biography of McLoughlin is Dorothy Nafus Morrison, *Outpost: John McLoughlin & the Far Northwest* (Portland: Oregon Historical Society Press, 1999).

[3] Archives Nationales du Québec à Montreal, N.W.C. Papers, H. Doucet, Notary, 4032.5, 29 Janvier 1817, Inventaire des papiers Pris par le Lord Selkirk au Fort William appartenanants [sic] à la Societé du Nord Ouest. (photocopy at OFW.)

[4] OFW Library. McCargo-Taitt family tree; also Brian Hotson, "The Stern Mr. Taitt", *The Courant* (Fall, 1989).

[5] Jean Morrison, "Alexander MacKay", *Dictionary of Canadian Biography*, Vol. 5, pp. 532-4.

[6] Archives of Ontario, Ms. 351. St. Gabriel Street Presbyterian Church (Montreal) Records. Microfilm copy at Old Fort William.

[7] "The 'Character Book' of George Simpson, 1832" in Glyndwr Williams, ed., *Hudson's Bay Miscellany, 1670-1870* (Winnipeg, Hudson's Bay Record Society, 1975), p. 219.

[8] Jean Morrison, "Peter Grant", *Dictionary of Canadian Biography*, Vol. 7, pp. 356-7.

[9] NAC, MG 19 E1(1), Selkirk Papers, p. 8672.

[10] Application of Laura Grey nee Bottineau, 1932 to U.S. Department of the Interior, Office of Indian Affairs. Photocopy at Old Fort William.

[11] See David M. Chapman, ed., "Fur Trade Rivalry on the Rainy River (1793-1797)" by Alma E. Henry, Thunder Bay Historical Museum Society *Papers and Records*, Vol. 28 (2000), p. 65. In "Fur Trade Rivalry" David Chapman has introduced and distilled the late Alma Henry's much longer manuscript by the same name. Based on the journals of the Hudson's Bay Company traders, John McKay and Donald McKay, Alma Henry's manuscript is in the Thunder Bay Historical Museum Archives. It, in turn, is based on the original journals at the Hudson's Bay Company Archives in Winnipeg.

[12] See Judy Petch, "Fort William Post Journals of the 1820's and 1830's: Some Extracts," Thunder Bay Historical Museum Society *Papers and Records*, Vol. 25 (1997) for scattered references to Masta and Dauphin. For Petch article also see below p. 139.

[13] L.R. Masson, ed., *Les Bourgeois de la Compagnie du North-Ouest,* Vol. 1 (Quebec, 1889), pp. 295-413.

[14] Old Fort William Library. Jean Morrison, "Pierre Masta: Teamster/Carter at Fort William" (1986).

[15] Agnes W. Turcott, *Land of the Big Goose: A History of Wawa and the Michipicoten Area* (Wawa: 1962), pp. 131-2.

[16] Mary Larratt Smith, *Prologue to Norman: The Canadian Bethunes* (Oakville: Mosaic Press, 1976), pp. 85-6.

[17] See Marion Elizabeth Fawkes, *In Search of My Father: One woman's search for the father she never know* (Toronto: Natural Heritage/National History Inc., 1994), pp. 9-30 for the author's discovery of her Daniel McKenzie-Margarette Graves antecedents. The father she never knew was Charles McKenzie Marten who was killed in France during World War I.

[18] The inscription ends with the following words: "Renovated in 1923 by the Local Historic Society in honor of these scions of the Houses of Rothsay and Cromartie Britain".

[19] More about William McGillivray's marriage to Susan and their mixed-blood children may be found in Marjorie Wilkins Campbell, *Northwest to the Sea: A Biography of William McGillivray* (Toronto: Clarke, Irwin & Company Ltd., 1975).

[20] Note that Simon, son of William and Susan McGillivray, was known as Simon McGillivray, Jr., to distinguish him from his uncle of the same name. For more information about William McGillivray's descendants contact Christi Anne Corbin, a teacher in Seattle, Washington, who is descended from Simon McGillivray, Jr. Corbin is a member of the Clan McGillivray Association (Inverness) and may be reached at *<cacor23@hotmail.com>*.

The Collin Family at Thunder Bay: A Case Study of *Métissage*

by Ruth Swan *University of Manitoba* and Edward A. Jerome *Hallock, Minn.*

Antoine Collin/Colin was a canoe-maker who was mentioned extensively in the fur trade journals in the early 19th century up to the 1830s. He and his descendants are of interest for the following reasons: 1) they represent the class of lower-ranked employees of the Montreal-based North West Company (NWC) who made the transition to the Hudson's Bay Company (HBC) and are well documented in the post journals and account books; 2) while some stayed in the Lake Superior area and moved into the Ojibwa communities after treaty, at least one son moved to the Red River valley and became "Métis"; 3) Antoine was Edward Jerome's great-great-great-grandfather.

Not a great deal is known about individual "voyageurs" who came from Quebec and settled in the Great Lakes communities, aside from the writings of Jacqueline Peterson (1978, 1981). W. J. Eccles (1987) provides useful information on the exploration of the old North West by French officials, and studies by geographers and historians of the fur trade and native history have contributed to our understanding of French expansion into the Great Lakes basin (Ray 1974; Campbell 1976; Gilman 1982, 1992; and White 1991). Theresa Schenck has produced a notable family study on the Cadottes of Lake Superior (Schenck 1994).

Edward Jerome, a descendant of the Pembina Métis in the Red River valley, has traced his ancestry back to Antoine Collin, the canoe-maker at Grand Portage and Fort William. This microstudy of a particular family investigates the canoe-maker's origins, the place of the family in the social hierarchy of the fur trade post, and what their ethnic identity might have been. It is part of a larger study which traces another son to the Red River valley and shows how these descendants contributed to the development of the bison hunting culture at Pembina.[1]

Antoine Collin's ancestry is difficult to trace because of the paucity of records in the 18th and early 19th centuries. There were no church records for the Thunder Bay area until the late 1830s when Father Pierz, based at Sault Ste. Marie, Michigan, went around Lake Superior to visit the Ojibwa and fur trade communities.[2] He listed an Antoine Collin (son of Joseph), born in 1766, and an Angelique Collin born in 1767. A Métis genealogy suggests that Antoine Collin was born in 1780.[3] His son Michel swore in an affidavit in 1874 that he had been born at Fort William in 1799. Since his father worked for the North West Company and it did not move from Grand Portage to establish the new rendezvous until 1804, it seems more likely Michel was born at Grand Portage where his father was stationed (Arthur 1973:xlv, 63).

Since it has not been possible to identify Antoine Collin's mother, it is difficult to say definitely that he had biracial heritage. However, Elizabeth Arthur described the Collin family as long-established residents: "The Collins were in the Fort William area from the beginning of the nineteenth century... some were halfbreeds; almost all married Indian girls" (1973:xliv–xlv). Campbell (1980:40) characterized the Collin family as different from the local "Indians" because of their occupation as "freemen" within the fur trade hierarchy.[4]

In his affidavit for halfbreed scrip in 1878, Jean Baptiste Collin listed his mother as "Mishaha Weyers (Latour)" without an ethnic designation (NAC, Affidavits, v. 1319). This suggests she may have had a French voyageur father, but was raised by her mother's Ojibwa family.[5] Since Jean-Baptiste was eligible for scrip as a "Halfbreed head of family", at least one of his parents had Aboriginal ancestry, possibly both.

Tanguay's *Dictionnaire généalogique* (1871–90, 3:109–112) shows that the first Collin (Mathurin) married in Quebec in 1668; thereafter, there are numerous references to the name, with Antoine's being baptized in 1736 and 1743. There is no baptism for an Antoine in 1766 as per Father Pierz's notes (Maurice, personal

---

*From David H. Pentland, Ed., *Papers of the Twenty-ninth Algonquian Conference* (Winnipeg: University of Manitoba, 1998), pp.. 311-327. Reprinted with kind permission of authors and publisher.

Marie Jeanne Collin and Alexandre Jerome with children at their farm at the entry of the Two Rivers in Hallock Township, Kittson County, Minnesota. Marie-Jeanne was the great-grand-daughter of Antoine Collin, the canoemaker at Fort William and of Alexander Henry, the Younger. Henry's daughter Betsy married Antoine's son Jean-Baptiste Collin in Red River; their son, Antoine Collin of Pembina (North Dakota) was the father of Marie-Jeanne whose husband, Alexandre Jerome, was the grandfather of Edward A. Jerome, co-author of this article. Photo courtesy of the Edward Jerome Family Collection.

communication, 1998), suggesting that Antoine the canoe-maker was born around Lake Superior. There is an Antoine Collin who had three children born 1792–94, one at Repentigny, Qué., but he cannot be connected with the voyageur.

Evidence from the voyageur contracts suggests that there were at least ten men by the name of Collin dit Laliberté in the Great Lakes area during the 18th century; for example, there was a Pierre Colin dit Laliberté at Detroit by 1713, an Antoine Colin at Michilimackinac by 1752 and a Claude Colin at Kaministiquia (the future site of NWC Fort William) by 1752 (MHS, QAR). They may have been the canoe-maker's grandfather, uncle, or cousins. There was a contract for Joseph Laliberté dit Colin to go to Michilimackinac in 1753 (MHS, QAR #263, 12 juin 1753), and contracts for Joseph Colin dit Laliberté to go to Michilimackinac in 1754 and to Grand Portage in 1758 (MHS, QAR #283, 19 mai 1754, and #361, 21 janvier 1758). Since Father Pierz listed Antoine's father as "Joseph" and his birth date as 1767, this Joseph was in the right place at the right time to be his father.

The evidence is circumstantial as we did not find a contract for Antoine Colin between 1780 and 1799; nevertheless, it appears likely that he was born around Lake Superior and had an Ojibwa mother; he may have been born at Grand Portage as he worked there in 1799. Usually, the contracts lasted three to five years and the French voyageurs took native wives according to the custom of the country.[6] Since many of the voyageurs listed in the genealogical dictionaries disappeared from the Quebec records and appear in Great Lakes communities, it appears that they formed the basis of mixed-blood communities around the Great Lakes, such as

The Collin Family at Thunder Bay

Detroit, La Baye (Green Bay), Chicago, Sault Ste. Marie, La Point and Grand Portage (Peterson 1978, 1981, 1985). Richard White's claim that "a separate people, the *métis*, …mediated between French and Algonquians and became of critical importance to the area" is debatable because they used the term "Freemen" rather than "métis" (White 1991:74).

The records of the fur trade provide the most information on the men of the Collin/Colin family. The earliest records from the North West Company show that Antoine Colin was at Grand Portage in 1799 with an annual wage of 600 livres (Masson 1889–90, 1:66). The NWC Ledger Book of 1811–21 includes Antoine Colin and his sons Michel and Jean-Baptiste; most of Antoine's income derives from canoe-building.[7] He also had an 1816 NWC account; against his annual wages (implying that he was a contract employee and not a freeman), he purchased on 19 November a 3-foot gun, 95 lbs. of flour, 3 lbs. of powder, 10 lbs. of shot, 4 flints, and 1 worsted belt. Against the income of a canoe on 20 November, he obtained two quarts of high wines mixed and a large horn comb. There are only four dated entries for 1816–17, suggesting that Antoine's family was fairly self-sufficient. Michel only appeared in two entries for 6 and 7 September 1816, with such items as blankets, strouds, yew-handle knives, tobacco, portage strap, silk handkerchief, and six yards printed calico.[8] During the Fur Trade War when the NWC and HBC were involved in fierce competition, the HBC Thunder Bay (Point de Meurons) post journal noted Antoine's unhappiness with the NWC and his offer to switch allegiances:

> This afternoon, Colin the Canoe Maker of Fort William came here with a Macock of Sugar to trade — he complains greatly of the usage he has met with from the Nor-Westers and has made one an offer of canoe bark which he says he will send the latter end of this month. [HBCA, B.231/a/4, 2 June 1818]

There was no further reference to this offer, suggesting that Antoine Collin changed his mind about defecting from the North West Company's service.

The fur trade journals and account books of the Hudson's Bay Company after consolidation in 1821 provide the greatest amount of information on these former employees of the North West Company and are the source of information for the manual for park interpreters at the modern "Old Fort William" (Judge n.d.) and Campbell's study (1976). In fact, the manual suggests that "Antoine Collin… is the head of the family in the period we portray at Old Fort William" (Judge n.d.:9). The post journal of 1826–27 by senior Chief Trader Roderick McKenzie and his son Benjamin provides a good example. Antoine Collin and his son Michel both appear frequently in the journal, but evidently had different responsibilities. Antoine was treated as a respected freeman who operated on a seasonal round, being assigned to specialized activities involving wood-working: canoe-making, barrel-making, making fence posts, laying cedar roofs and fishing. He did not live all year round at the post, but came and went depending on where he was needed. Michel, his son, seemed to be one of the post labourers who was assigned daily chores like the other men, but was also an apprentice to his father and often assisted him in specialized activities. By 1828, Michel too is described as a "freeman" in the journals (HBCA, B.231/e/5).

Examination of the HBC post journals and account books shows that ethnic identity was not often used in the fur trade records (including some NWC sources in the HBCA). The clerks keeping the journals usually distinguished between "Indians" and "freemen", suggesting that those with French names had more responsibility and higher social status in the eyes of the officers. For example, on 25 June 1837, "Two boats arrived from Michipicoten in charge of Baptiste Visinau [Vezina, another well-known freeman family] and Louis Rivet. The crews were all Indians. They brought Provisions & Salt for the current outfit" (HBCA, B.231/a/17, fo. 3). The freemen were usually named and were known to the clerk; the Indians were nameless, unless the head of a family: "Michel Collin and the Indians have housed 8 cart loads of hay in the stable lofte" (HBCA, B.231/a/16, fo. 4d). It was mainly the Indian trading captains or (male) heads of families who were known to the clerks and named; these were men who lived and hunted outside the post and not nameless labourers. However, they socially interacted with the freemen who engaged in a seasonal round and often hunted or fished with the local Ojibwa families: "The Spaniard (Chief) with old Peau de Chats arrived from the Grand

Portage. They report that there are a great number of Freemen with their families fishing on Isle Royale for the American Fur Company" (HBCA, B.231/a/17, fo. 7d). Antoine is often identified as "Old Collin" and his son simply as "Michel" because they were so well-known to HBC personnel: "Old Collin with an Indian went off to fish for himself at the Small Islands on the west end of the Pattie [or Pie Island]" (HBCA, B.231/a/17, fo. 11d). He and his son were often referred to as "freemen": "Old Collin the freeman went off to make Martin Traps somewhere about the Petit Marais" (HBCA, B.231/a/17); "Michel Collin the freeman & Cedar the Indian went off along with the men to hunt about Lac la fleche" (PAM, MG1, C1, 28 February 1830).

Only rarely did the HBC clerks use the racial epithet of "Halfbreed" for these men as in the description of the fray between "the Halfbreeds and the sailors" on New Year's Day 1838 in which Michel Collin was involved:

> All the Servants of the Company & Freemen paid us a visit this morning agreeably to the custom of the country, treated them with as much Brandy as they choose to drink and with Butter Cakes. The women also with cakes & Wine and lastly the Indians with a Couple of Glasses of Wine. There was some blows & a squabble between the Cooper & Michel Collin the Freeman which was very near occasioning a general Fray between the Halfbreeds and Sailors. [HBCA, B.231/a/17, fo. 17]

The earliest reference to a "halfbreed" was on 26 May 1831: "Solomon the Half Breed, The Canard & Petit Corbeau's step-son arrived" (PAM, MG1, C1); this group sounds like several Ojibwa hunters rather than a reference to a French freeman.

Thus, at this early period, the HBC journals reflect that biracial heritage was less significant than the type of work done and the relationship to the post, even though many of the freemen from Quebec did marry Ojibwa women and hunted, fished and sugared with their "Indian" relatives. Brown (1980*a*:218) demonstrated how the concept of "patrifocality" operated in the fur trade. If the father stayed in the community with his native wife and family, the sons would be more likely to identify with the father and maintain an ethnic identity connected to the fur trade post; whereas, if the father were absent and the son grew up in the Northwest, he would be more likely to be identified as "halfbreed" or "métis": "As buffalo hunters, suppliers, or workers in other subservient capacities, they tended to constitute the lower classes of the fur trade, while maintaining a separate group consciousness that went back to the earliest days of Red River." [Brown 1980*a*:219]

Brown did not discuss how this process affected the development of biracial consciousness in the Great Lakes area before the Red River settlement was established; historically, a separate "métis" identity did not develop there as it did in Red River. Because the treaties were established in 1850, 20 years earlier than in Red River, many of the freemen who had married Ojibwa women and their descendants took treaty when the opportunity arose. As a result, people with French names (Pelletier, Boucher) or anglicized French names (Collins) still live at the Fort William First Nation, adjacent to the city of Thunder Bay (Maurice, personal communication, 1998).

As Peterson (1978, 1981, 1985) has shown, there were large enough groups of biracial French and Indian men (with French names and Ojibwa mothers and wives) that they provided a separate class of "freemen" in the fur trade hierarchy. They did not come from Quebec, and had no intention of going to Quebec, but they were treated by company bourgeois as separate from their native kin. Some of these men such as

Family of Alexander Jerome and his wife, Marie Jeanne Colin Jerome, daughter of Antoine Colin of Emerson/Pembina area, and his wife Margariet Godin, c.1895. Two daughters Mary, age 3, and Caroline, age 2. Marie Jeanne Colin was born in 1872 so she was about 23 when this photo was taken. Photo courtesy: Edward Jerome Family Collection.

younger son Jean Baptiste Collin, who moved to the Red River valley in the 1820s and married a mixed-blood woman, were parents of some of the Pembina Métis and in fact made application for scrip themselves as "Half-breed Heads of Families" in 1878 (NAC, Affidavits, v. 1319). This process of Métis ethnogenesis did not evolve in the Great Lakes as it did in the Red River valley. As a result, the Collin family who remained near Thunder Bay became "Indians" and the ones who moved west became "Métis".

An overview of the seasonal round demonstrates the Aboriginal economy and culture in which the freemen of Thunder Bay participated. We argue that these freemen in fact spent much of their time in subsistence activities supporting their families from country produce; that they were not "dependent" on the post, but only traded for luxuries such as alcohol and cloth and the occasional tool; and that they spent a good deal of their time with their Aboriginal relatives. The fact that these freemen had French names somewhat disguises the Aboriginal side of their culture and the close interaction they enjoyed with the local Ojibwa, many of whom were their relatives or their wives' relatives. The seasonal round, well known to anthropologists, generally involved the following cycle of economic pursuits: maple sugaring in the spring, building canoes in the summer, fishing in the fall, and hunting with the families inland away from the lake in winter (Danziger 1978, Hickerson 1988, Peers 1994, Schenck 1997). The following are examples from the 1826–27 season:

> June 30. A. Collin, his Son, Scandagance & Petit Ours arrived from rising Canoe Bark, brought 99 rolls.
>
> July 5. Collin began to put a new bottom to Governor Simpson's Canoe, ditto a [canot de] maitre with the assistance of his son.
>
> July 7. Collin finished mending Governor Simpson's Canoe. Two canoes of the Land Arctic Expedition arrived from the Interior with dispatches for Montreal.
>
> July 8. Collin repaired one of the Land arctic expedition Canoes.
>
> July 11. Collin began a north Canoe, his Son and Masta assisted him.
>
> July 16. Michel Collin & 3 Indians went up the River to seine for Sturgeon, but only brot 3 small ones.
>
> July 18. Collin & his son began to put the Laths & Timbers in the Canoes that he made last week.
>
> Aug. 23. Collin making a fishing canoe.
>
> Sept. 8. Bouchard & Deschamps went & brought barrels to Collins fishing Isles Seiners — Shaeling and Michel at small jobs around the post.
>
> Sept. 18. Gambois [Grandbois] went off along with [Antoine] Collin for fall fishing.
>
> Sept. 19. Michel Collin & Deschamps went off for the fall fishing. The men with the Boat brought barrels to the Welcome Islands.
>
> Oct. 19. 3 men went off with the Schooner Boat to Rabbit Island, Michel's fall fishing to bring him barrels & to take home some of the fish.
>
> Oct. 24. Late at night, the men arrived in a small canoe from Rabbit Island, with the news that the Boat was broken open on the Island in the gale of Monday — so much so that she could not be repaired.
>
> Oct. 28. Set the men with the Boat to bring Collins fish.
>
> Oct. 30. The men arrived from Collins fishing with 16 Barrels fish. Sent the men off to the Pate [Potter or Pie Island] to bring Collins fish.
>
> Nov. 1. Collin & Bouchard arrived from the fishing. [Collin Sr. disappears from view until the spring, suggesting that he has gone inland to hunt during the winter.]
>
> Nov. 8. The men went to the Welcome Islands, brought 5 barrels of fish. Our fish is now all home. The women of the Fort began Knitting Nets.
>
> Dec. 2 . Sent off an Indian boy to where Michel is encamped to know if he will go up to Lac la Fleche along with my men [to investigate American competition].
>
> Dec. 3. Michel arrived along with the Indian boy.
>
> Dec. 11. Dompierre & Grandbois went to the Monte with the old mare to bring Michel's wife's Rabbits.

Mar. 10. Michel Collin & his family went off to their sugar bush to hunt Rabbit.

Mar. 15. Michel [and men] went off to Lac la Fleche with corn.

Mar. 19. The men went to the monte with Collin to bring his baggage.

Mar. 26. Robidoux went with Madam Collins Baggage to the Monte.

Apr. 3. Dominique & Oisina [Vezina] making bars for Governor Simpson's canoe. [Note that Collin Sr. is brought in for the specialized work.]

Apr. 5. Madame Collin paid us a visit.

Apr. 30. Collin, his old lady & the Little Englishman arrived from the Sugar Bush... I was informed that the Americans were in search of Indians along the lake and that they had been four days ago at his tent [note his dwelling].

May 1. Collin & his old lady went off for the Sugar Bush.

May 2. Collin arrived from his sugar bush, intends beginning a north canoe tomorrow for Governor Simpson.

May 5. Collin & Dompierre at their usual occupation. The women of the Fort served [assisted] at the canoe.

May 6. Michel Collin went off for his sugar bush.

May 13. Collin finished stretching a new canoe... Michel Collin, his mother and Oisina's [Vezina's] wife arrived from the sugar bush.

May 15. Brisebois, Michel Collin with the Indian women sprouted potatoes up at the Root House.

May 16. Michel & 3 Indian Boys went off to seine at the Rapids for suckers. Sheling [Shaeling] began painting the Governors Canoe.

May 17. Collin with the Indian women finished cleaning & sweeping out the Fort. Michel arrived from the Rapids, brought 95 suckers.

May 22. Mrs. Alex. McTavish arrived from Lake Nipigon in a north canoe with 4 men.

May 23. Collin & the Nipigon men began a north canoe for Mr. McTavish.

May 26. Gov. Simpson, my father & Mr. Ross arrived from Michipicottan.

May 27. At 2 am this morning, Gov. Simpson and Mr. Ross started for the interior in 2 north canoes.

May 28. [Some of the men] started for the Pate [Pie Island] to bring some canoe wood that has been cut there several years. Mr. Alex McTavish went off.

May 31. Collin making small repairs to the Governor's large canoe [last entry for the year].

[PAM, MG1, C1]

As the chief canoe-maker, Antoine Collin enjoyed the patronage and attention of Governor George Simpson who depended on good transportation to get around Rupert's Land quickly. As a reward, Simpson ordered him a special present. On 18 July 1829, the clerk noted: "As old Collin has nothing to do til Monday, I gave him a Gallon of Rum which Governor Simpson desires me to give him" (PAM, MG1, C1).

The above entries show the seasonal round of the canoe-maker, the people he worked with, the importance of family involvement in economic activities and his relative independence from the Company's structure and control. Carol Judd described the changes that occurred for native people in the company structure after the 1821 consolidation: "Often Indians both built and paddled the canoes which transported the trade goods and furs between the inland posts and the bayside... Indian canoemen were highly paid for their services, and they also had the winter free to trap fur-bearing animals if they wished" (Judd 1980:306). She noted that, in the pre-1821 period, Indians were not subject to "prejudicial treatment" as labourers; the main difference between them and regular HBC servants was that the latter worked on three- to five-year contracts with security and fixed annual salaries while the Indians worked seasonally as required. After 1821, when there was a surplus of labour, the status of Indians declined and the hierarchy of the company became more rigid and conservative.

Campbell described the NWC social hierarchy at Fort William and distinguished three groups of labourers based on ethnic heritage: (1) descendants of the "original French settlers"; (2) the "(Métis) sons of the voyageurs"; and (3) "native tribes" (Campbell 1980:34). She based her classification on a description by Nor-Wester Ross

Cox who wrote a memoir of his experiences trading in the Columbia. Cox did not use the word *Métis* — he calls Baptiste LeBlanc "a half-breed hunter" (Cox 1957:93) — Campbell must have it.

These categories described by Cox and Campbell are problematic in terms of ethnicity, suggesting differences in backgrounds which may not have been true. The first group were the "Pork-Eaters" from Quebec who only came as far as the Great Lakes; Campbell assumes they were non-Aboriginal which may not be accurate. She inserted "(Métis)" into the second category although that was not a term used at that time by anglophone writers in the fur trade. It is difficult to know what name they used for themselves as most of them did not write. It is also a term which is usually connected with the people at Red River and not around the Great Lakes.

In the HBC records, clerks usually differentiated three categories based mainly on occupation and life-style: "servants", "freemen" and "Indians".[9] It is quite possible that people of biracial ancestry belonged to all three, but were distinguished by their lifestyle and nature of their work.

Campbell also distinguished between the NWC terms *engagé* and *freeman*. She stated that the former were contract employees and the latter were men who stayed in the Northwest at the expiration of their contracts, lived near a post with their native families and worked for the companies for short periods of time (Campbell 1980:34–36). However, this distinction is based on the category of labour and not ethnicity. Therefore, it may be unwise to assume "Métis" for the second category or non-Aboriginal for the first; the "Indians" may or may not have had European ancestors. Extensive intermarriage between fur traders and native women for at least a century in the Great Lakes area suggests that there were significant mixed offspring in all three groups.

Campbell described the "freemen" and the "Indians" at Fort William as if they had different lifestyles from their Aboriginal neighbours. She cites the Collin family as one of the long-standing residents of the area "whom one must rank among the first settlers of the area" (Campbell 1980:40; cf. Arthur 1973:lxiv); in fact, the Collins might have been at the French posts around the Great Lakes for several generations by 1799. She includes a census of 1828, showing that Michel Collin (Freeman) had one wife and five children and Antoine Collin (Freeman) had one wife and one child. Although she acknowledges that the men at the post married the local Ojibwa women, she implies that HBC regulations (after 1821) pressured these families to assimilate into the non-Aboriginal community. Our research suggests that, with the Collin family, and probably with other freemen, the opposite occurred.

By the 1830s, some of the post journal entries were not so complimentary to "Old Collin" and his family. In September 1836, the clerk wrote that "Old Collins wife went off and left all her children with him… She is a worthless character, most likely she is gone to find the Americans at the Grand Portage" (HBCA, B.231/a/16, fo. 9d). A week later the family was reunited. "Old Collins wife did not go far — the old man was informed that she is with the people who are fishing at the Welcome Islands where he immediately went for her" (HBCA, B.231/a/16, fo. 10). The journal writer was incorrect in speculating that Mme. Collin had defected to the opposition; she was probably staying with relatives at the fishery. It is doubtful that this wife is the woman who Jean-Baptiste Collin identified as his mother, Mishaha Weyers (Latour), who was too old to have an infant in 1836, but no first names are given. There are also allusions by the writer to Collins' drinking bouts and a question of paternity of a grandchild; Michel's daughter Mary had a son whose father she refused to name (Campbell 1980:41). These references suggest increasing intolerance on the part of the fur trade writers. As time progressed, more cultural distance emerged between the post clerks and the labourers and freemen who adopted an Aboriginal lifestyle.

Cultural manifestations suggest that the mixed-heritage people of the Great Lakes fur trade posts combined elements from the local Ojibwa and French voyageurs before the time of treaty in 1850. For example, their dress was somewhat distinctive, such as the hide coat pictured on the cover of the "Where Two Worlds Meet" catalogue from the Minnesota Historical Society. Author Carolyn Gilman wrote: "Skin coats modelled on the European cloth coats sold by traders were made by the Ojibway, Cree and particularly the Red River métis in the early 1800s" (Gilman 1982:107). It is likely that, in the Great Lakes region, cloth coats were used more extensively because the voyageurs who were spending much of their time in canoes did not like leather which became stiff when wet (Gilman 1992:9). To disguise his English identity, Alexander Henry the Elder adopted "Canadian" (i.e. French-Canadian voyageur) dress consisting of a loose shirt, a molton or blanket coat and a large red worsted cap:[10] "I had the satisfaction to find, that my disguise enabled me to pass several canoes, without attracting the smallest notice" (Henry 1969:35). He does not mention the famous Assomption sash or "ceinture fléchée" which voyageurs brought to the Great Lakes region, but these were adopted by Indian groups in the region (Hartman 1988:115 and cover photograph).

Floral beadwork was another manifestation of *métissage*, combining elements of Ojibwa art forms, decoration of utilitarian objects and French materials. Unfortunately, as Ted Brasser has pointed out, "Red River métis culture and its artistic expressions flowered and withered before the ethnologists began their systematic collections of documented artifacts" (Brasser 1985:221). The same could be said for the fur trade culture of Lake Superior (see for example the undated photograph of the beaded tikanagen or cradleboard in Danziger 1978:41). From one of the American Chippewa communities in Minnesota, probably Grand Portage, this artifact shows the complexity of design in 19th-century Ojibwa beadwork, combining French and Aboriginal influences.

The catalogue from "Where Two Worlds Meet" shows examples of a woolen shirt decorated with floral embroidery and blue silk ribbon (Gilman 1982:68, 96), glass beads from Grand Portage in the late 1700s (Gilman 1982:14, 66) and an Assomption sash from the early 1800s from Montreal (Gilman 1982:45, 69). The catalogue does not include much beaded clothing and decorations, probably because it is based on archaeological collections and such items would not last well when buried. The artifacts illustrated were probably collected at a later date after the demise of the fur trade in Minnesota.

A painting by Eastman Johnson of Ojibwa women at Grand Portage in 1857 shows them wearing clothing made of trade blankets, cloth (ribbon decoration) and silver (Gilman 1982:72). It is likely that women in that area were wearing such clothes 50 years earlier at Grand Portage and Fort William. A woollen hood collected by Frances Densmore in 1930 at Grand Portage is made of grey wool decorated with yellow and black fringe and the text suggests it "resembles those in 19th-century paintings of Indian life" (Gilman 1982:96). Such an artifact from a 20th-century Ojibwa community on Lake Superior shows how the fur trade influenced Indian dress and how European styles were adopted by local women artisans and clothing makers.

Another important aspect of material culture was canoe-making, a good example of Aboriginal technology adapted to the fur trade.[11] Eric Ross (1970:58–59) identified St. Joseph Island, near Sault Ste. Marie, as a NWC centre for canoe-making around 1811, observing that the Ojibwa of that area were "noted for their skill in making canoes." However, Grand Portage and Fort William were important as well because of their geographic location: climate, vegetation and technical expertise meant that local resources were available for this work. Simply put, large birch trees grew in abundance and local families — not only Ojibwa, but freemen like the Collins — developed the expertise and were in demand for their workmanship. The fact that Antoine Collin made canoes for Governor George Simpson demonstrates that he was considered the best canoe-maker in the area.

These examples of material culture show that there was extensive *métissage* or cultural mixing for probably most of the 18th and 19th centuries in the Lake Superior region. How to describe this process and the populations involved is more difficult. What cultural niches various descendants of the biracial communities chose in different places and at different times has fascinated historians. According to Jennifer Brown (1980b), it is difficult to find the appropriate vocabulary to describe such groups. However, through genealogies it may be possible to trace the historic process of *métissage* on a family-by-family basis. It would appear that the mixed Ojibwa and French material culture which occurred around Lake Superior and became identified in Red River as "métis" became part of what was later identified as the culture of the Ojibwa of Lake Superior, so that people with French or anglicized French names and manifestations of a mixed culture survive on Lake Superior Ojibwa reservations in the 20th century.

Jennifer Brown has described the importance of the woman as "centre and symbol" in the creation or "ethnogenesis" of Métis communities (Brown 1983:39–46). She used the term "matrifocality" to describe the process whereby the adult children of fur trade unions remained with their native mothers in the west when their fathers returned to Canada or Britain, thereby increasing the influence of the women on their progeny of mixed background. As with many of these families, there is nothing known of Antoine Collin's mother (probably Ojibwa) or his wife, Mishaha Weyers dit Latour ("Madame Collin") to know what influence they had over their sons. The HBC post journals suggest that Madame Collin enjoyed a close relationship with her son Michel who remained at Lake Superior with a multi-generational kin network. What influence she had on Jean-Baptiste, the son who moved west, is difficult to estimate, but obviously the Collin family do not represent the situation that Brown described as she was referring to mothers and children of fur traders who remained in the North West. The Collins were more like the people that Peterson described, moving as immigrants from the Great Lakes region into Red River and bringing aspects of their mixed French/Ojibwa culture with them. To some extent, *métissage* was imported into Red River from other populations which demonstrated cultural mixing.

Genealogical sources suggest that two women named Rosalie Collin and Hélène Collin were the children of Antoine and Josette Collin, possibly his second wife. These records come from Sault Ste. Marie, which was the closest community to Fort William with a Catholic priest in the early 1800s.[12]

There is no evidence that Antoine Collin went to Red River, but he threatened to, as described in the journal for 15 July 1824: "Old Collin got drunk yesterday and this morning came over to inform Mr. McKenzie that he means to go to the Red River. He returned the ct. [hundredweight] etc. thread he had purchased for making his nets for the fall fishery. However, this is not likely to last long being a drunken freak."[13]

While it appears that Antoine did not make good on his threat, his family did go to Red River on August 14: "Antoine Collins wife & some of his family went off with them [the Freemen] for Red River". Which wife this was is difficult to determine; however, if Mishaha Weyers dit Latour was still alive in 1824 and Antoine had another wife, Josette, with young children, the former may have moved to Red River with her younger son, Jean-Baptiste, when he decided to settle there. Since Antoine's wife is never called by her first name, it is difficult to determine which is which. With so little information on the wives and mothers of the freemen, it is difficult to analyze the influence of several generations of *métissage* had on this family in the Great Lakes region other than hints from the material culture.

To conclude, the examination of the family of freemen and canoe-makers at Thunder Bay (Baie de Tonnerre) shows that, despite their French name and labour for the fur trade companies, the Collins were closely connected to the local Ojibwa community. In his younger years, Antoine Collin may have been a dashing voyageur who grew up around the Great Lakes posts and made a living as a canoe-paddler, but, in his later years, he demonstrated a sufficient expertise in Ojibwa canoe-building and wood-working that he no longer had to continue such an arduous life-style and could pursue subsistence activities with his family for most of the year.

What ethnic identity did the Collin descendants who stayed at Lake Superior develop? A petition from the Fort William Indians to Sir John A. Macdonald in 1887 includes the names of three Collins: Baptiste, Simon and Michael (Arthur 1973:199). Genealogical information from the Fort William First Nations parish records suggests that descendants of Michel Collin (born about 1798–99) married local Ojibwa women and descendants with the name "Collin" still live in that community (Maurice, personal communication, 1998). There was no separate cultural niche for people of mixed heritage at Lake Superior fur trade communities and any incipient *métissage* demonstrated by cultural manifestations such as beadwork, clothing and fur trade technology did not develop into a separate ethnic identity as occurred at Red River. The signing of the Robinson–Superior Treaty in 1850 left local people with two choices: they could be either treaty "Indian" or non-Indian. Despite *métissage*, there were probably no "Métis" at the fur trade communities around Grand Portage and Fort William. The descendants of the freemen with French names became Ojibwa or French Canadian.

REFERENCES

Arthur, Elizabeth, ed. 1973. *Thunder Bay district, 1821–1892: a collection of documents*. Toronto: Champlain Society.

Brasser, Ted J. 1980. In search of métis art. *The new peoples: being and becoming Métis in North America*, ed. by Jacqueline Peterson and Jennifer S. H. Brown (Winnipeg: University of Manitoba Press), 222–230.

Brown, Jennifer S. H. 1980*a*. *Strangers in blood: fur trade company families in Indian country*. Vancouver: University of British Columbia Press.

-----. 1980*b*. Linguistic solitudes and changing social categories. *Old trails and new directions: papers of the 3rd North American Fur Trade Conference*, ed. by Carol M. Judd and Arthur J. Ray (Toronto: University of Toronto Press), 147–159.

-----. 1983. Woman as centre and symbol in the emergence of Métis communities. *Canadian Journal of Native Studies* 3:39–46.

Campbell, Susan. 1980. *Fort William: living and working at the fort*. Toronto: Ontario Ministry of Culture and Recreation.

Cox, Ross. 1957. *Adventures on the Columbia*, abridged ed. Portland, Ore.: Binfords & Mort.

Danziger, Edmund J. 1978. *The Chippewas of Lake Superior*. Norman: University of Oklahoma Press.

Eccles, W. J. 1987. La mer de l'Ouest: outpost of empire. *Essays on New France* (Toronto: Oxford University Press), 96–109.

Gilman, Carolyn. 1982. *Where two worlds meet: the Great Lakes fur trade*. St. Paul: Minnesota Historical Society Press.

-----. 1992. *The Grand Portage story*. St. Paul: Minnesota Historical Society Press.

Hartman, Sheryl. 1988. *Indian clothing of the Great Lakes: 1740–1840*. [no place]: the author.

Henry, Alexander (the elder). 1969 [1809]. *Travels and adventures in Canada and the Indian territories*. Edmonton: M. G. Hurtig.

Hickerson, Harold. 1988. *The Chippewa and their neighbors*, ed. by Jennifer S. H. Brown & Laura Peers. Prospect Heights, Ill.: Waveland Press.

Hudson's Bay Company Archives (HBCA). B.231/a/4–17. Fort William (Point de Meurons) post journals, 1818–38.

-----. B.231/e/5. Report of District, 1828.

-----. E.7/8. Fort William (NWC) account book.

-----. F.4/32. North West Company ledger, 1811–21.

Judd, Carol. 1980. Native labour and social stratification in the HBC Northern Department, 1770–1870. *Canadian Review of Sociology and Anthropology* 17:305–314.

Judge, Rob. n.d. Farm building kit for Old Fort William: manual for interpreters. MS.

Kent, Timothy J. 1997. *Birchbark canoes of the fur trade*. [no place]: the author.

Masson, L. F. R. 1889–90. *Les bourgeois de la Compagnie du Nord-Ouest*. 2 v. Québec: A. Coté. [Facsimile reprint New York: Antiquarian Press, 1960.]

Minnesota Historical Society (MHS). Quebec Archivist Reports.

National Archives of Canada (NAC). RG15. Dept. of Interior, Manitoba Halfbreed Affidavits, v. 139 (microfilm C14926).

Peers, Laura. 1994. *The Ojibwa of Western Canada, 1780–1870*. Winnipeg: University of Manitoba Press.

Peterson, Jacqueline. 1978. Prelude to Red River: a social portrait of the Great Lakes Métis. *Ethnohistory* 25:41–68.

-----. 1981. The people in between: Indian–White marriage and the genesis of a Métis society and culture in the Great Lakes region, 1680–1830. Ph.D. thesis, University of Illinois at Chicago Circle.

-----. 1985. Many roads to Red River: Métis genesis in the Great Lakes region, 1680–1815. *The new peoples: on being and becoming Métis in North America*, ed. by Jacqueline Peterson & Jennifer S. H. Brown (Winnipeg: University of Manitoba Press), 37–71.

Provincial Archives of Manitoba (PAM). MG1, C1. Fort William Collection (FWC).

———. Red River Census, 1835.

Ray, Arthur J. 1974. *Indians in the fur trade: their role as trappers, hunters, and middlemen in the lands southwest of Hudson Bay, 1660–1870*. Toronto: University of Toronto Press.

Ross, Eric. 1970. *Beyond the river and the bay*. Toronto: University of Toronto Press.

Schenck, Theresa M. 1994. The Cadottes: five generations of fur traders on Lake Superior. *The fur trade revisited: selected papers of the 6th North American Fur Trade Conference, Mackinac Island, Michigan, 1991*, ed. by Jennifer S. H. Brown, W. J. Eccles & Donald P. Heldman (East Lansing: Michigan State University Press; Mackinac Island: Mackinac State Historic Parks), 189–198.

———. 1997. *"The voice of the crane echoes afar": the sociopolitical organization of the Lake Superior Ojibwa, 1640–1855*. New York: Garland Publishing.

Sprague, D. N., and R. P. Frye. 1983. *The genealogy of the first Métis nation*. Winnipeg: Pemmican Publications.

Tanguay, Cyprien. 1871–90. *Dictionnaire généalogique des familles canadiennes depuis la fondation de la colonie jusqu'à nos jours*. 7 v. Montréal: Eusèbe Senécal & Fils. [Facsimile reprint Montréal: Editions Elysée.]

Thunder Bay Historical Museum Society. Fort William journal, 1823–24.

Van Kirk, Sylvia. 1980. *"Many tender ties": women in fur-trade society in western Canada, 1610–1870*. Winnipeg: Watson & Dwyer.

Wallace, W. Stewart, ed. 1934. *Documents relating to the North West Company*. Toronto: Champlain Society.

White, Richard. 1991. *The middle ground: Indians, empires, and republics in the Great Lakes region, 1650–1815*. Cambridge: Cambridge University Press.

NOTES

[1] This is the Ph.D. dissertation of Ruth Swan, "A history of the Pembina Métis".

[2] We would like to thank Father William Maurice, St. Anne's Church, Fort William First Nation, Thunder Bay, for genealogical information and Eric Angel for his assistance.

[3] Sprague and Frye (1983, Table 1) give birthdates of 1780 for Antoine and 1783 for his wife.

[4] HBCA, B.231/e/5. An 1828 census lists both Michel and Antoine Collin as "freemen".

[5] "Weyers" is not a known French voyageur name, but it might be a misspelling of "Sayer". John Sayer was a North West Company bourgeois in the Fond du Lac district of northern Minnesota. He was born about 1750 and had a fur trade licence for Michilimackinac by 1780 (Wallace 1934:497); he could have had an Ojibwa daughter born about 1783 who had a son at Grand Portage by 1799.

[6] "The bourgeois' control over their men was also continually limited by the latters' willingness to choose the option of remaining in the country as freemen instead of either returning to Montreal or pursuing their fur trade duties. Equipped with wilderness skills and often unwilling to return to the more constrained life of their home society, a considerable but undetermined number left their employers to settle with their native families in the Northwest where they subsisted partially independently and partially by income gained from work as guides, suppliers or hunters for fur trade company men in their area" (Brown 1980*a*:86); see also Van Kirk (1980:28).

[7] HBCA, F.4/32, fo. 231 (Antoine), 248 (Michel), 148 (Baptiste). The data included here are based on research in the HBCA by Jerome and Swan before we saw the work of Judge (n.d.) and Campbell (1980).

[8] HBCA, E.7/8, fo. 140 (Michel), 141 (Antoine). There is some confusion over this record as someone has written "R.R.S." (Red River Settlement) at the top of each page; however, the handwritten title of the journal is "Fort William", and the archives' new finding aid correctly identifies it as the "Fort William Account Book".

[9] For example, "The Company's servants, free men and Indians paid us their usual visit this morning according to the custom of the country" (PAM, MG1, C1, 1 January 1830).

[10] See the oil painting "The Voyageur", by Abby Fuller Abbe (about 1860), illustrated in Gilman (1992:70).

[11] A comprehensive history and catalogue, *Birchbark canoes of the fur trade*, by Timothy J. Kent (1997), documents its

importance.

[12] Mary Black-Rogers (personal communication, 1997) reports that Rosalie married François Desmarais at St. Boniface on 20 September 1825, and genealogist Heather Armstrong (personal communication, 1998) reports the marriage of Hélène Collin to her second husband Joseph Biron at Sault Ste. Marie, Mich., in 1847; Hélène was born about 1814 and died in Sault Ste. Marie, Ont., in 1903. We would like to thank Andrea Hanibal-Paci for her assistance.

[13] Thunder Bay Historical Museum Society, Fort William Journal (1823–24); this journal is not available in the HBCA or PAM.

Angelique and Her Children

by Elizabeth Arthur

Fur trade records kept by European businessmen offer only an occasional glimpse of the Indian women they married, and the glimpses that do exist often tell more about the social attitudes of the men who kept the records than about the role of women in fur trade society. Sylvia Van Kirk has called these Indian wives "the women in between"[1], the representatives of a "host" society remaining to some extent within their traditional environment, but living at the forts built by the European "visitors". One such woman was a Nipigon Indian whom the Europeans called Angelique. According to the story told by her grandchildren, she was abducted about 1803 by the North West Company clerk, Roderick McKenzie.[2] The implication is that the customary Indian marriage rites were omitted, but this is highly unlikely. Amicable relations between the visitors and their Nipigon hosts demanded the acceptance of Indian custom, and there is every reason to believe that the McKenzies' was a marriage *à la façon du pays*. Nearly forty years later, Angelique McKenzie, baptized and married according to Christian rites, appears in the official church records. Earlier, she was referred to as "a woman of the Indian country."[3]

What then can be discovered about this woman's life? Her place of residence was that of her husband — Nipigon for the first twenty years of the marriage, Fort William for about seven years, Isle à la Crosse in northern Saskatchewan for another twenty years, then the Red River Settlement in old age. The records show her burial in St. Andrews cemetery near Lower Fort Garry on November 19, 1859, aged seventy-five.[4] They also record the baptisms of her children, eight of whom seem to have been born at Nipigon, three at Fort William, and one at Isle à la Crosse. The general role of Indian women as "an integral if unofficial part of the fur trade work force"[5] makes it likely that her skills in moccasin and snowshoe making were exploited to the full. The long period of residence near her relatives gave her an opportunity to serve as an agent in the development of trade relationships between the Nor'westers and the Nipigon Indians. By the beginning of the 19th century there was evidence elsewhere of increasing friction between the races and, by 1806, the North West Company forbade its employees to marry Indians;[6] after that date, it was the mixed-blood daughters of fur traders who married *à la façon du pays* or, after the union of the fur trading companies in 1821, by a contract insisted upon by the Hudson's Bay Company. Regulations by that time also made sure that wives and children of traders would not be maintained at Company expense.

The increasing restrictiveness of Company policy and the appearance of missionaries who tried to deny women like Angelique any status meant that her position over the years depended entirely upon the attitudes of the man she had married. Roderick McKenzie's career might, at first glance, seem to parallel many others in the fur trade — educated in Scotland, clerk north of the Great Lakes by the 1790's, Chief Trader under the Deed Poll of 1821, promoted to the rank of Chief Factor in 1830. But there is one remarkable fact about him — he never returned to Scotland even on furlough;[7] there are references to his occasional presence in Montreal in the early years, but no indication that he ever travelled east of Lake Superior in the last forty years of his life. To show the importance for Angelique of this commitment to the north west, one has only to note the careers of her predecessors in the Lake Superior District. When Alexander Stewart was transferred from Fort William to Island Lake in 1823, he left behind him his Indian wife and their daughters; only the sons accompanied him.[8] For a time, McKenzie's superior was John Haldane who, on his retirement to Scotland in 1827, promised financial support for his country wife, Josette Latour. As the years passed, he conveniently forgot the arrangement,[9] and Josette was living a wretched existence near Sault Ste. Marie as late as the 1850's.

Haldane's conduct drew so much unfavorable attention that it must have been unusual, but so was Roderick McKenzie's. His generosity to his wife and family were well known. Letitia Hargrave at York Factory reported

---

*Thunder Bay Historical Museum Society *Papers and Records*, 1978, pp. 30-40. All attempts to locate copyright holder of this article by the late Dr. Arthur have failed; republished with permission of TBHMS.

Hudson's Bay Company post at Nipigon. While stationed at Nipigon as a North West Company clerk, the future Hudson's Bay Company Chief Trader Roderick McKenzie met Angelique and married her around 1803. Eight of their twelve children were born during their twenty-year sojourn at the post. TBHMS 974.2.530.

scaling down the orders for clothes from England to what she thought "old Rory" could afford.[10] (She was meddling quite unnecessarily as his financial records make clear, but her own ideas of what was a suitable standard of living for Indians and mixed-bloods influenced her also.) Roderick McKenzie's determination to remain in an environment where Angelique could be content shines through all his letters on the subject of retirement. Briefly, he thought about the upper Ottawa or perhaps Sault Ste. Marie. He inquired about the possibilities of Norway House or Cumberland. At last, he settled reluctantly in Red River, fearing that the diet and the intrusion of "civilization" would not make for happiness for an old Indian trader or his Indian wife.[11]

McKenzie was by no means unique in resisting European pressure upon him to marry according to the rites of a church. Many old Nor'westers felt that a religious ceremony would depreciate the position their wives had held for decades. Was not marriage *à la façon du pays* binding and permanent? They also saw something ridiculous in these long-delayed rites, and commented caustically when their contemporaries hobbled to the altar, surrounded by a crowd of children and grandchildren. Just why Roderick changed his mind after repeated assertions that he would never do so is not clear.[12] His two wills, one drawn up some years before the 1841 marriage, and one considerably later,[13] show his awareness of the changed status in law, but both provided for Angelique and her children, so that concern over the disposition of property does not seem to have been the reason for his change of attitude. It seems more likely that consideration of retirement and of the degree of acceptance Angelique would find in a settled community influenced his decision. Undoubtedly the Rev. James Evans, who visited Isle à la Crosse in 1841, put these points forcibly.

The earlier will had divided the property more or less equally among Angelique and the children but, by the 1850's, four of the children had died, and the size of the estate had increased greatly from what it had been twenty years before. In his second will, Roderick made provision for Angelique and for several dependent grandchildren, included nominal sums for each of the surviving sons, then left the bulk of his estate to three daughters, and one granddaughter. Other factors may have influenced these decisions, but it is difficult to avoid the conclusion that Roderick found more cause to rejoice in his daughters than his sons. The history of the twelve children affords an extraordinarily vivid picture of the lives of mixed-bloods in the early 19th century, and it provides an opportunity to examine the contention that the women of these families possessed better changes for upward mobility than the men.[14]

With respect to the McKenzie daughters, it must be emphasized that their opportunities increased greatly over time. Among the older children, a traditional European view dictated that the boys would go to school, while the girls remained at Nipigon and learned the skills their mother could teach them. Nancy, the eldest daughter, married a French Canadian *engagé* from Sorel, Antoine Dutremble. She lived at Nipigon and at Fort William, then in Lower Canada. Her status in the fur trade society was far lower than the one her mother enjoyed; her husband's income was never large enough to maintain his family, and Roderick was supplementing the Dutrembles' meagre earnings both before and after Nancy's death in 1840. Eventually, the younger child went to live with her grandparents.[15] The second daughter, Catherine, never married. Until her death in her 30's, she was the one who cared for her father when he was ill.[16] Later, Nancy's daughter assumed the nursing responsibilities.

The three younger McKenzie daughters were all baptized at Red River on the same day, and that alone indicates the way in which institutional developments were to make their lives different from those of their older sisters. Mary and Margaret both married within a few years of this ceremony, so that it was the youngest, Jane, who arrived at Red River as a child, who could benefit most from educational opportunities available there. In 1838, Mary married Adam McBeath, of mixed blood like herself, a post master for the Hudson's Bay Company in the Mackenzie River District.[17] Her sister Margaret married a year later a young Scottish Canadian clerk who was to rise far higher in the Company service. James Anderson, according to the family friend who gave the bride away, acquired a mail order bride.[18] By this time, missionary influence in the north dictated a formal ceremony but, in other respects, Margaret's early married life was remarkably similar to her mother's. For several years, her husband was a clerk at Nipigon, just as her father had once been. Anderson also rose to the rank of Chief Factor and, although his career led him to the remote north and to the Labrador coast, his links with Upper Canada remained. It was to Sutton West, on the shore of Lake Simcoe, that he chose to retire in the midst of his relatives.[19] It was to that society that Margaret learned to conform.

When Roderick McKenzie died, it was the task of Sir George Simpson, as one of the executors, to acquaint his heirs with the details of the will. Letters to the three sons-in-law informed them of their wives' considerable legacies, and slight variations in the wording make it very clear what Simpson considered the social position of each in 1859.[20] Anderson ranked highest and McBeath lowest. But, in spite of his judgement, it was Jane, whose husband was ranked between the other two, who represented the most interesting example of upward mobility.

Educated at the Red River Academy, remaining there to teach, referred to as "accomplished", she found herself so highly valued by her father that her matrimonial chances seemed slight. Her choice was a young Scot, recently arrived in Rupert's Land, also called Roderick McKenzie. Her father considered his rank and salary too low,[21] and it is obvious that it was these criteria rather than racial ones that were being applied. It is also evident that the expectations of the *pater familias* had altered enormously over the years since Nancy and Mary had married. Some friends privately made the revolutionary suggestion that Jane should be allowed to choose for herself,[22] and in the end she did, but only after her Roderick had received a promotion. Her mother's views of the proceedings, as usual, went unrecorded. But if cultural conflict over the upbringing of the children did indeed cause anguish to Angelique as it did to others,[23] if the Red River Academy did indeed separate children from their Indian heritage, Jane was the daughter farthest removed from her mother's traditions and closest to the European model of the time.

Among the seven sons, all of whom became employees of the Hudson's Bay Company, a somewhat different pattern emerges. Six of them received an education, usually calculated by their father in number of years, and ten years in school seems to have been the objective. The older sons were sent to Montreal; at least one attended school briefly in Upper Canada, and the youngest ones were educated at Red River. It was Samuel, the third son, who was never sent to school, and only learned to read and write when he was twenty-four.[24] It is impossible to discover why one was treated so differently from the rest. His father's letters and journals make frequent reference to "poor Samuel" who was described as sickly, at least in his youth, but the reader is left in doubt as to Roderick's meaning; poor heath, poor ability, or merely poor opportunities. It is gratifying to find that this was the son who rose highest in the Company service, and when the last Council of the Northern

Department of Rupert's Land met in July, 1870, one of the most experienced men present was Chief Trader Samuel MacKenzie.[25]

The possibility of any of his sons rising as he had done apparently never occurred to Roderick McKenzie. Unlike some fathers who denounced the Company's discriminatory treatment of mixed-bloods, he always placed the blame for lack of promotion on his sons' failure to measure up to reasonable and objective standards. He regarded the oldest, Roderick Junior, as the most reliable and the evenest in temper,[26] if not the most intelligent. It was all the greater shock when this son killed an Indian in a drunken brawl near Lake Nipissing in 1844.[27] He was acquitted on the murder charge, but his excessive drinking brought about his dismissal from the Company service shortly afterward, and he died destitute in a shanty near Mattawa in 1850.[28] The second son, Benjamin, was usually regarded as the cleverest,[29] but his father claimed that only harsh discipline had saved him, and Samuel as well.[30] Both these young men began in the Company service in the Lake Superior District, departed, discontented, for Lower Canada, suffered hardship, and then moved west to increasing success. Benjamin was still a clerk when he died in Hawaii in 1838, and his father assumed the responsibility for educating his three small children.

During the 1840's, Roderick's concern about his younger sons dominated most of his private letters. Patrick entered the Company service in the Saskatchewan District in 1839,[31] failed to give satisfaction to his employers, and was transferred to the Columbia. There Chief Trader. John Tod dismissed him, and the news filtered back to Isle à La Crosse that he was suffering severe hardships as a farm labourer. His father mourned the young man's carelessness and inattention to duty,[32] refused him financial aid, but relented so far as to appeal (unsuccessfully) to have him reinstated by the Company. "He is not a drunkard, Roderick wrote to Governor Simpson, obviously selecting the best that could be said, "but a good-natured lad, but they say rather timid with the Indians."[33] Far more disappointing were Ferdinand's wasted opportunities. He was apprenticed to a Dr. Elliot of Edinburgh, but neglected his work, ran up large debts with his tailor,[34] and was eventually dismissed. The Hudson's Bay Company then engaged him as a clerk, over his father's objections. "Let him engage as an apprentice sailor before the mast, too good a situation for such a vagabond," Roderick thundered in the same letter in which he threatened to cut Ferdinand out of his will.[35] The threat was never carried out and a reconciliation was effected before Ferdinand was sent to the Columbia District.[36] In view of the problems with both of these boys, Roderick suggested rather nervously that he had two others just finishing school and looking for work.[37] Both Alexander and James entered the Company service and apparently gave satisfaction, although their father always seemed to be awaiting poor reports of them. In his agony over Ferdinand, he did make a point explicitly that seems to have underlain his troubled relationship with his sons. "None of these unfortunate half-breeds will ever give satisfaction in any other country than their own, and even in their own very seldom."[38]

The changing pattern of life throughout the years of the McKenzie marriage can be traced through the relationships with the children, the improving financial position, and the intensified European cultural impact of later years. Nancy's children retained their link with French Canada, and grandfather McKenzie dispatched a wedding present of £100 to the new Mme. Pontbriant in 1848.[39] They, and probably Roderick Junior's family as well, were Roman Catholic. The western branch of the McKenzies became Protestant, although Samuel's children were closely linked with the Saskatchewan Métis community. Benjamin's children included an Anglican missionary to the Indians, a Cambridge graduate who became superintendent at Kildonan.[40] Two of Jane's sons achieved sufficient prominence to be included in Morgan's *Canadian Men and Women of the Time*, one a physician in Portland, Oregon, the other a lawyer-politician representing the English minority in Quebec.[41]

When one looks at the distances geographical and cultural that divided the McKenzies, one is amazed at the sense of family that bound them together. Unlike some parents of mixed-blood families, Roderick and Angelique did not erect insuperable barriers between their children, educating some for life among Europeans and leaving the others to fit into Indian society if they could.[42] (If this has been the original plan for Samuel, it miscarried.) In one sense, unity could be seen as imposing an even greater strain on Angelique, but her communications with her children never snapped, even though news had to come by way of letters to her husband. The tragedy of children sent to distant schools, pining away, and dying there was not part of this family history. The McKenzies were a sturdy lot and schools killed none of them, but, particularly, for the sons, the sense of belonging to neither their father's culture nor their mother's must have been overpowering. Both Roderick Junior and Benjamin left brief journal records of their work at Nipigon where their Indian relatives came to trade; it is evident that their education had made them careful to identify themselves with their father's tradition and, of course, with the attitudes of their employers.[43] Also, the knowledge that, in the view of most Hudson's Bay Company officials, the Nipigon Indians were especially violent and unreliable put particular pressure on ambitious young men to dissociate themselves from their uncles and cross cousins (that is children of Angelique's brothers).[44] According to Ojibwa custom, such cousins would be regarded as non-kin in any case; close ties would normally have been maintained between the children of sisters, and it is not known whether Angelique had any sisters.

At what cost the McKenzie sons maintained this illusion of being European while they worked with Indians, yet were repeatedly confronted by European prejudices against themselves can only be guessed. The tortured life of Roderick Junior offers the strongest clues. He was the only one of the family old enough to experience employment with the North West Company and to observe, before he was out of his teens, the change in attitude in the new Hudson's Bay Company. He did not have access to the documents, but he must have been aware of the difference between the reports given by his father's old friend, John Haldane, and the comments of the new governor, Sir George Simpson. There is a vast difference between "a promising young man"[45] and, "Tolerably steady for a half-breed, manages a small post but has no right to look higher."[46] Roderick's own agony of spirit was expressed in a letter to his superior,[47] but he decided to remain in the Company service, apparently finding some satisfaction, and earning some praise[48], in his years at Sturgeon Lake. When that post was closed down, however, he was moved to a completely new area in which there was competition for Ottawa valley lumbermen and groups centred in Goderich and Penetanguishene.[49] On the fringes of what was called civilization, his life disintegrated, and he provided the Hudson's Bay Company, and even his own father, with further support for their belief that the mixed-bloods would inevitably fail. The strength of the Company prejudices is revealed in a different way in the death of the youngest McKenzie in 1859. James lost his way en route from Pembina to Fort Garry, and froze to death. There was shock expressed, but also wonder that a "first rate traveller, and accustomed from early boyhood to such work"[50] should have ventured out in December so lightly clad and should have failed to find his way. The Indian heritage was supposed to be of some use, and even it had failed at a crucial moment.

But the social pressures and the social judgments of the mid-19th century did not destroy the McKenzie family. One has only to look at the actions of the daughters whose social position had given them an opportunity to separate from the rest. Jane, within a year, offered a home to Roderick's daughter Magdalene, a niece she had never seen.[51] The last reference in the Simpson correspondence to another McKenzie granddaughter, Katherine Dutremble, has her spending her money lavishly, and rather ironically, on furs and preparing to visit her Aunt Margaret in Sutton, Canada West.[52] This sense of family was obviously in part the legacy of Roderick, the Highland Scot, but, especially in view of his own ambivalence, it must also have been the legacy of Angelique, the Nipigon Indian. The picture of her in old age is one of elegance and tranquility, serving tea from the silver service hallmarked 1830, in the stone Georgian cottage her husband had built as their retirement home.[53] It was a long distance from the life of her youth, travelled with a man imbued with the Puritan conviction that one must always expect the worse, who mourned every sign of weakness on his children's part and seemed to regard his affection for them as a sign of weakness on his part. In more respects than Sylvia Van Kirk intended the phrase, Angelique must have been "the woman in between".

NOTES

[1] Sylvia Van Kirk, "'Women in Between': Indian Women in Fur Trade Society in Western Canada" in Canadian Historical Association, *Historical Papers*, 1977, p. 31.

[2] Margaret A. MacLeod (ed.), *The Letters of Letitia Hargrave,* (Toronto, 1947) Liii.

[3] Hudson's Bay Company Archives (HBCA), E 4/2 Baptismal records, Red River Sept. 3, 1841, baptism of James McKenzie. Contrast earlier Red River records for Alexander, Apr. 13, 1838, for Margaret, Mary and Jane, Apr. 19, 1835.

[4] Public Archives of Manitoba, St. Andrews records.

[5] Van Kirk, p. 32

[6] W. S. Wallace (ed.), *Documents Relating to the North West Company,* (Toronto, 1934), p. 211.

[7] MacLeod, p. 169. Letitia Hargrave to Mary Mactavish, Sept. 12, 1843. Minutes of Council contain frequent references to his eligibility for leave at various times, and the reversion to some other office as he failed to take advantage of it.

[8] Robert McElroy & Thomas Riggs (ed.) *The Unfortified Boundary: a diary of the first survey of the Canadian boundary line from St. Regis to the Lake of the Woods by Major Joseph Delafield* ... (New York, 1943), p. 402, Delafield's journal entry from Fort William, July 9, 1823.

[9] HBCA, D5/20 fol. 308, George Keith to Simpson, Aberdeen, Sept. 25, 1847. Keith was a witness at Michipicoten twenty years before when Haldane promised an annuity of £60.

[10] MacLeod, pp. 168-9. Letitia Hargrave to Mary Mactavish, Sept. 12, 1847.

[11] HBCA, D5/20 fol. 370, Roderick McKenzie Sr. to Sir George Simpson, March 4, 1844 D5/14 fol. 116, Same to same, July 1, 1845; D5/27 fol. 53, finally accepts Red River as the place to "pitch his tabernacle", but let it be somewhere near Lower Fort Garry.

[12] Ibid., D5/7 fol. 199d, Donald Ross to Simpson, Norway House, Aug. 15, 1842.

[13] Ibid., A/36, Will of July 21, 1835 superseded by one of June 27, 1855 leaving a sizeable estate including life tenancy of the Red River home and £1000 to Angelique, about £3000 to each of the surviving daughters and the granddaughter who looked after him and Angelique, and lesser amounts to sons and children of deceased sons.

[14] Sylvia Van Kirk, "The Economic and Social Role of Women in the Fur Trade" (Unpublished Ph.D. thesis, University of London, 1975), pp. 270 ff.

[15] HBCA, B149/2/11, Nipigon Journal entry records 1829 marriage, also gives indication of the Dutrembles place in the Company hierarchy. D5/8 fol. 351, McKenzie to Simpson, July 8, 1843 gives details of financial dependency.

[16] Ibid., B89/a/23 Isle à la Crosse Journal, Sept. 7, 1844; D5/33 McKenzie to Simpson, June 22, 1852 re Catherine's death of "consumption".

[17] Ibid., E4/1b, Record of marriages, May 25, 1838 at Fort Simpson by M. McPherson, magistrate. McBeath's position and salary throughout the years can be traced in B239/G volumes. As a post master, he earned £60; then as a clerk in the 1850's, he was earning £75. By 1857 he head left the far north for Swan River, where his position could readily be compared with that of his wife's relatives in adjacent districts. By that time, another generation of McBeath's was represented in the HBC records (D4/51, fol. 85, Simpson to Adam McBeth [sic] June 11, 1856). The spelling of the name had undergone change by this time.

[18] G.P. de T. Glazebrook (ed.) *The Hargrave Correspondence, 1821-1843,* (Toronto, 1938), p. 313, William Nourse to James Hargrave, May 1, 1840. "I had the satisfaction last fall of acting Pere for our worthy friend R. McKenzie C.F. — and giving away his daughter Margaret to my friend Mr. James Anderson of Lake Huron — which I think tho' something of a singular choice as he had not seen the lady is likely to be a happy one— he is a fine young man and the Captain's fortunate in getting such a son-in-law."

[19] Ontario Archives (OA), James Anderson Papers, include material on Anderson's role in the search for the Franklin party, also some material from his son, James M. Anderson of Ainslie Hall, Sutton West, Ontario.

[20] HBCA, E4/55 fol. 156, Simpson to James Anderson, Feb. 10, 1859; the other letters are in a different file, D4/84b fol. 71, Simpson to Roderick McKenzie, June 17, 1859 and fol. 74, on the same day to Adam McBeath.

[21] Ibid., D5/34 fol. 269, Roderick McKenzie to George Simpson, Aug. 19, 1854.

[22] National Archives of Canada (NAC), MG 1944, Charles McKenzie to his son, Hector Aeneas, Lac Seul, Sept. 13,

1851; same to same, May 1, 1854.

[23] Van Kirk, "Women in Between", p. 39; "The Economic and Social Role of Women in the Fur Trade", p. 270.

[24] HBCA, D5/8 fol. 351, Roderick McKenzie Sr. to Simpson, July 8, 1843, A 32/42, Servants' Contracts, includes a contract at Lachine, March 13, 1837, signed by the 23-year-old Samuel with an X. The contract was cancelled at Norway House July 27, 1838 and Samuel signed his name.

[25] Douglas MacKay, *The Honourable Company* (Toronto, 1966), p. 285. Although the first recorded signature used the same spelling as his father, Samuel later adopted a different spelling.

[26] HBCA, D5/14 fol. 116, Roderick McKenzie Sr. to Simpson, July 1, 1845.

[27] OA, Cameron Papers, James Cameron to Angus Cameron Timiskaming, Jan. 29, 1845; HBCA D4/32 fol. 78d, Simpson to Duncan Finlayson, London, March 28, 1845; D4/33 fol. 87,

Simpson to Hector McKenzie, Lachine, Oct. 29, 1845.

[28] NAC, MG 19 A44 Charles McKenzie to his son, Sept. 13, 1851; HBCA, D4/42 fol. 160, Simpson to Roderick McKenzie Sr. Dec 10 1850.

[29] Ibid., A 34/2, Simpson's Character Book, 1832.

[30] Ibid., D5/10,, fol. 370, McKenzie to Simpson, March 4, 1844.

[31] Ibid., B89/1/18, Isle " La Crosse Journal, Jan. 26, 1839.

[32] Ibid., D5/8 fol. 351, McKenzie to Simpson, July 8, 1843; D5/10 fol. 310, Same to Same, March 4, 1844.

[33] Ibid., D5/22 fol. 372, Same to Same, June 29, 1848.

[34] Glazebrook, p. 366 Alex. Christie to James Hargrave, Dec. 10, 1841; HBCA, D5/13 fol. 163, Dr. Elliot to Simpson, Feb. 20, 1845.

[35] Ibid., D5/14 fol. 116 McKenzie to Simpson, July 1, 1845.

[36] Ibid., D5/21 fol. 110 Same to Same, Jan. 17, 1848.

[37] Ibid., D5/16 fol. 64, Same to Same, Jan. 8, 1846 re Alexander; D5/18 fol. 56, Same to Same, July 20, 1846, departure of Alexander for his post in Mackenzie River District; D5/327 fol. 53, Same to Same, Jan. 8, 1850 re James, who had an appointment at York Factory by 1851 (B239/G/91).

[38] Ibid., D5/6 fol. 181, McKenzie to Simpson, July 30, 1841.

[39] Ibid., D5/22 fol. 372, Same to Same, June 29 1848; D4/42 fol. 160, Simpson to McKenzie, Dec. 10, 1850 reports delivery of the gift.

[40] Thomas C. B. Boon, *Anglican Church from the Bay to the Rockies*. (Toronto, 1962), pp. 69-88; HBCA, A/36 Will of Roderick McKenzie.

[41] Henry J. Morgan, *Canadian Men and Women of the Time* (Toronto, 1912), pp. 700-01.

[42] MacLeod, p. 84, Letitia Hargrave to Mrs. Dugald Mactavish, Dec. 1, 1840. "Some people educate & make gentlemen part of their family & leave the others savages. I had heard of Mr. Bird at Red River & his dandified sons. One day while the boats were here a common half breed came in to get orders for provisions for his boatmen. Mr. H. called him Mr. Bird to my amazement. This was one who had not been educated & while his father & brothers are Nobility at the Colony, he is a voyageur & sat at table with the house servants here. Dr. MacLoughlen [sic] one of our grandees at great expense gave 2 of his sons a regular education in England & keeps the 3rd a common Indian."

[43] HBCA, B149/a/11 Nipigon Journals 1828 include Benjamin's report of activities while he was in charge during part of the summer of 1828. His brother Roderick kept the summer journal the previous summer, B149/a/10.

[44] Charles A. Bishop, *The Northern Ojibwa and the Fur Trade* (Toronto, 1974), pp. 49-50.

[45] HBCA, B231/3/1 Nipigon Correspondence Inward, Roderick McKenzie (Jr.) To Alex McTavish, Sturgeon Lake, Apr. 1, 1827.

[48] Ibid., B211/a/2-4; 7-9 Roderick McKenzie's Sturgeon Lake Journals.

[49] Elaine A. Mitchell, *Fort Timiskaming and the Fur Trade* (Toronto, 1977), pp. 189-90

[50] J.J. Hargrave, *Red River* (Montreal, 1871), p. 65.

[51] HBCA, D5/52 fol. 100d, Roderick McKenzie (Jane's husband) to Simpson, May 20, 1860.

[52] Ibid., D5/50 fol. 521, Katherine Dutremble to Simpson, Montreal, Dec. 19, 1859.

[53] MacLeod, pp. liii, lvi.

Part Six
The Hudson's Bay Company's Sway on Lake Superior

Part Six: The Hudson's Bay Company's Sway on Lake Superior

Until 1821 the North West Company had almost complete dominion over those areas of the Lake Superior and Rainy Lake watersheds that lie within the present boundaries of Northwestern Ontario. All that changed in 1821. Two former Nor'westers had charge on the ground but as officers of the Hudson's Bay Company: Chief Factor Dr. John McLoughlin at Rainy Lake and Chief Factor Alexander Stewart at Fort William. At Michipicoten, a Hudson's Bay Company writer, Andrew Stewart, was given charge as Chief Trader. While trade goods for, and furs from, the Lake Superior District were immediately routed through Michipicoten, that post became headquarters of the Lake Superior District only in 1827 with Chief Factor George Keith in charge.

John Weiler's report on post-1821 Michipicoten is yet another example of historical research conducted for public purposes, in this case for the Ontario Ministry of Natural Resources as "an aid in formulating directional interpretative planning alternatives for the Michipicoten Wilderness Reserve". Covering many aspects of Michipicoten's role as district headquarters, transhipment point and fur trade post, the report provides the context for the Fort William Post Journals of the 1820's and 1830's edited here by Judy Petch. By carefully reading these entries of daily life and work at Fort William, one can sense the Fort's decline from its former glory and its new subservient relationship to Michipicoten.

When the Hudson's Bay Company absorbed the North West Company in 1821, the status of two Lake Superior establishments changed dramatically. The NWC's imposing inland headquarters, Fort William, became a subsidiary of what was once a much lesser post, Michipicoten which almost immediately served as the entrepôt or supply centre for the HBC's entire Lake Superior District and by 1827 as its administrative centre.

While little known beyond the agency for which it is written, this historical study by John Weiler has much relevance to this volume. Not only does it concern developments in the fur trade at Michipicoten after 1821 but also in much of Northwestern Ontario. It also shatters some myths about the decline of the Lake Superior-Great Lakes route under the Hudson's Bay Company.

What follows is a large portion of Weiler's original report. Commissioned by the Historical Sites Branch, Ontario Ministry of Natural Resources in 1972 as "an aid in formulating directional interpretive planning alternatives for the Michipicoten Wilderness Reserve", it was also intended as a guideline for future archaeological and historical research. The Historical Sites Branch is now the Heritage Branch, Ministry of Culture while the park, now the Michipicoten Post Provincial Park, is operated by the Ministry of Natural Resources. It has no visitor facilities but is a good spot for nature viewing and hiking.

The original Hudson's Bay Company journals are among the many historical treasures in the Thunder Bay Historical Museum Society's Archives. The citizens of Northwestern Ontario are fortunate to have documents like these preserved for future generations.

The Hudson's Bay Company's Michipicoten Post, 1821-1904*

by John Weiler

Preface

The mouth of the Michipicoten River was utilized as a fur trade site for nearly two centuries. This was a direct consequence of Michipicoten's geographic position at the crossroads of water routes north to Hudson Bay and east to Montreal: the two historic transport-communications systems in the Canadian fur trade. The first post was established by the French, from 1725 to 1763, on the southwest bank of the Michipicoten River opposite its confluence with the Magpie River. Thereafter, posts were operated here successively by independent traders from 1767 to 1783 and later by the North West Company from 1783 to 1821.

The Hudson's Bay Company's presence at Michipicoten dates from 1797. The company established a post on the north bank of the Michipicoten River, opposite the North West Company site, with the intention of directing the fur trade to Hudson Bay and away from the Nor'westers' Montreal route. In 1803, however, the Hudson's Bay Company abandoned its Michipicoten establishment as part of an agreement with the North West Company concerning trading territories in the hinterland between Hudson Bay and Lake Superior.

After the North West Company transgressed this agreement, the Hudson's Bay Company re-established itself on the north bank of the Michipicoten River in 1816. [*In 1816 Lord Selkirk, of the Hudson's Bay Company, seized Fort William and then ordered detachments of De Meurons, his mercenary soldiers, to occupy NWC posts at Michipicoten, Lac la Pluie and Fond du Lac. ed.*] The rival companies then renewed competition until their their coalition in 1821. During the summer of that year the Hudson's Bay Company moved its operation to the buildings of the former North West Company post on the southwest bank of the Michipicoten River. The history of the Hudson's Bay Company's Michipicoten Post, from 1821 to 1904, was to proceed from this site.

I. Administrative History

Following the assimilation of the North West Company in 1821, the Hudson's Bay Company reorganized its fur trading territories into administrative departments. Each department was divided into sub-administrative units called "Districts". Michipicoten was located in the Lake Superior District of the Southern Department, with district headquarters at Fort William and departmental headquarters at Moose Factory. In 1827 Michipicoten replaced Fort William as the headquarters of the Lake Superior District.[1]

General supervision of the Southern Department was under a Governor and a Council consisting of at least three Chief Factors.[2] Alter 1826 one of the Chief Factors on the governing council was stationed at Michipicoten.[3] In 1821 William Williams was appointed Governor for the Southern Department. However, by 1826, Williams was recalled and George Simpson, Governor of the Northern Department, was given the extra responsibility of supervision in the Southern Department. It was not until 1839, however, that the double office was formally conferred on him. Simpson was never stationed permanently within the Southern Department but he continually toured and held council in these territories. In 1827 he held his first council of the Southern Department at Michipicoten.[4]

The Lake Superior District, administrated through Michipicoten, was a strip of territory more than 300 miles in length and 130 miles in width, bounded by Lake Superior (South), Moose and Albany Districts (North), Sault Ste. Marie and the Lake Huron District (East), and the Rainy Lake District (West).[5] The posts of the Lake Superior District, besides Michipicoten, included the Pic, Long Lake, Red Rock, Lake Nipigon and Fort Wil-

---

*Research Report, Historical Sites Branch, Ministry of Natural Resources, 1972 (extracts). ©Queen's Printer for Ontario, 1972. Reproduced with permission.

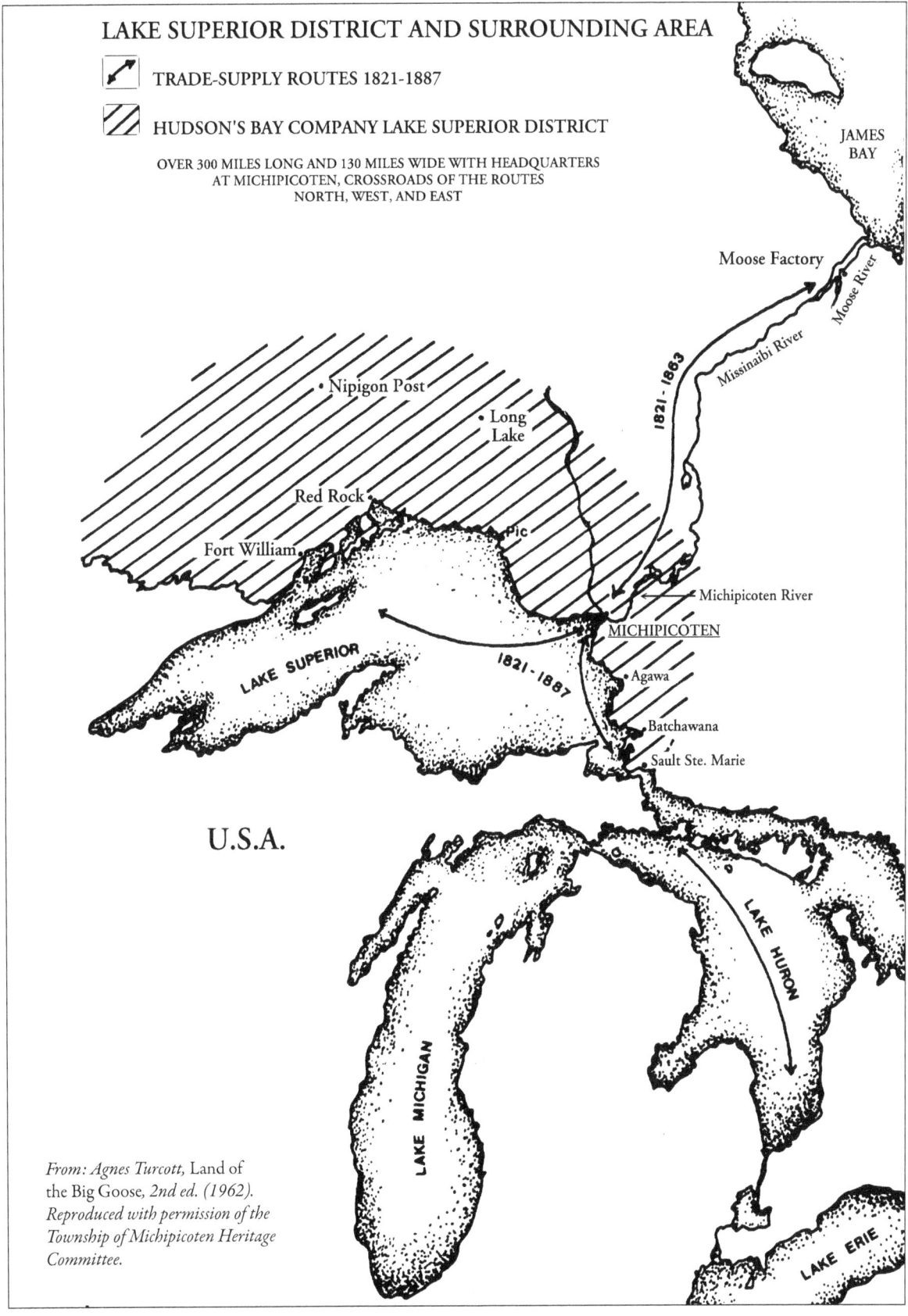

liam.[6] Temporary outposts were often operated from the Lake Superior District's permanent establishments. Michipicoten's outposts were at Batchewana Bay[7] and Agawa Bay.[8]

The chief company officer at Michipicoten was the individual responsible for the vast majority of administrative affairs in the Lake Superior District. His duties included the keeping of the district's consolidated business records; reporting annually on the district's operations; supervising the company's "officers in charge" at the district posts; ordering the district's yearly "Outfit" (supply and provisions); shipping the district's "Returns" (furs); and generally conducting all the major business correspondence and transactions of the Lake Superior District.[9]

In 1863 the Lake Superior District was transferred from the Southern to the Montreal Department, with department headquarters at Lachine, Canada East (Quebec).[10] Michipicoten, however, continued to be the administrative centre for the Lake Superior District. It was to maintain this function until 1887.[11] By 1892 the Lake Superior District was enlarged to include the Nipigon and New Brunswick Districts with district headquarters at Red Rock. Michipicoten Post was closed from 1895 to 1903. After a brief re-establishment it finally ceased operations permanently in 1904.[12]

II. The Michipicoten Post and the Lake Superior District in the Hudson's Bay Company's Frontier Economic Strategy, 1821 to 1885

Before the coalition of 1821, the Hudson's Bay Company's policy in the Great Lakes basin had been directed at challenging the Northwesters and other traders based on Montreal, by pushing numerous posts further and further south from Hudson Bay. Though the coalition made it possible to reduce the number of posts and concentrate at a few well-sited establishments, it did not eliminate competition utilizing the Great Lakes-St. Lawrence system. Independent traders from Canada and the United States continued to penetrate the area, presenting a potential threat to the company's monopoly in Rupert's Land.

Consequently, the Hudson's Bay Company adopted a policy which viewed the southern border regions of Rupert's Land as a protective buffer zone, a highly competitive frontier. Along the frontier the company appointed its most active and experienced personnel to manage the trade. It also bettered the opposition's prices and continually encouraged the Native people to hunt for every available fur. Michipicoten and the Lake Superior District assumed an important role in this "frontier strategy".[1]

Competition infiltrated the Lake Superior District from Sault Ste. Marie and western Lake Superior. At the Sault, independent traders based in Canada and the United States invaded the immediate hinterlands of Michipicoten. During the 1820's and 1830's the Hudson's Bay Company faced direct competition at Batchewana Bay, one of Michipicoten's outposts.[2] From across the international border along the Pigeon River, the Hudson's Bay Company's Fort William establishment faced opposition from the American Fur Company until 1847 as well as from independent traders.[3] During the early decades of the nineteenth century the Hudson's Bay Company appears to have successfully challenged its opposition in the Lake Superior District. In 1832 the Chief Factor of Michipicoten reported to Governor George Simpson that both the American Fur Company around Fort William and the "petty traders" from Sault Ste. Marie had been effectively controlled.[4]

By the 1870's, however, the Hudson's Bay Company was confronted with opposition much more acute than before. In 1873, for instance, opposition was reportedly intense in the New Brunswick District, immediately north of Michipicoten.[5] At the same time competition was advancing rapidly towards western Lake Superior. By 1880, competition had become extremely serious, especially around Fort William. As Thomas Richards, in charge of Fort William, reported to P.W. Bell, the Chief Factor at Michipicoten, "Since my last note to you I have not received a single skin, the American fur buyers at hand collect all that comes in their way so that there is no chance of competing with them."[6]

During the later decades of the century, increasing competition, and the depletion of the fur resources which it entailed, gradually undermined the effectiveness of the "frontier policy" in the Lake Superior District. The

Hudson's Bay Company's posts on Lake Superior declined rapidly. By 1885 Michipicoten itself was no longer of any great consequence. It was maintained only for local trade on the lake and merely covered expenses.[7]

III. Michipicoten Post: Trade and Supply Entrepôt of the Hudson's Bay Company's Lake Superior District, 1821 to 1887

(i) The Basis of the Entrepôt: Trade and Supply Routes

Michipicoten's geographic location at the cross-roads of water routes north to Hudson's Bay and east to Montreal was undoubtedly the most fundamental causal factor in its two century existence as a fur trade establishment. From the French regime (1725) to the coalition of the North West and Hudson's Bay Companies (1821) a continuous rivalry existed between these two alternate trade-supply systems. The coalition or 1821 did not terminate the rivalry, it merely altered its character. Indeed, it was the very interaction of the northern and eastern routes which established Michipicoten as the trade-supply entrepôt of the Hudson's Bay Company's Lake Superior District.

Traditional historiography of the Canadian fur trade suggests that the coalition of 1821 pronounced the demise of the Great Lakes-St. Lawrence-Montreal system and the triumph of the Hudson's Bay route.[1] This was supposedly assured by the decision to terminate Fort William's operation as the vital depot of the east-west route, and the accompanying decision to direct the trade and supply of the Lake Huron and Lake Superior posts from Hudson Bay, via Michipicoten, rather than from Montreal.[2] The findings of this report, however, indicate that the traditional view is in need of significant revision. The eastern trade-supply route did not decline after 1821. It increasingly gained importance over the Hudson Bay route until the coalition decisions were dramatically reversed. By 1863 the northern route to Hudson Bay was abandoned in favour of the eastern route to Montreal. In short, though Michipicoten and the Lake Superior District were supposed to look north to Hudson Bay, they were inevitably drawn east to the Great Lakes and the St. Lawrence.

Following the coalition of 1821 fur returns of the Lake Superior District, as well as those of the Lake Huron District, were collected annually at Michipicoten, shipped north to Moose Factory and then on to England via Hudson Bay.[3] This fur shipping system was maintained until 1863 when Michipicoten and the Lake Superior District were transferred from the Southern to the Montreal Department.[4] Now, fur returns of the Lake Superior District were collected at Michipicoten and shipped to Montreal via Sault Ste. Marie.[5] A decade later this procedure was still in practice.[6] It is assumed that Michipicoten continued to function as the fur shipping centre of the Lake Superior District until its demise as district headquarters in 1887.

From 1821 to 1863, provisions and trade supplies for the Lake Superior District were imported into Michipicoten and then shipped to the various district posts. European made articles were procured from Moose Factory, not only for the Lake Superior District, but also for the Lake Huron District. Non-European goods were obtained almost exclusively from Upper Canada. Some goods, however, came from the United States. These were imported via Sault Ste. Marie.

The eastern supply network was vital to Michipicoten and the Lake Superior District. George Keith, Chief Factor at Michipicoten, continually reiterated that the major advantage of the Lake Superior District was its connection through Sault Ste. Marie to the supply sources of Upper Canada, and that the district could not sustain n the large expense of importing provisions from Moose Factory.[7]

Furthermore, by the mid-1840's, a considerable quantity of goods (both European and Canadian) were being imported from yet another source—the Montreal Department headquarters at Lachine, Canada East. Though Moose Factory continued as a source of supply, nearly two-thirds of the goods imported into the Lake Superior District now came from Canada and the Montreal Department headquarters.[8]

After the transfer of the Lake Superior District to the Montreal Department in 1863, Montreal replaced Moose Factory as the source of European supplies. These were imported to the district via rail and steamship connections from Montreal to Sault Ste. Marie. Other goods were also procured via Sault Ste. Marie, either from the Montreal headquarters or from a number of ports situated on the Great Lakes system including Sault Ste. Marie, Windsor, Sarnia, Collingwood, Detroit, Hamilton and Toronto.[9]

Michipicoten continued to administer the ordering of "outfits" for the district posts until 1887. However, after 1863, Michipicoten no longer acted as a distribution centre for imported supplies. The Lake Superior District was divided into a number of shipping sectors with each sector having its receiving centre for goods carried from Sault Ste. Marie. Michipicoten was the port of entry for itself and the outposts of Agawa and Batchewana Bay. The other receiving centres were at the Pic, Red Rock and Fort William. This supply system was to be maintained even after Michipicoten had ceased to be the administrative centre of the Lake Superior.[10]

(ii) Transport Technology

Transport techniques varied with time and circumstance. Essentially, however, there were two distinct methods employed; one for the Michipicoten-Moose Factory route (north-south) and another for the Lake Superior route (east-west). Each of these routes witnessed significant changes in means of transport as the nineteenth century progressed and technological development increased.

The Michipicoten-Moose system was utilized as a major trade-supply route from 1821 to 1863. During June of each year the fur returns of the Lake Superior and Lake Huron Districts, along with provisions from Sault Ste. Marie for Moose Factory, were shipped out of Michipicoten via the Michipicoten and New Brunswick Rivers to Long Portage. Here the fur returns and goods were unloaded and conveyed by another team operating from Long Portage to Moose Factory, with the latter post as base. Then, the return cargo of European supplies from Moose Factory, for the Lake Superior and Lake Huron Districts, were transported by the Michipicoten crew back to Michipicoten Post. This procedure was to remain unchanged throughout the entire period of the route's employment.[11]

The Michipicoten-Moose route was never an efficient transport system. The major disadvantage was the inconvenience and expense of an operation which required a double set of transport servants, one based at Moose Factory, the other at Michipicoten.[12] Also, the shallow and rugged nature of this river system presented continual navigational problems, particularly as the bulk and quantity of goods carried increased.

Originally, light, maneuverable North Canoes were used on the route. The brigade travelling from Michipicoten in 1827, for example, consisted of six canoes manned by four servants each.[13] Canoe transport, however, soon became inadequate for handling increasingly heavy cargoes. Consequently, in 1828 the Hudson's Bay Company, under the direction of Governor George Simpson, decided to adopt a new form of transport vessel — "keel boats" [a variation of the "York boat". ed.] Three of these vessels were constructed at Michipicoten in 1828-1829 and were employed for the first time in 1830. No detailed description of these vessels has survived other than the notation that they were thirty feet in length and a modification of the river boat style used in the Northern Department.[14] "Keel" boats continued thereafter as the principal means of transport on the Michipicoten-Moose route. In 1858, for example, the brigade embarking from Michipicoten for Long Portage consisted of four keel boats manned by a total of thirty servants.[15]

The Michipicoten-Moose Factory system, however, continued to present navigational problems. Some efforts were made to improve portage routes and often batteaux were unloaded, with goods transferred to canoes, at particularly dangerous sections of the river passage.[16] On one notable occasion the Hudson's Bay Company attempted to alter the course of the Michipicoten River. In 1880 the Chief Factor at Michipicoten decided to divert the Michipicoten about two miles above the post to avoid a long, time-consuming bend in the river. This was accomplished by cutting a small ditch across the narrow neck of land (less than 100 feet), separating the river's meander bend and letting the spring floods cut a new channel in a more direct north-south line. The bend became an oxbow known as Dead River.[17] By this period, however, the Michipicoten-Moose system had long since been abandoned as a major trade-supply route. It was used now only by fur hunters and for inter-post communications between New Brunswick and Michipicoten.

The Lake Superior system was utilized throughout the entire history of Michipicoten Post and the Lake

Michipicoten Hudson's Bay Company post, from a painting by William Armstrong. Based on a late 19th-century photograph.

Superior District. After 1863 it became the exclusive trade-supply route. Initially, large lake boats or batteaux were employed to carry goods between Michipicoten and the various Lake Superior posts as well as the supply centre at Sault Ste. Marie. Canoes (both North and Montreal canoes) were also used; but usually to accompany a brigade of batteaux.[18] However, in 1836 the Hudson's Bay Company built a schooner, the *Whitefish*, at Pointe aux Pins near Sault Ste. Marie and pressed it into service for the Lake Superior District in 1837.[19] Thereafter, lake boats and batteaux continued to be used for smaller cargoes. Canoes were increasingly phased out, almost disappearing from use on the Lake Superior trade-supply route.[20]

A "professional" crew for the company schooner was procured from Europe in 1838. The crew consisted of a sailing master and three sailors. They were sent from Moose Factory via Michipicoten to Fort William, where the *Whitefish* was docked for the winter.[21] The *Whitefish* served the Lake Superior District until the early 1850's.[22] In 1851 a new schooner, the *Isabel*, was constructed to replace the *Whitefish*.[23] The *Isabel* was reportedly built "in the old English style of ships" and was of "eighty-six tons burthen".[24] This new schooner was wintered, repaired and outfitted at Michipicoten.[25] In 1856 it had the distinction of being the first Canadian vessel to pass through the newly constructed ship canal at the Sault.[26] The *Isabel* remained in service for the Lake Superior District until about 1867.[27]

Around the mid-1860's, the Hudson's Bay Company began to utilize the steamboat services of various transportation concerns operating on Lake Superior and shortly afterwards abandoned the use of its own schooner craft.[28] The steam vessels which served Michipicoten and the Lake Superior District included the *Isabel*, the *Collingwood*, the *Algoma*, the *Manitoba* and the *Chicora*. In 1872 the exclusive contract for transporting the Lake Superior District fur returns was awarded to the Beatty Company. Beatty steamboats carried the furs to Sarnia where they were consigned to the Grand Trunk Railway and shipped to Montreal.[29] It is not known precisely how long this contract was maintained after 1874. Steamboats, nevertheless, continued to function as the primary means of transporting trade and supply goods for the Lake Superior District even after the demise

SS. Algoma. The Algoma, *a sidewheeler, made its first trip into Lake Superior in 1864 and its last in 1874. Carrying passengers, mail and freight, it stopped at Michipicoten and other Lake Superior ports, including Prince Arthur's Landing. TBHMS 981.38.289.*

of Michipicoten as district headquarters in 1887.[30]

The Michipicoten River, besides presenting difficult navigational problems for the Michipicoten-Moose system, also created a hindrance for the Lake Superior transport route. Sand bars constantly choked the mouth of the Michipicoten River making navigation of schooner craft extremely troublesome between the lake and the Michipicoten Post wharf. Often cargoes had to be partially unloaded at the river's mouth to permit a vessel's progress to the post.[31] Steamboats never attempted to dock at Michipicoten Post. Their cargoes were unloaded at the village of Michipicoten Harbour.[32]

(iii) **Provisions and Supplies**

Provisions and supplies imported into Michipicoten were largely of two general categories: European Goods and Canada Goods. The former were procured through Moose Factory until 1863 and thereafter from Montreal. The latter were mostly procured from Southwestern Ontario and Sault Ste. Marie. A few articles, however, were obtained from supply centres in the United States.[33] Unfortunately, most of the useful documentary evidence detailing the character of provisions and supplies is restricted to the post-1850 period. Nevertheless, the available sources do permit relatively informative generalizations concerning the kind and character of goods imported into Michipicoten throughout the nineteenth century.

Articles imported from Europe consisted mostly of clothing and clothing materials, dry foods, assorted domestic utensils, firearms and gunpowder, alcoholic beverages (mostly brandy and rum) and sundry luxury goods. As the nineteenth century progressed, many of these articles were supplied from Canada. European supply goods, therefore, gradually decreased in quantity. This was especially true after the transfer of the Lake Superior District to the Montreal Department in 1863.[34]

Canada goods were primarily foodstuffs. The major foods imported were salt, salt pork, flour, oatmeal, cornmeal, and "high wines".[35] Construction and manufacturing raw materials were also significant among the goods imported from Canada, particularly during the latter part of the century when the Hudson's Bay Company increasingly brought in materials for construction and repair of post buildings.[36] The most important goods imported from the United States were tobacco and traps. Both articles appear frequently in the "Lake

Superior District Accounts Books" after 1865. Tobacco was procured from New York City; traps from the Oneida Community in New York State.[37]

(iv) Furs and Fur Trade Practices

Though the Lake Superior District was definitely not one of the more lucrative of the Hudson's Bay Company's territories, there is no evidence, before 1840, that the company was disappointed with the district's fur returns.[38] After mid-century, diminishing fur resources, competition and decreasing market demands, caused a gradual decline in the Lake Superior District trade. At the time of writing it is impossible to describe accurately the economic status of the Lake Superior District without undertaking an extensive study of the company's accounts. Further research is most definitely required in this area.[39] Also, because no systematic economic study exists of the Hudson's Bay Company's nineteenth-century establishments in Ontario, it is impossible to compare the Lake Superior District with contemporaneous districts in the province. The most that can be said concerning the productive capacities of the Lake Superior District is that fur returns were at their zenith from 1821 to about 1850.

Among the Lake Superior District establishments, Michipicoten was not particularly outstanding in fur production. Although no figures are available, it is relatively clear, from the Lake Superior District annual reports to 1837, that Michipicoten was not given special significance with regards to productive potential. At best, Michipicoten probably matched the individual outputs of the district's major posts.[40] There is considerable evidence, however, that by the late 1850's, Michipicoten's own fur returns were beginning to slip behind those of the other establishments.[41] Nevertheless, conclusive statements concerning Michipicoten's fur productivity are not possible without further research.[42]

The fur species produced by the Lake Superior District remained relatively constant throughout the nineteenth century. bear, beaver, otter, mink, muskrat, fisher, lynx and martin were the major furs listed in the records of district returns. The most abundant species were muskrat and martin. Michipicoten followed the district's general pattern almost exactly.[43]

The fur trading practices of Michipicoten post were representative of the Hudson's Bay Company generally. Fur hunting was undertaken by the native Ojibwa peoples. The hunters were advanced provisions on credit by the company in August, travelled to their respective hunting grounds for the winter months and returned in spring with their fur returns.[44] Hunters' returns were supposed to balance with the value of provisions credited them. However, since both the cost of provisions and the price of furs paid by the Hudson's Bay Company varied, the economics of this credit system were in continual flux.[45]

There is no record yet available in Canada before the 1860's of hunters' accounts with the Hudson's Bay Company at Michipicoten. It is therefore impossible to determine [at time of writing] just how efficiently this system operated for most of the nineteenth century. By the latter part of the century, the "Michipicoten Indian Debt Books" indicate that native hunters were often in arrears to the company.[46] This was a reflection of gradually declining fur production in the Lake Superior District. Furs brought in at Michipicoten during the spring months were sorted by species and quality, packed and pressed, and prepared for shipment. These operations were conducted by contracted employees of the Hudson's Bay Co. stationed at Michipicoten.[47] There is no evidence to indicate that there was anything "unique" in Michipicoten's processing of furs. Fur returns were shipped out of Michipicoten annually, during the month of June.[48]

IV. THE HUDSON'S BAY COMPANY'S MICHIPICOTEN POST, 1821-1887: SUPPORT AND SUBSIDIARY FUNCTIONS TO THE FUR TRADE [EXTRACTS]

(i) Food Supply

Though Michipicoten relied heavily upon imported food provisions, it was the policy of the Hudson's Bay Company to be as self-supporting as possible. Consequently, the potential food resources of the Michipicoten environs were exploited to the limited of their productivity. Food producing activities at Michipicoten were, in order of importance: fishing, agriculture and hunting.

(a) Fishing

Fishing and fish processing were the most important support and subsidiary functions of the Michipicoten fur trade establishment. The fisheries produce was not only vital to Michipicoten's food supply, but it also supplied other Lake Superior District posts. For nearly two decades, the Michipicoten fisheries were thus an important commercial enterprise.

The fisheries were conducted from early spring to late fall with the major species being whitefish with trout a close second. From September to late October, fisheries for Michipicoten were conducted along the shores of Lake Superior at Gros Cap, Gargantua Bay and off Michipicoten Island.[1]

Fish processing was an important activity at Michipicoten Post. Most of the fisheries production was salted and barrelled for future use. A separate area of the post site was reserved for dressing and packing fish as well as for storing and repairing nets.[2] Besides supplying its own needs, Michipicoten often furnished salt fish to other Lake Superior posts.[3] Michipicoten was not, however, the exclusive producer of this commodity. The other district posts located on Lake Superior also engaged in fishing, especially Fort William.[4]

(b) Agriculture

Though agriculture at Michipicoten was never very extensive, its products were very important for the post inhabitants' diet. Because of soil conditions and a short growing season, the only crop which could be effectively cultivated was the potato.[5] Potatoes were an important dietary supplement for the large amount of salted foods consumed by the post's employees and their families. Besides potato cultivation, Michipicoten always maintained a small assortment of livestock providing the post with meat and dairy products. In 1828, for example, the post had six cows, two heifers, one bull and eight sheep. Feed for the post animals consisted mainly of hay cut "across the river from the post".[6]

(c) Hunting

With the notable exception of rabbit snaring, hunting was not a very important food source for Michipicoten post. Rabbit was particularly vital to Native peoples during the winter months.[7] This mammal was probably the major winter-time source of fresh meat for Hudson's Bay Company personnel at Michipicoten. A careful daily record of rabbits snared was kept, for example, in the Michipicoten Post Journals for 1858-1859.[8]

(ii) Commercial Fishing: 1839-1860

Commercial fishing was Michipicoten's most important subsidiary enterprise and a significant adjunct to the fur trade in the Hudson's Bay Company's Lake Superior District. The Company commercialized its already well-established fisheries largely a a defensive response to competition.[9] Beginning about 1830 fishermen from the Sault, Cleveland and Detroit established stations on the north Shore of Lake Superior.[10] More importantly, the American Fur Company commenced large scale fishing operations on the lake in 1835, with headquarters at La Pointe [on the largest of the Apostle Islands, southwest Lake Superior].[11] One of the American Fur Company's fishing stations was at the Montreal River, only a short distance from Michipicoten.[12] The influx of American fishermen was doubly dangerous to the Hudson's Bay Company. Fishing concerns often engaged in periodic fur trading with the Indians and often diverted the Natives from the fur trade by employing them in fishing.

The American Fur Company was definitely the worst threat, especially by discouraging the Indians from fur hunting. This was clearly evident around Fort William by 1836.[13] Consequently, the Hudson's Bay Company entered the commercial fishing business to counter these threats to the fur trade and was further encouraged by the fact that the American market offered profitable returns for its fisheries produce.

V. THE HUDSON'S BAY CCOMPANY'S MICHIPICOTEN POST, 1821-1904: AN INSTITUTIONAL ESTABLISHMENT OF 19TH-CENTURY EUROPEAN TECHNOLOGICAL CIVILIZATION ON THE NORTH SHORE OF LAKE SUPERIOR

(1) Indian Annuities Distribution Centre, 1850 - c.1880

In 1850 William B. Robinson was appointed by the Canadian government to negotiate a treaty with the Indians on the north shore of Lake Superior from Batchewana Bay to the Pigeon River and inland to the height of land which separated the territory from regions held by the Hudson's Bay Company charter.[1]

Robinson recognized the attachment of Native populations to Hudson's Bay Company establishments and depended on company officers to arrange conferences with them.[2] More importantly, the HBC was utilized as an agency for distributing yearly annuities granted by the subsequent Robinson-Superior Treaty. Annuities distribution centres were established at Michipicoten and Fort William. Reserves of land set aside for Native habitation were also created by the treaty and one of these was located near Michipicoten at Gros Cap. Significantly, the treaty was witnessed by John Swanston, the HBC's Chief Factor of Michipicoten.[3]

The Robinson Treaty was directly beneficial to the Hudson's Bay Company. It was a relatively effective method of alleviating a long-standing Indian-trade problem. As early as 1827, many Michipicoten Indians had often travelled years to Manitoulin and Drummond Islands in Lake Huron for government gratuities and while there engaged in fur trading with independent entrepreneurs.[4] Now with annuities distributed at Michipicoten, the Natives were encouraged to remain in the vicinity of the post and trade there exclusively. It is not known precisely when the HBC's Michipicoten post ceased to function as an annuities distribution agency. However, records have been found of annuity money received at Michipicoten from the provincial Indian office in Toronto as late as the mid-1870's.[5]

VI. THE HISTORICAL SIGNIFICANCE OF THE HUDSON'S BAY CCOMPANY'S MICHIPICOTEN POST, 1821 TO 1904.

The Hudson's Bay Company's Michipicoten Post was a fur trade establishment of both provincial and regional historical significance. It was provincially significant, from 1821 to 1863, because of its relatively unique role as an entrepôt simultaneously utilizing both the traditional trade-supply routes of the Canadian fur trade, the northern route to Hudson Bay and the eastern route to the Great Lakes-St. Lawrence. It was regionally significant for several reasons. Firstly, from 1827 to 1887, Michipicoten was the most important fur trade establishment on Lake Superior. It acted as the administrative headquarters and, until 1863, the trade-supply entrepôt of the Hudson's Bay Company's Lake Superior District.

Further to its fur trade functions, the post became a communications link between a growing Ontario and its northwestern frontier as well as a focal point for other historical developments. These included commercial fishing from 1821 to around 1860, missionary activities, Indian annuities distribution after the Robinson Treaty of 1850; and from 1897 to 1904 government regulation of mining operations by the Michipicoten Mining Division of the Ontario Bureau of Mines.

NOTES

Weiler's principal sources were microfilms of Hudson's Bay Company Archives (HBCA) records held at the National Archives of Canada and the Fur Trade Collection at the Archives of Ontario (AO). The HBC reels are now available on inter-library loan from both the Hudson's Bay Company Archives and the National Archives of Canada. A description of reels related to Michipicoten may be found at *www.gov.mb.ca/chc/archives/hbca/resource/post-rec/post8.html#129*.

Since the manuscript descriptions of the Ontario Archives Fur Trade Collection have been revised since this article was written in 1972, every attempt has been made to provide updated references. A full description of this material may be found at *www.archives.gov.on.ca*.

SECTION I
[1] Reel 1M779, B129/e/4; B129/5; B231/e/3.
[2] E.E. Rich, *History of the Hudson's Bay Company*, Vol. III: 1821—1870 (Toronto: McClelland and Stewart, 1960), p. 406

[3] Reel 1M779. B129/e/5.
[4] Rich, pp. 438-9.
[5] Reel 1M779, B129/2/5 to B129/e/13.
[6] *Ibid.*; AO, F431, Accounts and invoices for the Lake Superior District of the Hudson's Bay Company. 1850-1901 (MU 1386 – MU 1389).
[7] A former North West Company outpost north of Sault Ste. Marie on Lake Superior, Batchewana was taken over by the HBC in 1821.
[8] Reel 1M779, B120/a/19.
[9] Reels 1M184; 1M520-5; 1M779-80; AO, MU 1386-MU 1389.
[10] "Agawa Post". Report prepared for Ontario Department of Lands and Forests, nd.
[11] AO, F431 24098 (1952).
[12] M.J. Shchepanek, "A Report on the Early History of the Michipicoten Trading Post Sites", Ms. prepared for Ontario Ministry of Natural Resources, 1972.

SECTION II

[1] J.S. Galbraith, *The Hudson's Bay Company as an Imperial Factor, 1821-1869* (1957), p. 433; Rich, p. 433; p. 464.
[2] Reel 1M779, B129/e/5.
[3] Reel 1M779, B129/e/5-B129/e/13;
[4] J.H. Baker, "Lake Superior: Its History, Romance of the Fur Trade, Its Physical Features", *Minnesota Historical Society Collections*, III (1880), pp. 342-4 Reel 1M184, B129/b/6.
[5] AO, F431, Box 2, Enc. 5.
[6] *Ibid.*, Box 2, Enc. 6;
[7] Reel 1M779, B129/c/16.

SECTION III

[1] See, for example, E.E. Rich, *The Fur Trade and the Northwest to 1857* (Toronto: McClelland and Stewart, 1967), p. 242; Rich, *The Hudson's Bay Company, 1670-1870*, Vol. III, p. 412.
[2] Rich, *The Fur Trade*, p. 242.
[3] HBCA, Reels 1M779-80, B129/e/5 - B/129/4/13.
[4] See Section I above: "Administrative History".
[5] AO, F431, Box 2, Encl. 2. "Letter Sault Ste. Marie to John McKenzie, Michipicoten 1863".
[6] *Ibid.*, Box 2, Encl. 5 "Letter J. Bissett, Montreal to P.W. Bell, Michipicoten, 1873.
[7] HBCA, Reels 1M779-1M780, B129/e/5 - B129/4/13.
[8] HBCA Reel 1M521, B129/d/4.
[9] Reel 1M522, B129/d/21.
[10] AO, F431, Boxes 2,3,4 and 5.
[11] HBCA Reel 1M779, B129/e/6.
[12] HBCA Reels 1M 779-1M780, B129/e/5-B129/e/13.
[13] HBCA Reel M779, B129/3/6.
[14] HBCA Reel 1M184, B129//6/1.
[15] AO, F431, Michipicoten Post Journals, 1858-1859.
[16] HBCA Reel 1M184, B129/b/3.
[17] Ontario, *Bureau of Mines Report 1898*, p. 192.
[18] HBCA Reel 1M79, B129/a/12.
[19] HBCA Reel 1M184, B129/6/11; Reel 1M521, B129/d/11.
[20] Lake boats and batteaux were used for small loads on short runs such as between the Pic and Michipicoten. Canoes were rarely employed except between Michipicoten and its outposts at Batchewana Bay and Agawa.
[21] HBCA Reel 1M152 ,B231/a/17-18.
[22] HBCA Reel 1M521, B129/d/10.
[23] HBCA Reel 1M521, B129/6/6.
[24] Rev. John Ryerson, *Hudson's Bay; or, A Missionary Tour, in the Territory of the Hon. Hudson's Bay Company* (Toronto: 1855), p. 2.

[25] HBCA Reel 1M521, B129/d/9.
[26] Grace Lee Nute, *Lake Superior* 91944), p. 130.
[27] HBCA Reel 1M522, B129/d/18.
[28] AO, F431, MSS Box 2, Encl. 3.
[29] *Ibid.*, Box 3, Encl. 5.
[30] It would be interesting to study the effect of the Canadian Pacific Railway's completion in 1885 on the trade and supply system of the HBC on Lake Superior. [Arthur J. Ray touches on the coming of the CPR across Northwestern Ontario in his *The Canadian Fur Trade in the Industrial Age* (Toronto: 1990), pp. 78, 88-90. With the railway came increased competition and a increasingly marked change in transportation patterns towards Winnipeg and Montreal and away from Moose Factory. ed.]
[31] AO, F431. Michipicoten Post Journals
[32] AO, F431, Box 2, Encls. 3 and 5.
[33] See Section 3 (i) above, "Trade and Routes".
[34] HBCA Reels 1M520-1M525; AO F431, Boxes 2-5.
[35] HBCA Reel 1M184, B129/6/1.
[36] OA, F431, Boxes 2-5.
[37] HBCA Reel 1M522, B129/d/21.
[38] HBCA Reel 1M779-1M780.
[39] See "Conclusions" above.
[40] HBCA Reel 1M779-1M780.
[41] OA, F431, Boxes 2-5.
[42] See "Conclusions" above.
[43] HBCA Reel, 1M779, B129/e/5; Reel 1M521, B129/d/3-4; AO, F431, Box 2, Encl. 6.
[44] HBCA Reel 1M779-1M780, B129/a/12-B129/a/20; See also Louis Agassiz, *Lake Superior* (Boston: 1850), pp. 62-3.
[45] For fur tariffs, see HBCA Reels 1M 520-1M525; AO, F431, Boxes 2-5
[46] HBCA Reel 1M522, B129/d/16; B129/d/24; Reel 1M524, B129/d/28.
[47] HBCA Reels 1M79-1M80; AO, 431.
[48] See Section III (ii) above

SECTION IV
[1] HBCA Reel 1M780, B129/e/10; AO, F431, MU 1385.
[2] HBCA Reel M79, B129/a/19; Agassiz, *Lake Superior*, p. 69; AO, F431, MU1385.
[3] HBCA Reel M79, B129/a/19; Agassiz, *Lake Superior*, p.60.
[4] HBCA Reel 1M152, B231/a/18.
[5] HBCA Reel 1M184, B129/b/4.
[6] HBCA Reel 1M9, B129/a/1'2; AO, F431, MU 1385.
[7] George de T. Glazebrook, ed., *Correspondence of James Hargrave* (Toronto: Champlain Society, 1938), p. 296.
[8] AO, F431, MU 1385.
[9] See Section 4 (1), a. "Fishing".
[10] Galbraith, The Hudson's Bay Company, pp. 40-41.
[11] Grace Lee Nute, "The American Fur Company's Fishing Enterprises on Lake Superior", *Mississippi Valley Historical Review* (1926), p. 487.
[12] *Ibid.*, p. 493.
[13] HBCA Reel IM152, B231/a/16.

SECTION V
[1] AO. Copy of the "Robinson Treaty made in the year 1850 with the Ojibewa Indians of Lake Superior'. [Text of the Robinson Superior Treaty is available on the internet.]
[2] AO. "Diary of Visits of William B. Robinson to the Indians.... 1850".
[3] Robinson Treaty.
[4] HBCA Reel 1M79, B129/a/12; Galbraith, *The Hudson's Bay Company*, p. 43.
[5] AO, F431, MU 1385.

Fort William Post Journals of the 1820s and 1830s: Some Extracts

Introduced and edited by Judy Petch

Several years ago an academic colleague, knowing of my amateur interest in local history and the fur trade, directed my attention to two Hudson's Bay Company (HBC) post journals which were written at Fort William in the 1820s and 1830s and are now in the possession of the Thunder Bay Historical Museum Society (TBHMS).[1] These journals, dated October, 1823 to September, 1824 and October, 1835 to May, 1837 respectively,[2] were the first primary documents I had ever read on the fur trade. I was intrigued by two things: the sense of eavesdropping on what first seemed to be a private community diary, and the strange yet familiar references to local geography, travel patterns, and economic activities. There were a few expressions (like *cavreau*[3]) which I couldn't define in context; and a diverse cast of characters, almost all of whom were unknown to me. However, as I began to read more widely to understand the background of people, places, and activities discussed in the journals, I came to the conclusion that, with appropriate editing and marginal comments, the journals, even if only in an extracted form, have some value to the general public as a window into Thunder Bay's early history and its role in the Canadian fur trade during the HBC era.

By way of introduction, there are several questions about the journals which need to be answered. Why were they written? Precisely who wrote them? What is their provenance? Then there are the more general questions: What are the principal features of these journals? What is their intrinsic historical value?

Post journals are similar to ships' logs. They are an official record of the activities of the post and its personnel during a certain period. Daily entries by the post manager, like those of the ship's captain, justify administrative decisions, report on the success of transactions and activities, account for the deployment of staff, and specify how policies are being carried out in the name of the company. HBC policy obviously required the keeping of post journals, as can be seen in the vast number of extant HBC post records from the early 1700s to well into the 1900s. Most of these are located in the Hudson's Bay Company Archives (HBCA) at Winnipeg.

Exactly who wrote these two Fort William journals is still a mystery. There were obviously several different writers since the original journals appear in different handwriting. Alexander Stewart, Chief Factor at Fort William from 1821 to 1824 possibly recorded the 1823-24 journal with Roderick McKenzie (the chief trader appointed to succeed him in 1824) a less likely choice. William Nourse (a clerk who had charge of the post in 1835), and his successor in 1836, chief trader Donald McIntosh,[4] may have kept the 1835-37 journals.

Another fascinating mystery is the provenance of these two journals. As seen above, many of the HBC post journals that survive today are with the HBC Archives at the Provincial Archives of Manitoba in Winnipeg.[5] To establish the "routine" provenance of HBC documents, let's return to the analogy of a ship's log for a moment. Assume that the period of the ship's particular mission is complete. The daily logbook of noteworthy and routine occurrences is passed on to head office. If the company is a commercial one, then corporate business strategy and investment decisions would probably be based in part on field information which the log or journal has imparted. When executive perusal is complete, the log, along with associated documents such as account books and correspondence, most likely would be transferred to the company's private archives, which in turn might eventually be handed over to a public archival institution.

Since the above process is what happened with most HBC records, how then did these two particular Fort William post journals come into the possession of the TBHMS and not the HBC Archives in Winnipeg? No donor is listed for these journals when they were catalogued for the then Thunder Bay Historical Society

---

*From Thunder Bay Historical Museum Society *Papers & Records*, 1997, pp. 45-63 (with slight revisions). Reprinted with kind permission of the author.

(TBHS) in the early 1940s. The only fact we know for certain is that the journals came into the TBHS collection before that time. Thorold J. Tronrud, of the Thunder Bay Historical Museum Society, speculates that the documents may have escaped shipment to the HBC head office in London, England. The company's records were held there until 1974 when they were transferred to Winnipeg. The journals, Tronrud surmises, may have been overlooked in the Fort's buildings until the establishment was closed in the 1880s[6] and then taken into personal possession by yet unconfirmed individuals. Brent Scollie, a retired librarian and historical researcher now living in Ottawa (but originally from Thunder Bay), has brought to my attention many HBC documents concerning the Fort William post which were donated to the TBHS by Dr. Charles Napier Bell, secretary of the Manitoba Historical Society. These donations are listed in *The TBHS Papers of 1912-13*, p. 36, *The TBHS Papers of 1920*, p. 33, and noted in "Fort William in the Middle of the XIX Century" by Alexander L. Russell, D.L.S. (Dominion Land Surveyor) in *The TBHS Papers of 1915*. The latter article refers to "souvenirs" from the Fort William post given to Russell in 1883 by HBC clerk Thomas Richards (then overseeing the Fort's closure after John McIntyre's retirement in 1878), and Russell's subsequent donation of these items to the Manitoba Society. Although the 1823-24 and the 1835-37 journals are not mentioned in any of these references, the journals may be part of the "souvenirs" that were transferred from Thomas Richards to Alexander Russell, and then to Dr. Bell who, as Brent Scollie notes, "in turn gave them back to the [Thunder Bay Historical] Society [in 1908]."[7]

As a record of daily occurrences, these journals give a cumulative picture of an isolated and largely self sufficient community engaged in a seasonal round of economic activities in support of the HBC's larger commercial enterprise, the fur trade. Individuals and groups frequenting the Fort also emerge, as do observations on such diverse subjects as meteorology and protection of the Company's monopoly from the American Fur Company and independent traders. For example, the entry for Sunday, August 28, 1836 recounts a thunderstorm of seemingly apocalyptic proportions. A month later on Thursday, September 29, 1836 a domestic argument is reported between a freeman,[8] Antoine Collin, and his wife. She decamps for Grand Portage in the United States leaving her family behind but a week later it is revealed that she has proceeded only as far as the Welcome

Fort William, 1858. Although the fort has obviously deteriorated since its heyday before 1821, much has remained the same — Ojibwa birchbark wigwams across the river, transportation by birchbark canoe and schooner (seen in the distance). TBHMS 977.113.274

Islands and her husband takes a boat to go and get her.

The historical usefulness of these two journals is both strengthened and handicapped by their contemporaneity. They present descriptions of, and report reactions to what the writer knew as the recent past, or current events. Consequently, the journals are generally not distorted by the hazy filter of memory or loss of accurate detail, as often happens in memoirs or analyses written years after the events described. For the reader today, on the other hand, the journals can be maddeningly deficient in background information about the people and places mentioned in the entries. The journal writers apparently assumed that their executive readers were familiar with the people, places and situations noted in this record of daily events from having read other contemporary HBC documents.[9]

Two main conclusions may be drawn from reading the journals. Firstly, within two years of the HBC North West Company merger, Fort William had settled into the role of a minor fur trade post, with complementary functions as a commercial fishery, a way station and service centre for such noted happenings as Lieutenant Henry Bayfield's survey of Lake Superior, and a producer of agricultural products for local and regional consumption. Secondly, even in the 1820s, the beginnings of the long, slow decline of the Fort's infrastructure were evident.[10] These conclusions are not original to me, having been reported in many published sources. However it is profound to read the original documents for oneself, and slowly recognize in the recorder's comments, descriptions and observations, subtle evidence of historical processes at work.

These two journals are only a small part of the mosaic of primary sources from Thunder Bay's fur trade era, but they are a great help to reconstructing in one's imagination the fur trade past of Fort William. It's in the imagination that a true appreciation of history begins, and it was from these two journals that I began my understanding of the role that Fort William played in the history of this region.

For expediency in showing the annual round of activities while sampling from both journals, and keeping a sense of continuity in the narration, I have chosen to excerpt two periods: October 1823 to May 1824, and June 1836 to early October 1836. I have tried to be as faithful as possible to the spelling of the original, but have altered punctuation for clarity, and capitalization to reflect modern usage. I take full responsibility for all errors, flaws and omissions in the transcription, and this introduction.[11]

1823-24 JOURNAL

[Full text for] October 1823

18th Saturday   After breakfast sent off the light canoe with the express for the Governor and Committee in England via Montreal. Mr. Clarke Ross, who had been detained here from indisposition, since the 17th. ult'o, took his departure in company with Mr. Bourgnon.

About 2 p.m. the new schooner was launched in the presence of the officers and the men of the naval surveying party, and of the whole of the Company's servants at the Fort. She was named the "Recovery"[12], and went off the stocks in good style, under a discharge of nine guns from the Fort, and nine rounds of small arms from the men in the government employ, who were drawn out on the occasion.

In the afternoon Lieut. Bayfield[13] and the other officers dined with Mr. Haldane[14] and his party, and a regale was provided from the Company's store for the men in the service of the government, and those in the Company's employ. The day was closed in the utmost harmony, and to the satisfaction of all parties....

20th Monday   This morning sent 4 men and Peter McFarlane to fish with a seine at the rapids. No particular occurrence at the Fort.

21st Tuesday   Men employed as follows: the blacksmith arranging his tools; Masta ploughing; Magnus Brass working on the new schooner; Maurisseau attending to the cooking; Dauphin at various jobs. No particular occurrence.

22nd Wednesday   Papamasum's son and the two eldest sons of the Peau de Chat[15] arrived in the afternoon. In the evening, one of the sons of the Little Rat[16], arrived from Lac la Loge, to get some necessaries for himself and his father.

23rd Thursday   This morning Mr. Grant and two new men were sent along with the Little Rat's son, to give credits to the family and arrange with them in regard to their plans for the winter. Papamasum's son, etc. got a few necessaries and returned to their lodge. In the afternoon, two of Netomass's sons arrived for a few necessaries.

24th Friday   Snowing. Gave the two young Indians who arrived yesterday a little ammunition, and sent them to shoot ducks or partridges. They returned in the evening; had only three muskrats but saw no wild fowl. The people returned from the Rapids with 800 Whitefish.

25th Saturday   This morning Peter and Baron were sent off to the Grand Portage to discover if the Americans have any establishment there[17] ....

27th Monday   The Pechau arrived with a few furs; got a little credit, and returned again to his Lodge. Masta finished ploughing. Others variously employed.

28th Tuesday   Peter and Baron returned from the Grand Portage where there is no appearance of the Americans.

29th Wednesday   Peter, Masta and Melonie went up to Point Meuron with some of the horses to leave them there to pass the winter. On the way one of the horses got ruptured so badly that they were obliged to shoot her. Cameron's brother in law (an Indian, so named) arrived with a few skins.

30th Thursday   Peter and 2 men with 2 Indian women went off to skin and bring home the flesh of the horse which was killed yesterday. The Indian who arrived yesterday got some ammunition and went away.

31st Friday   No outdoor employments as it rained all day, but employed four of the men in hulling barley. Blacksmith and others as before.

[Excerpts from] November 1823 [and months following]

2nd Sunday   As the river nearly frozen and the season far advanced, sent 5 men with the boat to fetch home the casks of fish from Antoine Collin's fishing....

4th Tuesday   Hard frost last night; a great deal of snow upon the ground. Michel Collin and Robert returned from their fishery; have 11 casks salted fish which makes in all from Michel's fishing, twenty casks.

Peter and the men returned with 14 barrels fish from A. Collin's fishing.

5th Wednesday   The men went off with the boat this morning to go to M. Collin's fishery, but the wind being unfavorable, were obliged to return.

6th Thursday   The men succeeded in crossing to M. Collin's fishery.

10th Monday   Michel Collin went over to the Island to look after the people who went off on Thursday last, as they appear to be a long time in returning.

11th Tuesday   River nearly frozen over. A. Collin and Ross returned from their fishing. They have procured in all this fall, 31 casks fish, besides some which they have hung up to freeze. Michel Collin also returned, and about 1/2 past ten p.m. the men with the boat arrived with the fish from Michel's fishery. They were obliged to leave the boat at the bottom of the river as the ice is too strong to allow them to bring it farther.

12th Wednesday   This morning Masta went down with the horses and sleys [sic] and brought up the casks of fish.

17th Monday   Sent the men to put the boat in a place of safety for the winter.

[In the next two weeks several domestic animals are slaughtered for meat, and women of the Fort go out snaring rabbits.]

29th Saturday   Commenced with the following rations for the men: 3 1/2 days salt fish and potatoes at 5 lb. salt fish and 1 gall'n potatoes pr. day; 2 days rations fresh fish at 9 lb. pr. day; and 1 1/2 days corn and grease at 1 quart corn and 1 1/2 oz. grease pr. day, for 1 weeks rations to each man. But Magnus Brass receives per. week 3 1/2 lb. pork, 5 1/4 lb. bread, 17 lb. salt fish and 3 1/2 gals. potatoes. In lieu of the two last, he received for this week (ensuing) 3 1/2 lb. fresh fish. He at first refused to take fresh fish, but finding that Mr. Haldane would make no alteration, he complied.

December 1823

1st Monday   Mr. Haldane having received information, that some of the men under the command of Lieut. Bayfield, had been attempting to trade furs, etc. from the freemen resident at this place, called upon Lt. B. this morning, and stated the circumstances to him; Mr. Haldane informed him, at the same time, that although these freemen were not in the Company's permanent employ, they derived the whole of their support from the Company, and that in every estimate made for the supply of the Indians, the necessaries required by these people were always included. In consequence of which, they were to be considered as on the same footing as the Indians, and any clandestine trade carried on with them, as an infringement of the Company's rights. Mr Haldane concluded by stating, that it was his desire to afford Lt' Bayfield every assistance in his power, to make him and his party comfortable during their residence here; and to forward any business connected with the survey under his direction and command. On the other hand he had been led to anticipate that Lt' Bayfield would discountenance any interferance [sic] with the Company's trade by any of his party.

Lieut Bayfield replied that he certainly perceived the impropriety of what Mr. Haldane now informed him and perfectly agreed in the necessity of putting a stop to such proceedings. He had, therefore, determined to issue public orders to his men to that effect, to avoid all complaints in future.

15th Monday   Pucquitchininies arrived from the Grand Marais, about 40 miles beyond the Grand Portage. He came to give information of the Americans being established there for the purpose of trading with the Indians. This place is upon the Americans' territories, but on the communication by which many of the Indians of this [place] pass.

20th Saturday   ...There are now the following Indians and their families, encamped here, who expect support from the Company according to the old custom, viz: Ackiwainsie, his son, and L'Homme de Sault[18] and a family of [space blank]

From the state of affairs, owing to the vicinity of the American traders, etc., it is found impossible to refuse support to these Indians and their families, without great hazard of displeasing them and perhaps losing them altogether.

There are likewise, some Indian old women, who, either from innability [sic] to support themselves, or from their connection with some of the best hunters belonging to this quarter, look for some support from this establishment, which cannot be well refused to them without danger of discouraging the Indians to whom they are related. In consequence of this, Mr. Haldane has been under the necessity of allowing them rations of fish and potatoes, until the season becomes sufficiently advanced to admit the possibility of their procuring their livlihood [sic] hunting.

24th Wednesday   This afternoon, gave each of the men 2#[19] beef, 1# flour and a little butter, etc., as a Christmas regale. Gave the Petit Vieux[20] also a little beef and flour. This is a good Indian, and an excellent hunter....

January 1824

1st Thursday   All the men, according to custom, were treated with drams, etc., this morning, and received each 2# beef, 1# flour, 1/2 pint barley, and a little butter, and a pint of rum as a regale.

The Indians also received presents of a little rum, etc. And the Petit Vieux, on account of his being a good hunter and a faithful Indian, received 2# beef, 1# flour and a little butter, as a regale.

A little before noon, three men (Bellehumeur, Ducharme and Gilbeau) arrived from Lac La Pluie [Rainy

Lake] by way of Lac des Bois Blanc. They brought letters from Dr. McLoughlin[21] and Mr. Simon McGillivray[22], requesting a supply of a few articles of trading goods for the former post....

2nd Friday   The men were allowed this day to complete the holidays.

3rd Saturday   Got the few articles of trading goods intended for L.L.P. assorted and packed, and gave out the sleds to the men to arrange for their voyage. Dampierre and La Tulip sawing firewood. Dauphin and Fanneant cleaning away snow from before the dwelling houses and stores. Robert threshing barley....

5th Monday   Early this morning, the three L.L.P. men (Bellehumeur, Ducharme and Gilbeau) were despatched with the goods required for that post, with the exception of the latter man's load (consisting of 1 capot, 4 ells [of cloth?], 1 chiefs coat, 5 blankets, and 1 pr. [strouds?]) which he was unable to take with him, being sick. It is therefore left until they can send from L.L.P.for it....

6th Tuesday   Petit Vieux and family went off highly pleased with his treatment whilst here. He received a present of a little rum and tobacco, to take with him. Also some fish and potatoes for his voyage.

7th Wednesday   ...Blowing very much all day. Magnus Brass working at various jobs, and in the afternoon getting boards, etc., in readiness for making a large chest for putting in one of the stores in which Mr. Haldane intends to put the Indian corn in order to secure it from mice and other small animals, which have hitherto destroyed a great deal, from the corn not being properly secured.

14th Wednesday   ...Robert finishing threshing the grain making in all, for the produce of the farm last autumn, 23 bushels pease, 24 1/2 bus. oats, 23 bus. Barley, and 10 1/2 bus. oats and barley mixed.

[During the rest of the month, various Indians bring in furs from their winter hunt, a packet is sent off containing letters for the Governor at Moose Factory, Montreal agents, and other company officials.]

29th Thursday   This forenoon two men...arrived from Pays Plat with [a] letter from Mr. Corcoran. They came for a supply of corn, etc., to enable them to pass over the remainder of the winter. Mr. C. has procured about 100 skins from the few straggling Indians in that quarter....

February 1824

1st Sunday   The Indians (Attineau, Oshickatusk and Waheskakiwansie) received some more credit and Cheobeting, also wishing to go off at the same time, got a few necessaries. After breakfast, having arranged their things, Mr. Haldane gave them a keg of 2 gal. h[igh]. wines, some tob'o, etc., and 6 qts. corn, some fish and potatoes, with which they departed, apparently much pleased with their reception.

Blowing all day and very cold.

5th Thursday   This morning sent off Baptiste Showenonscan and Laurent Richard, with a supply of corn, etc. for the post at Pays Plat. Very cold.

19th Thursday   At 10 o'clock A.M. Fanneant and La Tulip arrived with a packet from the Governor of [the] Southern Department at Moose. They went no farther than the Pic where they found this packet and the despatches, which they conveyed from hence for the Gov'r at Moose. They left with Mr. McTavish who will forward them on.

[Much of the work at the Fort this month consists of cutting cordwood, and hauling it, and clearing snow, with the blacksmith at work making beaver traps.]

March 1824

4th Thursday   Continued rain all day. Dauphin and Melonie employed cleaning the drain to carry off the water.

Pacutchininie came in with the heart and tongue of a carribou [sic]. The Petit Vieux has also killed one.

5th Friday   Raining hard all last night and today; indeed there has hardly been an abatement since it commenced on the 3rd. inst., and such a fall of rain as this at this season has not happened before in the remembrance of any one here.

9th Tuesday   ...Memo: a cow calved.

15th Monday   Masta and Fanneant were sent off with two horse sleds to get ice from the lake for the purpose of filling the ice house. Dampierre and Dauphin assisting at placing the ice in the ice house. Others employed as on Saturday, except the blacksmiths who were making fire steels.

17th Wednesday   Two men...arrived from Mr. Corcoran's with despatches from Moose Factory, and from Montreal. By the packet for Moose, the different documents for arranging the accounts of this department, were received.

Finished filling ice house.

22nd Monday   Several of the Merino ewes have had lambs within the last few days, but very few of them live above a day or two, owing perhaps, to the earliness of the season.

30th Tuesday   Three men (Rouleau, Fanneant, and Melonie) were sent off this morning to take provisions, etc, to the sugar bush for the party who are going there tomorrow to make sugar.

April 1824

1st Thursday   Rouleau, Fanneant and Melonie returned from the sugar bush, having erected a lodge and cut firewood, for the sugar makers.

2nd Friday   Fanneant was sent off this morning to the sugar bush with kettles, etc. Melonie assisting the blacksmiths; Dauphin and Rouleau picking out all the spoilt potatoes in the cavreau....

[Travellers arrive from Lac la Pluie to await the opening of navigation on Lake Superior before continuing further east; fishing is done with lines and nets under on the ice of the bay; migratory waterfowl are hunted; blacksmith and carpentry chores are done on the *Recovery*; wood is secured for canoe building.]

24th Saturday   ....Louis Ross arrived this evening from White Fish Lake with a letter from Mr. Grant, requesting the few necessaries for the Indians there. He says the Americans have been trading with Scandagance and Hawaytask.

26th Monday   Early this morning sent Ross back to White Fish Lake with the articles requested by Mr. Grant. Masta attending the cattle in the meadows to prevent them from crossing the river. Felix and Rouleau spreading the snow about, that it may be the sooner thawed.... Pierre, the Iroquois, and La tulip securing the boats laying in the river to prevent them from being carried off by the ice when the river breaks up.

30th Friday   It froze very hard last night; cold weather during most part of the day.... The blacksmiths finished 51 steel traps this morning, and got iron and steel to make more. Fanneant went to visit his lines, and to kill ducks.

He returned with 5 trout and 4 ducks. He took up his lines as the ice is now very weak. The men finished storing the canoe wood, and afterwards hauled in some logs to mend the observatory. Rouleau and Masta mending the fences....

[1836 JOURNAL]

[Excerpts from] May 1836 [and following]

Sunday 1st   Thermo was at the freezing above this morning. The river has broke up in several places & they say that the ice has drifted down opposite to the sugar bushes. The men who were there yesterday evening cross'd over to this side in a canoe. Weather clear wind from the eastward. There were a good many bustard & ducks flying above.

Wednesday 4th   Thermo was 20E above 0 [Fahrenheit] this morning. The men commenced to prepare the stockades in order to put them up in the front of the Fort. The river is clear of ice. It disappeared in course of the night. Wind from north. Weather clear.

Saturday 7th   Thermo was 27E above 0 this morning. The men put up the stockades on the east side of the Fort door. Severals [sic] families arrived from the sugar bush. It has been a pretty favourable season for the sugar. They made as much as the preceding spring....

Monday 9th   ...Old Collin commenced to tighten the timbers in one of the light canoes. Blowing a high gale from sw. which broke up the ice in the bay to Sheep Island.

Wednesday 11th   ...Cloudy weather. Wind unsteady. Boucher and Camaviaire commenced gumming the canoes....

Thursday 12th   Fine clear weather. Blowing a heavy gale from north east, which shattered the ice in the bay a good deal.... The canoe maker tightened the timbers of three light canoe[s].

Friday 13th   ...Old Collin finished tightening all the canoes that will be required for the Northern Department.

[Ice breaks up in the bay, and is driven out to the open Lake; canoes are gummed; several Indians arrive to trade the proceeds of their winter hunt; barley is sown.]

Thursday 26th   ...Governor Simpson[23] & Messers Dease[24] and McIntosh[25] arrived in two canoes at 4 O clock pm.   The men were cutting seed potatoes.

Friday 27th   ...The Governor and Mr. Dease proceeded on their to the interior in two light north canoes. Send two Indians to the Pic with a packet from the Governor to Mr. C. F. [Chief Factor] Bethune.

Sunday 29th   ...The men and two Inds arrived from Nipigon in a fishing canoe they came here for a heifer calf and a north canoe. Old Collin started for the Sault. Indians are starving.

Monday 30th   Fine clear weather. The men sowed 45 bushels of potatoes. Blowing a light breeze but changeable.

June 1836

Wednesday 1st   ...wind from southwest. The people sowed all the potatoes, say 160 bushels. The Spaniard[26] and step son arrived and brought 140 skins of prime furs.

Monday 6th   Very warm weather. The grass & all other vegetables are scorched for want of rain. The men were employed making and preparing pack[s]. Wind from north east.

Monday 13th   It rained all the afternoon. The nets & seine produced 30 white fish. A son of Mr Flette a farmer from Red River with a half breed from the Sault arrived in a fishing canoe Mr. Flette is not arrived. He crossed over to Pattie [Island] on account of the wind being too high. They are now on their away to Red River. Wind from south.

Tuesday 14th   Blowing a high gale from north which prevented the people from setting out for Michipitcoten. I finished my dispatches & closed the business of outfit 1835. The nets produced 40 white fish. Scandagance brought us six sturgeons.

Thursday 16th   Raining still all day. Mr. Flette arrived, with the rest of his family this afternoon. He finds himself in a rather unpleasant dilemma with respect to his journey from hence to Fort Frances for want of proper vsouts[sic=voyageurs?] to take the bow & stern of his canoe as well as to carry it in the portages. The river is very high in consequence of the late heavy rains. Hence they will have some difficulty with such inexperienced hand[s] in rapids.

Saturday 18th   Mr. Flett & his family set out on their journey to the interior in a north canoe & a fishing canoe. They were very much incumbered [sic] on account of the number [of] passengers. Including men women acc[ounte]d there were 18 on board of the north canoe & two Indian[s] who went to guide and assist them were in the small fishing canoe. We had several light showers in course of the day. Weather calm.

Friday 24th ...Old Collin arrived he did not go farther than Michipicoten. The old Brisbois departed this life this afternoon. She was a poor infirm creature and as helpless as a child and had been so for several years past. She was only a few days sick.

Saturday 25th Fine clear weather. Wind south west. Interred the old woman that died yesterday. The nets and seine produced 50 whitefish.

Thursday 30th Clear weather very sultry. The seine produced upwards of 700 whitefish. Salted two bbls [barrels] today and two yesterday. The men hoeing in the potatoes in the garden. Wind southwest.

July 1836

Saturday 2nd For want of rain ever [sic] thing in the garden is burnt or scorched, and the grass is short and very thin....

Saturday 9th Rained again all night. Cleared up about 12 o'clock. The canoe that old man [Antoine Collin] layed [sic] yesterday the women finished sewing the gunwales & the two large seams and he put the timbers in it to take their bent. Blowing a high gale from south west.

Monday 11th ...H Davilleau & Tremble were employed in the smith shop repairing half axes & capletes. Fontain was making rakes for the hay.

Wednesday 13th ...Michel Collin and family arrived from the Sault. Nothing particular from that quarter.

Friday 15th Fine clear weather. Wind from the south east.... Carleau and Stepson with the Canard & Illinois[27] 3rd son arrived & brought 13 rolls of good bottom bark.

Monday 25th ...about 2 o'clock p.m. Governor Simpson arrived from the Northern Department on his way to Canada....

Tuesday 26th ...Governor Simpson procede[d] on his voyage early on the morning. La Garde went off to return to Nipigon with a case of iron and sundry other small articles of supplies for that post. The people of the Fort and Indians were employed at the hay. Michel housed 6 cart loads today of hay. Wind from s[outh] west.

August 1836

Tuesday 2nd It rained for the most part of the day. Old Tremble is very sick; it appears to be the influenza. La Bete and his family arrived from Isle Millens. He killed only 3 rain deers [sic]. The mowers were employed as usual. But Michel and Indians secured none of the hay today. Blowing a heavy gale from south west.

Wednesday 3rd The weather clear and cloudy alternatively & light showers at intervals Michel and the Indians secured 6 cart load of hay in the remise.[28] Tremble is rather better: the pain in his side has left him, it is the head ache now that make[s] him suffer. Wind north east all day.

[Haying takes up most of the month, ending on the 24th.]

Saturday 20th It rained from the most part of the day which prevented the hay makers from housing the last of the hay that is mowed. Payed [sic] severals [sic] of the Indians employed at the hay with ammunition & tobacco. Wind from south.

Tuesday 23rd Fine clear weather. Light wind from the westward, the men were variously employed. The Indians who are encamped at the Point Brule waiting for the arrival of the outfit [supply of trade goods,

C. Graham. Hauling Nets on Lake Nipigon. In the 1800's, fishing was almost as important to the Hudson's Bay Company as the fur trade in its Lake Superior district which included Lake Nipigon and all Lake Superior posts. TBHMS 976.100.1kk (972.2.479)

etc. for the coming year] to take those necessaries for the winter, are starving and came to the place begging for provisions. The Indians at the place get a few fish in their nets. The seine & nets produced fish enough for the days consumption for all hands.

Thursday 25th   The two boats arrived at last. They brought the outfit & provisions in good condition. There are four men forwarded by the boats which I [am] instructed to send on without delay to Lac la Pluie, from thence they will proceeded to Red River where I understand they are to winter. Light wind & unsteady.

Friday 26th   Unbaled all the goods and found them in good order. Wrote my dispatches for Red River & Michipicoten in order to dispatch the above men hence to Lac la Pluie tomorrow & Jos. Fontain to Michipicoten.

Sunday 28th   There was a most dreadful thunder storm about 2 o'clock am. I never in my life experienced such flashes of lightening, it was most aweful [sic]. The thing it put me mind of was the general conflagration of the world as describe[d] in holy writ the last day....

September 1836

Thursday 1st   Rained at intervals. Wind from the westward. Despatched two young Indians to Michipicoten with a letter to acquaint Mr. C. F. Cameron that the American Fur Company are building at the Grand Portage. The sein [sic] and nets produced very few fish. The men reaped the field of barley.

Monday 5th   Hard grey frost last night. Wind high from south west. The nets & seine produced 200 white fish. Attenau & his son arrived   and brought a dozen of skins in rats. They took their usual advances for the winter and then went off to return thence they came....

Tuesday 6th   Sein & nets produced enough for all hands for the day. Weather cloudy. A high westerly wind during the day. The men housed all the barley say 340 sheaves. Attenau shot a bear this morning and brought the most of the meat to us.

Friday 9th   Michel Collin went off this morning in an old boat with one of the Company's servants, his son, and an Indian for the fishing at Shagoinna. He took 100 new casks that his father made & 19 barrels of salt. These as they are employed, he will also salt fish in them. Sent off 4 of the Company's servants & two Indians with a boat load of cord wood & empty casks to the fishing station at Rabbit Island....

Saturday 17th   Fine weather and calm. All the Montreal men, decharged [sic] servants, & families that arrived here from the Northern Dept. [last] Thursday evening in 4 north canoes proceeded on their journey downwards this morning in two Montreal canoes[29] much crowded with people. H Davilleau went off to fish a few days at point Brule. Boucher catched [sic] 29 trout in 4 nets he set at Sheep Island.

Wednesday 28th   We have seldom experienced such hard frost as we had last night at this season of the year.... The people could only begin to take up the potatoes in the afternoon owing to the ground's being froze. Therefore they only took up 40 kegs....

Thursday 29th   Cloudy weather & indicates snow. Blowing a heavy gale from the westward. Old Collin['s] wife went off in consequence of a quarrel with the old man. She left all her children even the one that was still on the breast. She is gone towards the Grand Portage to join the Americans. She is a worthless loose character....

October 1836

Thursday 6th   ...Old Collin[']s wife went only to the Welcome Islands where Visina is fishing. He (the old man) went for her there & returned from thence this morning....

ACKNOWLEDGEMENTS

The author would like to thank the following people for their advice and assistance in preparing this article: Tory Tronrud, Brent Scollie, and Shawn Allaire, former librarian at Old Fort William.

NOTES

[1]The Thunder Bay Historical Museum Society (TBHMS) also has in its collection one Fort William post journal from the 1870s, which is not included in this article.

[2]Each journal is bound with handwritten daily entries. The journal for 1823-24 contains 48 pages with dimensions 9.25 inches x 14.5 inches; the journal for 1835-37 has 92 pages with dimensions 8 inches x 12.75 inches.

[3]Cavreau means "cellar" which here refers to a root-cellar such as were used to store potatoes and root vegetables.

[4]Susan Campbell, *Fort William: Living and Working at the Post*, Thunder Bay: Old Fort William, Ontario Ministry of Culture and Recreation, 1980.

[5]When the HBCA's holdings are considered together with the TBHMS holdings, the Fort William post journals apparently run in sequence from 1823 to 1851, with the exception of September 1824 to June 1826, and a gap from 1840 to 1849. The HBC Archives also have other Fort William diaries from the North West Company period covering 1817-18, and 1818-21. TBHMS holdings also include a Fort William post journal from the 1870s.

[6]Thorold J. Tronrud, personal communication to editor, Thunder Bay, Ontario, April 4, 1996.

[7]Brent Scollie, personal communication to editor, Ottawa, August 20, 1997.

[8]A freeman was a fur company employee who had finished his contract but stayed on in the interior after his discharge. Freemen often lived near HBC posts and worked for the Company as labourers or tradesmen on a freelance basis.

[9]Since most people today have not had the privilege of reading all these documents, we can profitably examine secondary, analytical sources which draw together expository background to events and activities that are reported without comment in the journals. Three secondary sources that I have found particularly helpful are: *Fort William: Living and Working at the Post* by Susan Campbell (1980), *Thunder Bay District 1821-1892: A Collection of Documents* by Elizabeth Arthur (1973), and "The Anishinabeg and the Fur Trade" by Victor P. Lytwyn in *Thunder Bay: From Rivalry to Unity* (1995).

[10]Regrettably, it hasn't been possible to show the latter conclusion effectively in these excerpts. I refer the reader to the

[11] original texts in the possession of the TBHMS. See Elizabeth Arthur, ed., *Thunder Bay District* for first hand accounts of Fort William's decline.

[11] The TBHMS also has a carbon copied typescript of the 1823-24 Fort William Journal on onion skin paper. There is apparently no record of the name of the transcriber. I have transcribed directly from the original handwritten text of both journals, and used the 1823-24 journal's carbon typescript as a reference.

[12] The schooner *Recovery* launched in 1823 was 133 tons. The schooner was readied for service over the winter of 1823-24, and headed downriver to Lake Superior on May 23, 1824. The vessel was the second schooner of that name to serve on Lake Superior, the first *Recovery* being of 90 tons. (This first vessel was apparently also built at Fort William, and launched about 1809-1811.) As Jean Morrison recounts: "As the Hudson's Bay Company at first had little use for ships on Lake Superior, it chartered the Recovery [I] to the British admiralty for Lieutenant Henry Bayfield's survey of the lake which commenced in June 1823. The ten year-old *Recovery* must have been inadequate for Bayfield commissioned the ship which had been under construction at Fort William since 1816.... The Hudson's Bay Company decided to sell the *Recovery* [II] after the survey, not because it [the ship] had no use, but because of problems with the sailors...." (Central Information Access file "Schooners" pp 13-14 manuscript "Early Shipping on Lake Superior," Old Fort William, 1985) In 1828 the vessel was run down the St. Mary's River rapids to the lower lakes and sold.

[13] Lt. Henry Wolsey Bayfield was a British naval officer commissioned by the British Admiralty to complete a hydrographic survey of the Great Lakes, including Lake Superior. He and his party overwintered at Fort William in 1823-24.

[14] John Haldane was an HBC officer in charge of the Lake Superior district from 1823 to 1827.

[15] Peau de Chat was a prominent Anishnabeg (Ojibwa) at Fort William. He was brother to Grand Coquin. Lytwyn (31, 1995) notes that their "winter hunting grounds were located near Whitefish Lake." Arthur (14, 1973) states that: "Peau de Chat seems to have been a name applied to more than one Indian chief. In the late 1820s and 1830s there are references to an old Peau de Chat who appeared at posts as far east as Michipicoten, in fact carrying the news of the Papineau rebellion to the post at the Pic. It is probable that this was Joseph Peau de Chat, chief of the Fort William Indians in 1849." Lytwyn also points out that in 1850 "Chief Joseph Peau de Chat signed [the Superior-Robinson Treaty] on behalf of the Fort William Anishnabeg." (33, 1995)

[16] The Little Rat was an Anishnabeg leader "who lived near Lac des Milles Lacs." (Lytwyn, 31, 1995)

[17] During the 1820s, competition with American fur traders (particularly John Jacob Astor's American Fur Company) south of the border between Lake Superior and Lake of the Woods was a continuing problem for the HBC. The Americans' accessible locations and competitive prices for trade merchandise lured Indians away from HBC posts. A kind of "cold war" situation developed, with HBC personnel at great pains to spy out the activities and intents of the Americans, and discourage the Indians from taking their business to the Americans. (Lytwyn, 28, 1995) Monitoring the Americans, was, as Lytwyn notes, "an important reason for keeping Fort William open after 1821." (28, 1995)

[18] L'Homme du Sault had hunting grounds "near a place called Portage la Prairie." (Lytwyn, 31, 1995)

[19] # means a pound (in weight).

[20] Petit Vieu(x) was highly thought of by HBC officers because of his productivity as a fur hunter, and his loyalty to the Company. Journal entries for January 1837 (not included in these excerpts) describe his final illness and death at the Fort.

[21] Dr. John McLoughlin joined the North West Company as a physician and clerk in 1803, rose to be a partner in 1814, and was made a chief factor of the HBC at the 1821 amalgamation. He was assigned to the Rainy River district in 1822, and in 1824 HBC Governor George Simpson appointed McLoughlin superintendent of the Columbia District. McLoughlin played a major role in the development of the Oregon Territory.

[22] The Simon McGillivray referred to here is probably the son of William McGillivray and his native wife Susan. Simon joined the North West Company about 1803 as a clerk and was made an HBC Chief Trader in 1821.

[23] George Simpson (1787?-1860) was appointed Governor-in-Chief of the HBC in 1826 and held that position until his death. An extremely capable and energetic administrator, he was noted for his many, rapid inspection trips through HBC territories.

[24] Possibly Peter Warren Dease, who entered the fur trade about 1801 serving successively the XY Company, NWC, and HBC. He served in the Athabaska, Mackenzie and New Caledonia districts. George Simpson seconded him to

John Franklin's "Land Arctic Expedition" for outfits 1824-25, 1825-26 and 1826-27. Dease also played an important role in Arctic coastal exploration during the 1830s. He had two brothers, Charles and John, who were also in the fur trade.

[25] This is likely Donald McIntosh, who took charge at Fort William in 1836.

[26] The Spaniard, also known as "L'Espagnol" had hunting grounds south of the border but preferred to bring his furs to the HBC. He was an important leader and spokesperson among regional Indians in the period covered by these journals.(Lytwyn, 30-31, 1995)

[27] L'Illinois was an Anishnabeg leader "who wintered near Black Bay." (Lytwyn, 31, 1995)

[28] A remise is a shelter, possibly for wagons, and carts.

[29] HBC employees who had completed their contracts and elected to retire to Canada were sent eastward in convoys to facilitate travel. Some employees took with them the wives and children they had acquired while in the Northwest. Montreal voyageurs were engaged specifically to paddle between Montreal and Fort William (sometimes further inland), returning to Montreal at the end of the navigation season.

Postscript
The Modern Fur Trade

Postscript: The Modern Fur Trade

Many of the preceding papers on Northwestern Ontario's fur trade ended by recounting its gradual decline over the course of the nineteenth century. But what has been the fate of the fur trade since that time? Did it suffer permanent collapse or is it a viable industry today? A look at the fur trade in the present seemed like a fitting way to finish this book on aspects of the fur trade's past. Such an article would view the fur trade during the 1900's and conclude with its situation at the beginning of the new century. How many people work as trappers in Northwestern Ontario today and what is the ratio of Natives to non-Natives? Which species are most commonly trapped and in what quantities? What is the average price for various skins and where are they marketed? A ready-made research paper on these topics must surely be available for inclusion in this book.

Alas, this was not the case. Searches of on-line library catalogues and queries to such institutions as Lakehead University, the Thunder Bay Public Library and the Ontario Ministry of Natural Resources proved futile. No one knew of any research reports or theses related to the modern fur trade in Northwestern Ontario. Resort to the Internet, however, led to *Ontario Fur Managers Federation Online.* Use of its "contact" feature soon produced useful leads from the OFMF's administrative assistant Lisa Ouellette, including one to Steve Ball, Vice-President of OFMF's Northwestern Region. On Mr. Ball's suggestion I visited the Northwestern Trappers Association convention at Thunder Bay in February 2002. No one at any of the displays could help until someone suggested that I talk to Murray Monk whom I found skinning a beaver before several fascinated onlookers.

Sporting a very long beard, Murray Monk is a tall exuberant man whose enthusiasm for trapping and conservation (he sees no contradiction) cannot help but win over most doubters about the legitimacy of his occupation. Alongside Murray was his beautiful new wife, Rebecca, a trapper in her own right and a creator of gorgeous fur hats, some of which she had on display. Murray told me that he was the subject of a chapter in Charles Wilkins' *A Wilderness Called Home: Dispatches from the Wild Heart of Canada*, a compelling narrative of diverse experiences across non-urban Canada. Wilkins' account of Murray's life as a trapper in the Nipigon area should be read by all wishing to understand the complexities of one of Canada's most historic trades. The author has kindly granted permission to use the chapter in full or quote from it extensively but unfortunately space has allowed only a few references to a fascinating book which deserves to be read in its entirety.

At another booth I picked up some issues of *International Trapper* (North American Fur Auctions) and *Tales and Trails* (Ontario Fur Managers Federation) along with some data compiled by the Fur Institute of Canada. Someone suggested that Gary Forma, Tourism/Marketing/Partnerships Co-ordinator for Ontario Parks at the MNR headquarters in Peterborough, might point me in the right direction and this was right for he referred me to Chris Heydon, the MNR's Fur Program Biologist. Chris not only went out of his way to compile the chart on current fur returns in Northwestern Ontario [see page 161] but he also put me in touch with Lynda Jagros-May of the Furriers Guild of Canada. Besides supplying useful information, Lynda directed me to Tina Jagros, Executive Director of the North American Fur Association who mailed me some promotional material on today's fur trade as well as two stunning videos on the latest fur trade fashions: *Fur—The Fabric of a Nation* and *The Montreal NAFFEM* (North American Fur & Fashion Exposition).

Although my mind was reeling from discovering this multitude of organizations involved in today's fur trade, I recalled attending two ceremonies in Winnipeg, the first in 1987 when the Hudson's Bay Company transferred its fur trade operations to Northern Stores Inc. and the second in 1990 when Northern Stores became The North West Company. Information about The North West Company's operations in Northwestern Ontario, which obviously belongs in this chapter, kindly was supplied in telephone conversations with NWC staff at North Bay, Longlac and Poplar Hills and with Charlie Snow, manager of the NWC store in Thunder Bay until its closure around 1990.

One of Lise Ouellette's recommendations was a visit to the websites of the auction houses at *www.nafa.ca* and *www.furharvesters.com*. Not only did I fellow this advise but my computer's search engine brought up far more information about the modern fur trade world-wide than could possibly be processed. Till then my knowledge of Revillon Frères was sketchy at best but a reference on the internet led to the Revillon Frères Museum in Moosonee whose director John Rutledge put me in touch with Betty Dyck, the granddaughter of a Revillon factor. From the Internet I also learned of the National Film Board's *Traces d'une histoire oublizée* and of Robert Flaherty's memoir. The Internet (and hard copy publications) also brought the animal rights movement and the fur industry's response forcibly to my attention. It also yielded an abundance of information on such diverse aspects of the modern fur trade as Aboriginal trappers and the fur industry in Greece, Russia and China.

Thanks to the computer, this chapter on the modern fur trade has strayed far beyond Northwestern Ontario, its original geographical scope. Space and the editor's qualifications have allowed but a superficial glance at the interdependent worlds of the regional and international fur trades. Perhaps in the near future, someone more knowledgeable in the field will undertake an in-depth study of Northwestern Ontario's present-day fur trade and its trappers.

Much gratitude goes to all who offered information for this chapter, those named above or in the text, those whose information could not be used for reasons of space and those whose names have been inadvertently omitted. Any errors, of course, are my own responsibility.

Ups and Downs in the Modern Fur Trade*

by Jean Morrison

As the nineteenth century drew to a close, new economic activities were fast eclipsing the fur trade in the southern regions of Northwestern Ontario. North of Lake Superior and Rainy Lake, the Hudson's Bay Company conducted its trade much as before but without its old monopoly privileges. In urban areas, however, many Hudson's Bay trading posts became "sales" shops or retail outlets of general merchandise with more customers from new settlements than from Native communities. Many reasons can be offered for the fur trade's decline. Intrusions of settlement and agriculture and of lumbering and mining into wildlife habitat are among the obvious as is the bringing of industrialism into the region by modern means of transportation. With steam navigation by water and by rail, Fort William became once more the transhipment point for western staple products and eastern manufactured goods, a role now shared with Port Arthur. These changes also rendered obsolete the Hudson's Bay Company's north-south economic ties between James Bay and Lake Superior. Commerce now flowed east and west as it had under the North West Company.

The fur trade's increasing insignificance in the region after 1821 is revealed in *The Land Between: Northwestern Ontario Resource Development, 1800 to the 1990s* by W. Robert Wightman and Nancy M. Wightman (Toronto: 1997). The book's first fifteen or so pages concern the North West and Hudson's Bay Companies at the time of their merger in 1821 but after that the fur trade receives scant mention. And while its forty-nine tables feature a variety of economic activities in the region, none is related to the fur trade.

Oft-cited explanations for the trade's decline include the beaver's near-extinction from over-trapping and the wide use of silk rather than beaver felt for making quality top hats. Beaver had once counted for more than half the fur trade's annual returns, an amazing statistic considering all the steps leading to a finished product whose sole function was status not warmth.[1] Despite conservation measures mandated by the Hudson's Bay Company to regulate trapping, beaver populations became dangerously low. What kept the trade going was the wealthy classes' use of chinchilla, ermine, mink, marten, fox, and sable in fine clothing and accessories.[2] Overall, however, the fur trade continued on its downward fall throughout the nineteenth century as profits fluctuated with the whims of fashion and the state of the economy.

In Northwestern Ontario, this was particularly true in the southern regions where competition, development and settlement took their toll. According to a Hudson's Bay Company senior director, Edward Ellice, the fur trade along the southern frontier declined by one-half to two thirds between 1821 and 1857 owing to particularly severe competition with American and Canadian independent operators. In response, the Hudson's Bay Company negated its own conservation policy by ordering the destruction of all fur-bearing animals in the area, a measure which did not entirely succeed.[3]

The coming of the railway in the 1880s furthered the decline of animal numbers. Penetrating the wilderness, this symbol of the Industrial Age also brought small-time competitors into the heart of the Hudson's Bay Company's former preserve. Among these petty traders were the railways' own employees. Along the National Transcontinental Railway (the Canadian National), conductors paid the Aboriginals cash for their furs, a welcome change from trade goods. Near Lake Nipigon and Montizambert (now Mobert), Canadian Pacific Railway workers also traded in contraband beaver and otter.[4]

Wildlife populations are subject to cyclical ups and downs. Despite threats to their existence from human and natural causes, the furbearers survived as did the fur trade. As the twentieth century dawned, the trade experienced a rebirth and, despite its near collapse towards the end of the 1900's, it gives every sign of being very much alive in 2003.

---

*Paper prepared for this publication

What saved the business back in 1900 was a fashion innovation designed to stimulate consumer demand. That innovation was the fur coat. Until the late Victorian era, winter garments featured fur collars, cuffs, trim and linings. On fancy garments, the outer body could be of velvet or silk brocade but it was usually wool. Wool had long been the preferred fabric for winter wear, with or without fur trimmings. This was also true for Aboriginals whose willingness to shed their pelts (worn with the fur inside) for woollen blankets helped make the fur trade possible. Then in Paris some brilliant designers and marketers conceived the idea of making fur coats and jackets with the fur on the outside.[5]

The prestigious French furriers, Revillon Frères, are credited with introducing this sensation at their Paris fashion house around 1900. Couturier-designed coats of luxury skins immediately appealed to high society, the traditional market for fur, but less expensive furs also attracted the middle class, a rapidly growing market in the economic boom before World War I. The new-fangled open motor car contributed to the demand since fur coats gave not only protection from the elements but prestige to the wearer. Men of means also took to fur for both warmth and show as in the raccoon skin coat. Fashion furs, however, "slowly became the domain of women and children. On children they looked cute in coat trimmings, hats and muffs, but on women furs evoked wealth and privilege."[6]

This new vogue created such a demand that Revillon Frères soon by-passed its London and Leipzig wholesalers by collecting pelts directly at source, the Native trappers of Canada's far north. In 1903 the firm had 23 posts across the country with head office and warehouse at Montreal, a large distribution centre at Edmonton, and headquarters for its James Bay trade at Moosonee. Revillon also forged links to the Lake Superior watershed by opening a post on Lake Nipigon's far northeast shore and another at Nipigon River's entry into Lake Superior. Since ships were scarce during World War I, it forwarded supplies for the James Bay district by rail to Pagwa on a branch of the Albany River from where they were floated or towed down river.[7]

For over thirty years, Revillon engaged the Hudson's Bay Company in deadly combat for control of the Canadian fur trade but in 1936, during the midst of the depression, overtrapping and low prices forced the former to surrender. Selling out to its rival, Revillon closed its posts but maintained its raw and dressed skin business in Montreal until 1951. Some insight into the competition between Revillon and the Hudson's Bay Company is revealed by Philip Godsell, the Hudson's Bay Company's field officer at Long Lac. There he faced opposition from Revillon's trader, Ernest Herbert McLeod. McLeod had served Revillon at Nipigon from 1905 to 1907 before his transfer to Ombabika Bay on Lake Nipigon's north shore. Around 1913, the company ordered him to Longlac across the Height of Land, where he stayed until around 1917.[8] As Godsell recalled:

> My friend McLeod, the Revillon Trader across the lake was, however, getting more and more annoyed at the success attending my growing authority over my Ojibway charges. He was afraid by this time to touch "contraband" [furs prohibited by treaty to be traded] so I had a decided advantage there as I would not trade beaver or other from Indians who sold other furs to him. McLeod complained to me at last that the Indians refused to trade with him in the daytime lest I catch sight of them through my long-range telescope, or my spies report the matter to me. Even at night, they insisted on the blinds being pulled down so that the light would not shine across the lake...Then I received word one day from the [Hudson's Bay] company that Revillon's had decided to close their post and ship the goods to Ombabika...I felt sorry for McLeod when I saw him leave as he was very decent about everything, but only those who have worked for the Company can understand the feeling that existed against the average opposition trader, and the perhaps misguided sense of loyalty that would, literally cause a HB man to push even his own brother to the wall if he happened to be trading in opposition to the "Gentlemen Adventurers".[9]

Revillon's venture in Canada is now largely forgotten outside of academic circles and has no entry in *The Canadian Encyclopedia*.[10] Yet Revillon Frères left Canada a lasting legacy, one in which Thunder Bay takes particular pride. This was *Nanook of the North*, the world's first documentary film Issued in 1922 and financed by Revillon, this movie about an Inuit family's year-long struggle for survival was filmed and directed by anthropologist and explorer, Robert J. Flaherty, then a resident of Port Arthur, Ontario. As Flaherty himself explained, "The resources of the Revillon Fréres fur trade post at Cape Dufferin were at my disposal."[11]

Fur press at Long Lake (or Long Lac), early 1900s. This photograph shows the traditional way furs were compressed into "packs" for transportation. Packs shipped by canoe usually weighed 90 pounds; those going by larger vessels could be up to 120 pounds. TBHMS 972.66.8.

On Revillon's first Paris showings of the fur coat, the international fashion market embraced extravagant displays of fur as garments and adornments. Since Paris set the world's fashion trends then, as now, the new mode launched an unprecedented explosion in fur's popularity. In Canada fur manufacturing was concentrated in the garment districts of Montreal and Toronto where factories and workshops employed thousands of artisans to finish, dye, cut and piece skins into overcoats, stoles, capes, collars, cuffs, wraps, hats, and muffs.[12]

The craze for fur coincided with a phenomenal growth in the retail trade across New Ontario and Western Canada before World War I, brought on by the influx of some three million immigrants. Along the southern frontier, where most newcomers settled, the Hudson's Bay Company soon found retailing general merchandise more profitable than trading for fur.[13] In 1881 it opened its first modern store in Winnipeg, Manitoba, and by 1914, it had opened more department stores across the west, a harbinger of a far-off time when the Company would abandon the fur trade altogether. Until that unforeseeable event, the company combined its retail and fur business by collecting furs at its posts and selling garments and accessories created from these furs at its urban stores.

From the First World War to the Second and after, the demand for pelts never ceased. By portraying celebrities draped in animal skins, Hollywood movies and gossip magazines conveyed a new glamour to fur, a quality fans and admirers wished to emulate. A craving for fine fur, which wild fur's dwindling numbers could not satisfy, led to fur farming (or ranching), first in Prince Edward Island where the fox farming industry began in 1900 to be followed by mink farming ten years later.[14] But despite fur's appeal, fluctuations in supplies of various species, from natural and human causes, and unstable pricing made the fur trade a very tenuous business indeed. Then the industry suffered its greatest blow ever with the rise of the animal rights movement.

Although animal rights activists had long condemned all cruelty to animals, perhaps it was Brigitte Bardot's denunciation in 1977 of the baby seal hunt which launched a total war on fur.[15] Trappers, fur farmers, wholesalers, manufacturers, retailers and consumers all came under attack through concerted protests and publicity campaigns which often displayed gory pictures of slain animals. Anti-fur trade tactics at times turned violent. Fur retailers had

The latest fashions in fur, 1910-11. From Hudson's Bay Company Autumn & Winter Catalogue, 1910-1911.

their store fronts smashed and fur wearers had their garments splashed with red paint. Typical of the arguments against wearing fur are those given below by Global Action Network of Montreal, one of a plethora of animal rights associations world-wide:

> According to Statistics Canada, more than two million animals are killed each year by the Canadian fur industry. This figure does not take into account the estimated 9 million "trash" animals, including dogs, cats, birds and even endangered species, that are caught in the traps each year and then discarded because they have no economic value.
>
> Approximately 1 million of these animals, including minks, foxes and ferrets, are factory farmed under horrific conditions. They are kept in tiny, filthy cages, and are denied the most basic of care. These animals are killed by anal electrocution, gassing, neck-breaking and lethal injection.
>
> The other 1 million are caught in cruel traps, including the leghold traps, conibear traps, snares and the drowning trap. These animals are left, often for hours or days, with no food, water or shelter, in extreme temperatures. One in four animals will chew off their own limbs to escape, and will go on to die of gangrene or other secondary infections. When the trapper finally comes to collect the animals, they stomp or beat them to death to avoid damaging the pelt.[16]

A devastating blow to trappers, manufacturers and retailers alike was the European Common Union's prohibition in 1991 on importing furs from countries where "animal trapping methods fell below internationally accepted standards of humanity." The proscribed furs included beaver, otter, coyote, wolf, lynx, bobcat, sable, raccoon, muskrat, fisher, badger, marten and ermine. Although the ban was never implemented, it reflects the impact of animal rights activists on European public opinion.[17]

Suddenly fur apparel no longer was "in". Widespread hostility to wearing fur in the 1990s made it "fashion's biggest taboo for most image-conscious consumers".[18] In Europe, Asia and North America the fur industry almost collapsed. Accusations by People for the Ethical Treatment of Animals (PETA) of widespread cruelty to furbearers, whether trapped or farmed, forced the closure of nearly all fur specialty shops in England.

It probably would have happened without the slump in sales but in 1987 the Hudson's Bay Company quit the fur trade, the purpose for its founding in 1670, and sold its 178 Northern Stores, many going back to the company's beginnings. By 1987, these stores had evolved into modern retail outlets with only fifty still collecting furs. All had become an unprofitable nuisance to their owners whose focus now lay on more profitable metropolitan markets. The "Company of Adventurers of England trading into Hudson Bay" thus sold its northern operations to a consortium of merchants and investors who adopted the name Northern Stores Inc.[20]

The new adventurers launched their enterprise by presenting themselves as successors to Canada's fur trade heritage. On May 2, 1987, the same month and day as the Hudson's Bay Company charter of 1670, they finalized the agreement in Winnipeg on board the replica of the *Nonsuch*, the Hudson's Bay Company's first ship to venture into Hudson Bay. But to prove their historical legitimacy they did more than that. They named the consortium's holding company "The North West Company". The new North West Company's acquisition of the Hudson's Bay Company's Northern Department 166 years after the Hudson's Bay Company absorbed the first North West Company in 1821 had an ironic twist, one neatly encapsulated by Peter Newman as "The Nor'westers' Revenge".[21] In 1990, Northern Stores Inc. changed its corporate name once more. It was now "The North West Company Inc."[22]

In 2003, The North West Company describes itself as "the leading provider of food and everyday products and services to remote communities across northern Canada & Alaska". Its website makes no mention of the fur trade which is now but a minuscule part of its business. Most Northern Stores in urban centres have closed but 24 still operate in Northwestern Ontario with only two surviving south of the Height of Land. The Wawa store, near the old Michipicoten HBC post on Lake Superior, does not handle furs, but at Sioux Lookout, on Lac Seul in the English River system, the Northern Store conducts a considerable trade mostly with Native trappers as does the Nakina store east of Lake Nipigon.[23]

The Ontario trappers who deal with the North West Company sell their furs for cash either at a Northern store or to a company buyer. These furs then go to The North West Company's fur marketing department at North Bay, Ontario, for processing before being shipped to North American Fur Auctions in Toronto (NAFA). NAFA traces its origins to the birth of the Hudson's Bay Company in 1670 and to the early public fur auctions in London, England. When the Hudson's Bay Company got out of the fur trade in 1987, it also sold its Canadian auction business. In 1992 the new owners joined with the Hudson's Bay Company's New York auction house to form North American Fur Auctions, now the largest fur auction house in North America and the third largest in the world.[24]

Some trappers market their furs through Fur Harvesters Auction Inc. (FHA). Instead of paying cash, FHA takes furs on consignment for sale at its auctions held four times a year in North Bay. Fur Harvesters, Inc. is the successor to the Ontario Trappers Association (OTA) which ceased operations in 1991 at the depth of the fur trade's downward slide. Most members in the OTA were non-Native, but FHA is a partnership of First Nations and non-Native trappers, an alliance facilitated by the Ontario Union of Indians whose president is Cliff Meness, a former chief of the Algonquins of Pikwakanagan south of Algonquin Park.[25]

The use of "harvesters" rather than "trappers" in Fur Harvesters Auction's name is a subtle response to the animal rights movement. Harvesters manage and do not destroy renewable resources, is the implication; they conserve the wildlife on which their livelihood depends. Trappers actively justify their trade in the battle to regain public acceptance of fur. One example is this defense of fur coats by a Thunder Bay trapper, Patte Foreman-Doherty.

> Please tell me what you wear on your person each day. Is your footwear or outer clothing made of leather? If so, who did it previously belong to? If it is nylon, then how does your conscience allow you to sleep at night when you support the oil products moving across our waterways and causing unparalleled environmental disasters such as the one off the coast of Spain? Nylon after all is the product of oil. ....
>
> If you took the time to research the harvesting of wildlife you would learn that as with everything in our ecosystem it needs to be managed and regulated so that we can prevent disease and over-population so that it will be there for centuries to come.[26]

Murray Monk of Nipigon, Ontario is a well-known, but perhaps atypical, trapper who has taken a leadership role in many fur trade-related organizations. Originally from Southern Ontario, this former millworker and union representative became a full-time trapper by choice in 1990.[27] Four years later he was President of the Ontario Fur Managers Federation which administers the mandatory forty-hour course in Fur Harvest, Fur Management and Conservation for obtaining a trapping license in Ontario. As Past-President he urged its members to:

> .....keep focused on the continued attack of those intent on tearing apart what we have achieved. ... Some people, jealous, greed or kicking in understanding of our way of life, will not quit attacking us. ... None of our furbearers are in danger which proves that trappers are true creatures of nature.[28]

As President of the Canadian National Trappers Alliance, which aims to "promote the welfare of Canadian trappers, and maintain and enhance the heritage of the wild fur industry as a sustainable resource," Monk has reiterated his defense of trapping:

> It is in the best interest of our federal government, along with our provincial and territorial jurisdictions to get in the act financially, and possibly look into areas of heritage funding. It is, after all is said and done, the heritage industry of this country. A decent price paid for the beaver and raccoon, for example, would make better business sense, as an incentive to harvest the over abundance of these species, than the costs paid when they become a nuisance.[29]

Many other organizations are devoted to promoting Canada's fur industry and protecting the livelihood of its trappers. In Ottawa, the Fur Institute of Canada helps trappers hone their conservation skills and trapping methods. Founded in 1983 with federal and provincial government backing, its mission is to "promote the sustainable and wise use of Canada's fur resources". Responding to "concerns for improvements to animal welfare, the efficiency of animal capture devices and the conservation of wild life populations," the Institute has committees dealing with Aboriginal communications, trap research, international relations, conservation and funding.[30]

Also promoting the trade is the Fur Council of Canada of Montreal. Incorporated in 1964, this national, non-profit federation publicizes fur as "the fabric of a nation," and the fur trade as the "economic engine that drove adventurers to explore North America". To charges that furbearers are endangered, the council replies:

> Wild furs are abundant: endangered species are NOT used in the fur trade....the fur trade uses only a small part of the surplus produced by nature each year. This is what biologists call "sustainable use of renewable resources" – a principle that is now endorsed by all major conservation organizations.

As for claims of cruelty to farmed furs, it proclaims: "Farmed fur animals receive excellent nutrition, housing and care. This is the only way to produce the high quality of fur required by the market." Another rationale for continuing the fur trade is this: "When you buy wild fur, you support aboriginal trappers and other people who live close to the land – people who have a direct interest in protecting wildlife habitat."[31]

Canada has about 80,000 trappers. An example of the extent of fur trapping in Northwestern Ontario is seen at Sioux Lookout where fur management and harvesting are classed as important but secondary economic activities. Altogether the region has 225 registered trap lines and 1,400 licensed "Fur Harvesters".[32] Across Canada, trappers are divided about equally between Natives and non-Natives, although the proportion of Natives is greater in the north with the reverse true for southern regions.

Northwest Ontario‡ fur harvests, 1990-91 to 2000-2001†

Season	Type	Species Marten	Mink	Beaver	Otter	Muskrat
90-91	Native††	22,130	1,860	5,709	763	573
	Non-native	19,762	2,416	14,498	794	941
91-92	Native	15,626	1,248	5,444	744	866
	Non-native	16,266	1,745	12,616	758	442
92-93	Native	9,407	824	4,259	702	*
	Non-native	13,298	1,402	11,549	825	*
93-94	Native	11,445	1,241	6,581	1,170	164
	Non-native	11,873	1,812	14,290	1,200	25
94-95	Native	17,259	1,665	6,825	1,365	808
	Non-native	13,203	1,470	16,784	1,428	145
95-96	Native	18,787	704	4,310	847	1,187
	Non-native	17,071	964	10,730	815	640
96-97	Native	14,542	947	5,833	788	107
	Non-native	13,754	1,680	15,059	1,011	0
97-98	Native	16,140	1,708	8,086	1,569	*
	Non-native	21,323	1,685	14,590	1,265	*
98-99	Native	6,152	647	2,489	384	374
	Non-native	12,950	1,973	13,430	1,069	1,183
99-2000	Native	4,251	132	1,308	263	912
	Non-native	13,626	1,136	14,054	1,177	767
00-01	Native	3,418	103	1,068	235	
	Non-native	13,264	1,104	13,439	1,159	

‡Territory contained between the Manitoba border and the eastern boundary of the Nipigon District /Geraldton Area (coincides with town of Marathon).
†Data courtesy of Chris Heydon, Fur Program Biologist, Fish and Wildlife Branch, Ontario Ministry of Natural Resources.
††After Jan. 1, 1998, mandatory pelt sealing (stamping) by MNR was replaced with mandatory harvest reporting by trappers.
  Few native trappers comply with the harvest reporting requirement, while non-native compliance is close to 100%. Amounts reported by native trappers for 1998-99 onwards are therefore artificially lower than actual harvests.
*Data not available.

The above chart gives the numbers of animals trapped by Natives and by non-Natives but with one disclaimer. Since few native trappers comply with Ontario's harvest reporting requirement enacted in 1998, the chart's figures for numbers of furs trapped by Natives after that date is "artificially low".[33] Until the Native and non-Native partnership in Fur Harvesters Auction Inc., the two sets of trappers have had a somewhat uneasy relationship around such issues as quotas, trapping out of season and trap line locations. Aboriginals argue that their rights to the land have existed from time immemorial and that these rights are guaranteed by treaty.

A good example of the Aboriginal position is provided by Treaty #3 which covers the region lying between the Lake Superior watershed and Lake Winnipeg. In documents posted on its website, Treaty #3's Grand Council explains the evolution of trapping regulations since 1947 when the "Province of Ontario introduced the Registered Trap Line System. The trap line boundary areas were modeled after traditional family trapping grounds established by the Ojibway Nation, generations before. We continue to use these trapping areas today."[34] This arrangement was intended to protect Aboriginal trapping areas from non-Aboriginals

> because there were no controls or written records of the trapping lands traditionally used by native trappers. While Aboriginal peoples understood and respected traditional family trapping grounds, non-Aboriginal trappers began [indecipherable] indiscriminately displacing Indian trappers from their territories.

Native trapping rights are thus bound up with land claims and traditional land use areas. The good intentions of Treaty #3 to reach agreement with the Ontario Government is seen in a job posting for a Trapping

Coordinator to complete the agreement and develop Treaty #3's trapping law. This was but one of 24 positions advertised by Treaty #3 in 2002. Other postings show that the traditional fur trade is no longer the primary economic activity of the First Nations. They include an Aboriginal Business Service Network Site Coordinator, an Infrastructure Policy Analyst and a Land and Resource Earth Law Co-ordinator, all demanding advanced computer technology skills. It may not be too long before Aboriginal trappers themselves become an endangered species.[35]

In 2003, Canadian trappers, Aboriginal and non-Aboriginal alike, had renewed confidence in the future of the fur industry, and with good reason. As the Canadian Broadcasting Corporation reported on March 5, 2003, "Fur is flying again in fashion":

> Designers and manufacturers are flocking to Canada from all over the world to bid on furs and that's driving prices up. It's good news for trappers who have been suffering from an anti-fur backlash over the past decade. North American Fur Auctions says 2003 is turning out to be a stellar year for the industry. "A lot of things have come together for us. Fashion designers from around the world are using the product more than ever," says Tina Jagros of the association.[36]

Vigorous marketing of Canadian pelts and fur garments in Greece, China and other countries have helped revitalize the industry. In February, 2003, Fur Harvesters reported "remarkable" results. "Long haired goods saw tremendous advances as did beaver," with buyers mainly from Greece but also from "new Russian accounts". Lynx and Lynx Cat realized a ninety percent increase with most purchasers coming from Greece and Italy. NAFA's February 2003 auction also gave proof of the fur trade's recovery when forty-nine pelts sold at $850US each, the highest price for beaver recorded since 1670 when the Hudson's Bay Company held its first auction in London. The purchaser was George Gab of the city aptly named Kastoria, a major fur manufacturing centre in northern Greece. Record prices again were paid for otter and lynx.[37]

This dramatic turn-around in fur's fortunes has been repeated even in Britain where the animal rights movement has enormous influence. A December, 2002, report states: "Britain's fur trade is enjoying its strongest growth for 20 years, suggesting a dramatic softening of public attitudes towards wearing animal skins." Despite PETA's hold over British public opinion, London is still the world centre for fur buyers, according to the British Fur Trade Association.[38] Most of the world's fur production, however, takes place in the fur farms of Denmark and Finland. Eighty-five percent of the international fur trade, in fact, is in fox and mink farmed in ECU countries; fur farming in Europe is thus a very profitable business, indeed.[39]

Hudson's Bay Company store at 337-343 Simpson Street, Fort William, circa 1910. The HBC built this store in 1881 as a "sale shop" catering to the general public. In 1914, the building was destroyed by fire and not replaced. The company offices were located on May Street. TBHMS 974.103.81.

A huge contribution to the rising demand for wild and farmed fur is its gigantic market in Russia, China and Greece, a market aggressively cultivated by the Canadian fur industry. Besides Canada and the United States, other strong consumers of fur include Korea, Japan, Hong Kong, Italy and Germany. Back in 1814 the North West Company realized its longtime goal of a trans-Pacific trade with China with its first shipment of furs from the West Coast to Canton. Who then could have imagined the magnitude of the Chinese market for North American fur some two centuries later? In the opinion of NAFA's president Herman Jansen, China is the market of the future. A hint of its vastness appears in his report from just a few of many Chinese "fur towns" in 1997.[40] At Xin Ji, a large leather garment manufacturing centre, a single order for 100,000 jackets of domestic leather trimmed with North American fox was not unusual. At Sun Ing, one factory alone uses 500,000 squirrels annually. Most garments produced in the "fur towns" are for export, many to North America where most of the furs originated. China's expanding market economy has, in turn, created an expanding domestic market for luxury goods. In North China, for example, fur garments manufactured in Harbin are in much demand from local residents for warmth as much as for prestige. Harbin also has an immense export business in fur including a considerable "border trade" with Russia.[41]

The Russian market perhaps has even more potential than the Chinese for Canadian fur. It uses far more pelts than it produces since Russian consumers who are "often newly rich and profoundly ostentatious" keep what they can for themselves.[42] Most fur garments sold in Russia come from Kastoria, Greece, where some two thousand workshops make it the fur manufacturing centre of Europe. Kastoria's manufacturers buy their pelts at auction centres around the world, including Toronto and North Bay. In 1996, for example, Greek furriers bought at least seventy percent of North America's raccoon production.[43]

One source of fur's revived respectability is its association with North America's Aboriginal peoples especially with the many Europeans who are enthralled by Aboriginal culture but disturbed by Aboriginal poverty. Killing the fur trade not only destroys Native livelihoods but endangers the Native traditional way of life, runs a pro-fur trade argument. Wearing fur thus can help reverse impoverishment in Aboriginal communities by displaying support in public for Native trappers and Native culture. In 1987, the Chiefs of Ontario articulated this view as follows: "These [anti-fur trade] actions are threatening our livelihood and culture as aboriginal people and the success of these campaigns will mean severe hardship for our most traditional land-based people."[44] The anti-fur lobbyists, however, label this assertion as "Playing the Ethnic Card", one which

> has proved irresistible to the Canadian fur trade, especially in Britain where there is a strong residue of guilt over the country's historical treatment of natives in stealing their land, killing them with liquor and white man's diseases, corralling them into reservations, where once they were nomads... Ultimately, fur's real value for indigenous peoples is as a negotiating ploy in their long political and legal struggle for an equitable share of Canada's lands and resources.....At the same time, those same leaders recognise that their future – welcome or otherwise – lies not in killing beaver and muskrat but in big business.[45]

Some younger Aboriginals are, in fact, veering away from a way of life based solely on trapping and entering the world of industry and commerce. With federal and provincial assistance they are becoming entrepreneurs with savvy about business development and also building partnerships in the public and private sectors. In the realm of the fur trade, they now do more than trap furbearers. On the initiative of the North West Territories government, for example, furs trapped in district bear the label "Genuine Mackenzie Valley Fur" to show that "the fur was aboriginally harvested using humane methods." Furs so labelled fetch good prices at the NAFA auctions in North Bay.[46] In other Native groups, artisans actively create fur products and market them to the world through the internet. One example is Michikan Lake Crafts of Bearskin Lake, an Oji-Cree community in Northwestern Ontario, whose products include fur hats, moccasins and mukluks with beaver, otter, or rabbit fur trim.[47] In 2002, Prime Minister Jean Chrètien led a Team Canada Trade and Investment mission to Russia and Germany. Accompanied by the premiers of Nunavut and the Northwest Territories and delegates from First Nations and Inuit businesses, its purpose was to promote trade in products of the north including garments and crafts of fur designed and made by northern Aboriginals and adorned with Native motifs.[48]

The upswing in fur sales is driven largely by the international fashion industry whose designs appeal to a generation not adverse to wearing animal skins. To cite *The Observer*, "The children of the anti-fur movement are now rebelling against it. They are bored with being politically correct."[49] In May, 2003, the North American Fur and Fashion Exposition at Montreal effusively promoted the latest vogue: "The new light weight furs float like a butterfly with styling and colours that sting like a bee". Some garments had an "eclectic cross-cultural look" while "rapper-chic broadens the men's market."[50] Designers like Paula Lishman of Toronto also use fur as a yarn for knitting shrugs, stoles, biker tops, two-piece suits and coats. Innovative uses for fur abound. "Think sheared mink T-shirts and rugby shirts, sheared beaver blazers, sable-lined jean-jacket shapes and shearling stiletto boots. In fact, don't think of it {fur] as part of an animal at all: Think of it as a fabric." This quotation comes from "Stealth Fur", a full-page article by Deirdre Kelly in *Globe Style*.[51] Spanning the top of the page is a colour photograph of a lady's shoe, a pump in "rainbow-coloured sheared beaver, $1025 by custom order"; down the centre of the text a model displays a striped rugby shirt of sheared mink priced at $8,500.

The contrast in the life-style of those who trap beaver and those who buy "rainbow-coloured sheared beaver" pumps is daunting. Essentially, though, the modern fur trade differs little from that conducted by traders and trappers in the past when its primary purpose was the elegant beaver felt hat worn for ostentation not warmth. One century after Thorstein Veblen coined the phrase "the conspicuous consumption of luxuries" in his *The Theory of the Leisure Class*, the term still applies in the world of fur fashions. Admittedly, some clothing made with fur does have practical value by providing warmth and comfort in winter climes. This is true not only of coats and jackets but also of women's and men's over-sized fur hats which are practical and very much in vogue.

In the early years of the twenty-first century, the fur industry is optimistic as rising prices for pelts and soaring sales of fur garments give proof of a revived public acceptance of the trade in trapped and farmed animal skins. Yet confidence in the industry's triumph over the animal rights movement may be misplaced. In February 2003, "anti-fur protesters hijacked a fashion show as models paraded on the London catwalk" and in March PETA activists stormed three Paris fashion shows in a twenty-four hour period.[52]

At time of writing it seems that PETA will win on one front, one of much symbolic value. The garment targeted is a hat, not the beaver felt top hat which launched the Canadian fur trade nor the dashing Dr. Zhivago-style hat prized in 2003, but a hat steeped in British tradition. This is the tall bearskin hat adopted by five Regiments of British Army Foot Guards as part of their ceremonial uniform almost two hundred years ago. Weighing around 1½ pounds and requiring one or two bear skins each, the 18-inch high hat is worn, not for warmth, but as a symbol of British military might.[53] The military bearskin hat had its origins in 1712 but the hat worn by the Guards today was adopted to commemorate Britain's 1815 victory over Napoleon's forces at Waterloo where France's Imperial Guard had worn bearskins to appear more intimidating. Altogether the Grenadier, Welsh, Irish, Scots and Coldstream Guards regiments have 2,500 bearskins in service and require one hundred new hats each year.

In 1997, PETA launched its attack on the bearskin hat by proclaiming that "Bears are individuals who live in families and feel pain and terror when shot." Citing what it claimed was an Ontario Ministry of Natural Resources report, it stated that "as many as one in seven bears are not killed outright [when shot]t but escape wounded. Wounded bears who get away may die from blood loss, starvation or gangrene."[54]

The British Ministry of Defence defended the bearskin by claiming that bears must be 'culled' anyway but by 2002, the military succumbed to PETA's petition campaign directed to Her Majesty the Queen and is looking for a suitable synthetic substitute. So far none is satisfactory. In wet weather, some look "like a very bad hair day," according to one army officer. "This is no good, as the guards are on show."[55]

Despite international pressure from animal rights organizations like PETA, it would seem that the fur trade will survive. The protest movement, however, has made the industry more conscious of animal welfare, especially in North America. Is trapping a humane use of our natural renewable resources or is fur "still the product of a tortured and slaughtered animal"? The future of the fur trade may not entirely depend on who wins this argument. In the case of wild fur it may also depend on whether the snowballing inroads of industrialism into Canada's north can leave room for an environment in which furbearers and their trappers can survive.

NOTES

Most, though not all, of the documentation for this article comes from the Internet where an over-abundance of data awaits the researcher on almost any topic. This presents a problem of selecting the right amount of relevant information for a short article. For those who wish to pursue this topic more thoroughly, NAFA's website at *http://nafa.ca/industry/links* has links to Canadian and international fur trade organizations, expositions, media, fur trade history, wildlife agencies, and trapping and hunting associations

=========

[1] "Emporium for the Interior" in Jean Morrison, *Superior Rendezvous-Place: Fort William in the Canadian Fur Trade* (Toronto: Natural Heritage Books, 2001), pp 46-52 has more on fashion and fur trade logistics.

[2] R. Turner Wilcox, *The Mode in Furs* (New York: Charles Scribner's Sons, 1951) looks at furred costume through the ages.

[3] Harold A. Innis, *The Fur Trade in Canada*, rev. ed (Toronto: University of Toronto Press, 1956), p. 332.

[4] Arthur J. Ray, *The Canadian Fur Trade in the Industrial Age* (Toronto: University of Toronto Press, 1990), p. 150.

[5] Fur Council of Canada. "A Brief Fashion History of Fur". Extracted and adapted from Elizabeth Ewing, *Fur in dress* (London: 1981). <<www.furcouncil.com/english/industry/history/history1.htm#>

[6] *The Old Times*, Maple Lake, MN., May 2003... <www.theoldtimes.com/past/0102_2.html>

[7] Sexe, Marcel, *Two Centuries of Fur-Trading, 1723-1923: Romance of the Revillon Family* (1923); see also *Revillon Frères* (Moosonee: The Moosonee Development Area Board, 2002).

[8] Information about Ernest Herbert McLeod kindly provided by his granddaughter, Betty Dyck of Winnipeg.

[9] Philip H. Godsell, *Arctic Trader: The Account of Twenty Years with the Hudson's Bay Company* (New York, 1934). Reference supplied by Betty Dyck.

[10] See scattered references to Revillon in Ray, *The Canadian Fur Trade in the Industrial Age*. In 1999, the National Film Board issued *Traces d'une histoire oubliée* ("Traces of a forgotten story"), a documentary which "tracks Parisian furriers and fur traders, Revillon Frères, across the Canadian North."

[11] Robert J. Flaherty, F.R.G.S., "How I Filmed Nanook of the North" (1922). <www.cinemaweb.com/silentfilm/bookshelf>

[12] Fur Institute of Canada (FIC), *With Respect to the Fur Industry* (Toronto: 4-pgs. - no date)

[13] *Exploration, the Fur Trade and Hudson's Bay Company*... <www.canadiana.org/hbc/hist>

[14] FIC, "With respect to Fur Ranching", (Toronto: 4pgs. - no date)

[15] Brigette Bardot Foundation. <www.fondationbrigittebardot.fr/uk/histoire.html>

[16] Global Action Network, "Is Fur Really Back?" <www.gan.ca/en/gan>

[17] Trade and Environment Database (TED) Case Studies: EC fur ban. <www.gurukul.ucc.american.edu/ted/ECFURBAN.htm>

[18] "Fur flies as Christmas sales take off", *Guardian Weekly*, December 5-11, 2002

[19] Statistics Canada, Fur Production. <www.statcan.ca/english/Pgdb/prim46.htm> and Global Action Network. <www.gan.ca/en/campaigns/wildlife/fur/factsheets/is_fur_back.html>

[20] *Financial Post*, May 4, 1987.

[21] *Maclean's Magazine*, May 11, 1987.

[22] *Winnipeg Free Press*, March 17, 1990.

[23] Information supplied by Gordon Gray and Sherry Baldwin, The North West Company, North Bay, Ontario

[24] NAFA. Home Corporate Profile. <www.nafa.ca/home/corporate.asp>

[25] *Aboriginal Ontario*, May 2003. Also on the internet at <www.aboriginalontario.com>

[26] *Chronicle-Journal*, December 18, 2002.

[27] Murray Monk is the subject of Chapter Twelve in Charles Wilkins, *A Wilderness Called Home: Dispatches from the Wild Heart of Canada* (Toronto: Penguin, 2001), pp. 210-227.

[28] Ontario Fur Managers Federation. <www.furmanagers.com>. Winter, 2001.

[29] Canadian National Trappers Alliance. <www.ranger1.ca/cnta/news.html>

[30] FIC, <www.fur.ca/about>

[31] Fur Council of Canada. *Fur: The Fabric of a Nation* (Montreal: n.d., brochure). See also "Fur becomes politically correct," <www.furcouncil.com>

[32] <www.municipalityofsiouxlookout.ca/profile/wildlife.htm>

[33] "Northwest Ontario fur harvests, 1990-91 to 2000-2001". Data kindly supplied by Chris Heydon, Fur Program Biolo-

[34] gist, Fish and Wildlife Branch, Ontario Ministry of Natural Resources
[34] The Grand Council of Treaty #3, Kenora, Ontario. <www.treaty3.ca>
[35] The Grand Council of Treaty #3, . <www.treaty3.ca/pages/employment>. Thunder Bay *Chronicle-Journal*. December 18, 2002
[36] CBC. <www.cbc.ca/stories/2003/03/04/Consumers/fur_030304>
[37] NAFA Wild Fur Sales Report, <www.nafa.ca/sales/Feb25_2003_wildfur.asp>
[38] *Guardian Weekly*, December 5-11, 2002, "Fur Flies"
[39] British Fur Trade Association..<www.britishfur.co.uk>
[40] "China: Market of the Future", *International Trapper*, Fall, 1997.
[41] *International Trapper*, Fall, 1997.
[42] <www.furs.com/FUR/FurAge4.html>. See also "Keeping Warm in Style with Fur Fashions," *Metropolis: Moscow Times*. <www.tmtmetropolis.ru/metropolis/stories/2002/11/29/112.html>.
[43] See "Kastoria: Land of Furs.". <www.ctfurs.com/kastoria.htm>. Also "In Greece, fur industry thrives", *International Herald Tribune*, October 5, 2002. <www.iht.com/articles/72834.htm>
[44] Cited in *InFURmation Headquarters*. "Native Peoples", . <www.inFURmation.com>
[45] "Native Peoples", <www.inFURmation.com>
[46] *Northern News Services*, August 2002. <www.nnsl.com>
[47] Michikan Lake Business Centre. <www.arts.knet.ca/crafts/bearskin/>
[48] *Aboriginal Planet Online Magazine*. <www.aboriginalplanet/750/archives/july2002/art3_main-en.asp>
[49] *Guardian Weekly*, December 5-11, 2002.
[50] North American Fur and Fashion Exposition of Montreal. <www.furcouncil.com/naffem/main.htm>
[51] *Globe and Mail*, November 23, 2002.
[52] <www.petauk.org/news/0303/0303paris3.html>; also <www.europe.cnn.com/2003/WORLD/europe/02/20/fashion.fur/>
[53] "Bearskin hats 'cruel,' says group", <www.canoe.ca/CNEWS/World/2003/03/16/44510-ap.html>
[54] PETA. "Help us to convince Queen's Guards...". <www.petauk.org/feat/bear/>
[55] See Note 53.

Some Relevant Readings

Books and Articles:

Arthur, Elizabeth. *Thunder Bay District, 1921-1892: A Collection of Documents.* Toronto: The Champlain Society, 1973.

Bertrand, J.B., *Highway of Destiny.* New York: Vantage Press, 1959.

Gilman, Carolyn. *The Grand Portage Story.* St. Paul: Minnesota Historical Society Press, 1992.

Huck, Barbara. *Exploring the Fur Trade Routes of North America.* Winnipeg: Heartland, 2000.

Lund, Duane R. *Lake of the Woods.* Staples, MN: Adventure Publications, 1984.

Lytwyn, Victor P. *The Fur Trade of the Little North: Indians, Pedlars, and Englishmen East of Lake Winnipeg, 1760-1821.* Winnipeg: Rupert's Land Research Centre, 1986.

Morrison, Dorothy. Nafus. *Outpost: John McLoughlin and the Far Northwest.* Portland: Oregon Historical Society, 1999. (For McLoughlin's career at Fort William and Rainy Lake)

Morrison, Jean, ed. *The North West Company in Rebellion: Simon McGillivray's Fort William Notebook, 1815.* Thunder Bay: Thunder Bay Historical Museum Society, 1988.

———— *Superior Rendezvous-Place: Fort William in the Canadian Fur Trade.* Toronto: Natural Heritage Books, 2001

Nute, Grace Lee. *Rainy River Country* . St. Paul: Minnesota Historical Society, 1950.

———— *The Voyageur's Highway.* St. Paul: Minnesota Historical Society Press, 1941, 1969.

Peers, Laura. T*he Ojibwa of Western Canada, 1780-1870.* St. Paul: Minnesota Historical Society Press, 1994.

Turcott, Agnes W. *Land of the Big Goose. A History of Wawa and theMichipicoten Area 1622-1960.* Dryden, Ontario, 1962.

Waisberg, Leo G. and Tim E. Holzkamm, "Their Country is Tolerably Rich in Furs": The Ojibwa Fur Trade in the Boundary Waters Region, 1821-1871", *Actes du Vingt-Cinquième Congrès des Algonistes.* Ottawa: Carleton University, 1994. Also at <www.treaty3.ca/pages/pdfs/fur_trade.pdf>

Wilkins, Charles, *A Wilderness Called Home: Dispatches from the Wild Heart of Canada.* Toronto: Penguin Books, 2001(for Chapter 12 on Murray Monk, Nipigon trapper)

Relevant Articles in Thunder Bay Historical Museum Society *Papers and Records*

1973, I, 33-40. Susan J. Campbell. "Competitive fur trade tactics: Pointe de Meuron 1817-1821".

1974, II, 29-36. Gregg A. Young, "The organization of the transfer of furs at Fort William: A study in historical geography".

1975, III, 27-34. Kenneth C.A. Dawson, "Underwater search for lost fur trade goods in Northern Ontario".

1976, VI, 30-40. Elizabeth Arthur, "Angelique and her Children".

1979, VII, 1-5. Jean Morrison, "Old Fort William's fiddler Joe Harrison and his ancestral links with the Fort William of 1816"

1980, VIII, 32-42. David Kemp, "The impact of weather and climate on the fur trade in the Canadian North-West".

1981, IX, 1-6. Adelaide Taylor, "Reminscences of York Factory".

——— 7-13. Joe Winterburn, "Lac la Pluie bill of lading 1806-1809".

—---— 31-48. Elizabeth Arthur, "The de Larondes of Lake Nipigon".

1987, XV, 3-13. Thomas W. Dunk, "Indian Participation in the Industrial Economy on the North Shore of Lake Superior, 1869-1940"

1990, XVIII, 2-29. Patricia Jasen, "Imagining Fort William: Romanticism, Tourism and the Old Fort, 1821 to 1971".

1995, XXIII, 24-39. Jayson Childs, "Feeding the Fur Traders".

1997, XXV, 45-63. Judith Petch, ed. "Selections from the HBC Post Journals in the 1820's and 1830's".
1999, XXVII, 17-32. Jayson Childs,. "Stone Construction at Old Fort William".
2000, XXVIII, 49-71. Alma E. Henry, "Fur Trade Rivalry on the Rainy River, 1793-1797", ed. David M. Chapman.

RELEVANT PAPERS IN THUNDER BAY HISTORICAL SOCIETY *ANNUAL REPORTS* (1908-1928)

1911-1912, III, pp. 9-12. A. A. Vickers, "Treaty Making with Indians".
1912-1913, IV, pp. 27-30. Miss J. Robin, "The Story of Fort William Mission".
1915, VI, pp. 11-16. A. L. Russell, "Fort William in the Middle of the XIX Century".
1916, VII, pp. 23-24. M. V. Moberly, "Looking Backward: Recollections of an Old-Timer".
1917, VIII, pp. 27-29. "Unveiling of Tablet" (Re "Hudson Bay Memorial" at foot of McTavish Street).
1919, X, pp. 13-18. Eugene Robin, "The Founding of Fort William Mission and The Jesuit Missionaries".
1919, X, pp. 21-29. P. H. Godsell, "The Ojibway Indian".
1920, XI, pp. 19-24. N.M.W.J. McKenzie, "Hudson Bay Reminiscences".
1923-24, XV, pp. 13-22. A. J. McComber, "Some Early History of Thunder Bay and District".
1924-25/1925-26, XVI and XVII, pp. 66-68. Capt, J. W. Hall, "Lake Superior: Its Discovery and History".
1926-27/1927/28, XVIII and XIX, pp. 76-79. Miss Annie E. McIntyre, "John McIntyre".

Index

Aboriginal rights, 161
Agawa Bay, 130
agriculture, 20, 50, 110, 134, 146, 148, 149
Aitkin, William (AFC), 37, 53
Albany Fort, 28, 35
Albany, New York, 29
Albany River, 27
alcohol in the fur trade, 17, 31-2, 39, 62, 79, 81-82, 87, 89, 109, 112
Algonquian-speaking Indians (*see also* Ojibwa Indians), 26, 27
American Fur Company, 37, 38, 52-53, 80-81, 128, 134, 135, 145, 148
American traders, 37, 53
Anderson, Dean L , 13-4
Anderson, James, 119
Anderson, Margaret, 119, 11
Anderson, Thomas G., 40
animal rights movement, 158-9, 163-5
Anishinabeg (Ojibwa Indians), 25ff.
Arctic Ocean, 49
Assiniboine country, 95
Astor, John Jacob, 52, 94
Astoria (Fort George), 99
Athabasca country, 49, 59, 60-67, 69, 70, 100, 103

Bardot, Brigitte, 158
Batchewana Bay, 130, 135
Bayfield, Lieutenant Henry Wolsey, 37, 141-143
Beatty Company, 132
Beaulieu, Paul and Bazil, 51
beaver, 68, 69, 78, 79-81, 88-90, 111
beaver hats (*see hats*)
beaver returns, 49, 88-89
Bell, Dr. Charles Napier, 140
Bell, Peter Warren, 40, 129
Bethune, Angus, 37, 99-100, 146
Bethune, Rev. John, 99
Bethune, Louisa MacKenzie, 92, 99-100
Bethune, Dr. Norman, 100
birch bark, uses, 25, 26, 73, 77, 78, 86, 115 (*see also* canoes)
Black Bay (Lake Superior), 39
boats: *batteaux*, 107, 130-1; keel, 130; steam, 52, 54, 132
Bottineau, Charles, 97
Boucher, 146, 149
Bourassa's Fort, 86
Boyer, Charles, 50
Brass, Magnus, 142-4
British Fur Trade Association, 163

Brulé, Etienne, 15
Brunswick Lake, 89

Cadotte, Jean-Baptiste, Jr., 20
Cadotte, Jean-Baptiste, Sr., 20, 29
Cadotte, Joseph, 52
Cadotte, Michel, 20
Cameron, C.F. (Chief Factor; *see* John Dugald Cameron)
Cameron, Duncan, 71-2
Cameron, John Dugald, 53, 79, 80-81, 84
Canadian National Trappers Alliance, 160
Canadian Pacific Railway, 41
canoes, 30-31, 58-67, 68, 70-3, 77-8, 86, 89, 110, 112, 115
canoe brigades, 59-60, 67; cargoes, 58-67; crew, 59, 63-4; , 62-64; manufacturing, 84-5, 109, 112-113; repair, 86, 146-7; routes, 33, 74-75, 85; passengers, 64-5; sizes, 30-31, 59-60, 71, 110, 130-131, 147, 149
Carriere, Martin, 104
Cartier, Jacques, 15, 26
Carver, Jonathon, 82
celebrations, 5 0 , 84, 85, 108
Chaboillez, Charles, 32
Champlain, Samuel de, 15, 26, 27
Charles II, 28
China, 162-3
Churchill, Manitoba, 58
climate, 17, 58, 68-75, 86
cloth and clothing, 14, 26, 62, 79, 112-114
Collin (*also spelled* Colin, Collins), Antoine, 31, 37, 92, 105-116, 141, 146-149
Collin, Jean-Baptiste, 105-109, 111, 114
Collin, Joseph, 105-6
Collin, Marie Jeanne, 106, 108
Collin, Michel, 37, 107-110, 111, 114, 142, 147-149
Collin, Robert, 142, 144
Collin, Simon, 114
Company of the Farm, 18
competition: between HBC and French traders, 19-21; NWC and XYC, 32, 49-50; NWC and HBC, 35-6, 46, 49, 51, 77,79, 84, 89-89, 103, 107; HBC and AFC, 52; HBC and independent traders, 77, 81, 155; HBC and Revillon, 156-7
coureurs de bois, 15, 18, 21, 28
contracts (see also *engagements*), 92, 98, 106, 111

Courchene family, 92
Cox, Ross, 111
Cree Indians, 88
Cumberland House, 49
currency, 79

daily life and work, 37, 82, 84-5, 107 ff.
Dauphin, Jean-Baptiste, 99, 143-145
Dauphin, Marie, 99
Dauphin, Vincent, 99, 143-145
Davilleau, Hyacinthe, 147, 149
Dawson route to Red River, 54
Dawson, Simon J., 54
Dease, John Warren, 51
Dease, Peter Warren, 146
De Meurons (mercenary soldiers), 5, 51, 83
Detroit, 13, 21, 29
De Wattevilles (mercenary soldiers), 51
diseases (*see* epidemics)
distances, 21, 66, 69, 70, 81, 85, 88
Dompierre, 145
Ducharme, 144
DuLhut, Daniel Greysolon, 13, 20, 28, 46
Dutremble, Antoine, 119, 147, 149
Dutremble, Nancy, 119

Elizabeth II, 3, 163
Ellice, Edward, 155
engagés (*see also* voyageurs), 83-4, 98
engagements (contracts), 98
English (Upper Churchill) River, 59
epidemics, 27, 30
Erie Canal, 52
Espagnol (*also* L'Espagnol, the Spaniard), 38-9
European Common Union, 158-9
Evans, Rev. James, 118
exploration, 71, 74, 105

Fanneant (Fainiant), A.M., 144-145
Faries, Hugh, 50
Fawkes, Marion Elizabeth, 100, 103
Fidler, Peter, 51
fish and fishing, 20, 26, 31, 37, 39, 83-4, 107-111, 134-135, 141-142, 146-7, 149
Flaherty, Robert J., 157
Flette, Mr., 147
Fond du Lac, 53, 93
Fontaine, Joseph, 147, 149
food and drink, 31, 37, 69, 71, 74, 77-78, 82-83, 108, 143-146, 148
Foreman-Doherty, Patte (trapper), 160
Fort Alexander, 92

Fort Bourbon, 20
Fort Chipewyan, 70
Fort Dauphin, 20, 93
Fort Frances, 48, 59
Fort Garry (upper), 54
Fort Kaministiquia (*see also* Fort William), 3, 14, 19-20, 28, 33-34, 46, 98
Fort Maurepas, 20
Fort Paskoya, 20
Fort St. Charles, 20
Fort St. Joseph, 14, 20
Fort St. Pierre, 20, 47, 86
Fort William (post and depot), 3, 5, 33-42, 70-72, 74, 85, 92-95; 98,107, 109,111-116, 128-130, 134; 139-150; decline, 41-42; population, 39
Fort William (municipality), 3, 42
Fort William Historical Park (*see also* Old Fort William), 3 Franchère, Gabriel, 3
Franklin, Capt. John, 59-60
Fraser, Catherine McKay, 95
Fraser, Simon (trader), 95
freemen, 37 (*see also* Métis; mixed-bloods)
Fremiot, Father Nicolas, 41
Frobisher, Benjamin, 30
Frobisher, Joseph, 30
fur auctions, 159, 161, 163-164
fur-bearing animals, 39-40; 68, 78, 80, 111, 155; conservation; depletion, 21, 39, 53, 68, 77, 155
Fur Institute of Canada, 160
fur farming, 157-8, 160, 163
fur fashions, 156-7, 162, 164
Fur Harvesters Auction Inc. (FHA), 159
Fur Institute of Canada, 160
fur markets, 78, 162-164
fur prices, 18, 162
fur returns, 38, 54, 88-89, 99, 133-134, 161
fur trade, French, 12-22, 26-29, 46-48, 106
fur trade routes, 3-5, 156
fur trade society, 37, 78-79, 83-84, 92-95, 115,
Furriers' Guild of Ontario, 153
genealogy, 95-96, 105-116
George III, 32
Georgian Bay (Lake Huron), 15
Germany, 164
Global Action Network, 163
Gloucester House, 30
Godsell, Philip, 158
Graffenried, Friedrich von, 83
Graham, Charles, 73

Grand Coquin, 39
Grand Portage, 13, 20, 28-19, 30-33, 49, 70-71
Grant, Mr., 98
Grant, John, 98
Grant, Mary, 97-98
Grant, Peter, 83-4, 97, 98
Grant, Susan, 97-98
Great Lakes, 27
Great Lakes-St. Lawrence basin, 49, 66, 68
Grey, Laura Bottineau, 97
Groseilliers, Médard Chouart, 16, 27-28
Gulf of Mexico, 3

Haldane, John, 37-38, 117, 118, 141, 143-144
Hargrave, Letitia, 118
Harmon, Daniel W., 65-66, 71, 73
Harrison, Edward, 92-95
Harrison, Joe, 93, 94
Harrison, Thomas, 93-94
hats: (bearskin), 164-165; (beaver), 54, 68, 153; (fur), 153; (silk), 54, 153
height of land, 3, 46, 47, 88, 93, 156
Henry, Alexander (the Elder), 20, 29, 69, 70, 72, 73, 78, 88, 89, 112
Henry, Alexander (the Younger), 64, 70, 71, 88, 92
Hind, Henry Youles, 47, 54
Horse Lake Rat, 79, 81
Hudson Bay, 3, 49,
Hudson Bay watershed, 3-4
Hudson's Bay Company (*see also* Competition), 3-4, 20, 28, 37-42; 46, 47, 68, 83, 84, 89, 90, 95, 104, 114, 115; amalgamation with NWC, 35, 49-51; charter, 28; retail stores, 41, 155, 157, 159
hunters, Indian, 52, 73, 79, 81-82, 84, 105, 109, 134

Illinois (Chief Illinois), 39, 147
independent traders, 128, 143
Indian, middlemen, 15, 27
Indians, Conveyance of Land, Kaministiquia River (1798), 34
Indians, 75, 77, 78-82, 83-85, 88-90, 94-95, 103, 105, 108-111, ll4-116; Algonquin,15; Anishinabeg (*see also* Chippewa, Ojibwa, Saulteurs), 25-35, 37-42; Assiniboines, 20; Chippewa, 88, 97, 112, 114; Cree, 20, 88, 93, 95, 102-103, 112; Huron,15; Iroquois, 15, 26; Ojibwa, 25ff, 77, 87, 88, 112; Saulteur, 88; Sioux (Dakota), 47-48
Indians, Rainy River, population, 81
Innis, Harold A., 13, 21 58, 68-69
international border, 33, 53
International Falls, MN, 86
Isbester, James, 85

James Bay, 26, 27, 28
Jay's Treaty (1794), 33
Jerome, Alexandre, 105, 108
Jerome, Edward, 105
Jesuits, *see* Missions and missionaries
Johnston, George 52

Kaministiquia, *see* Fort Kaministiquia
Kaministiquia River, 3, 13, 28, 33, 47
Kastoria, Greece, l62, 163
Keith, George, 129

Lac la Pluie (*See also* Rainy Lake), 5, 39,47-58, 59-67
Lagimodière, Jean-Baptiste, 93, 94
Lake Athabasca (*see* Athabasca)
Lake Huron, 15, 71
Lake Huron District, 95, 129-130
Lake Michigan, 15
Lake Nipigon, 20, 27, 29, 33, 71
Lake of the Woods, 20, 28, 46-48, 49, 71
Lake Superior, 3-4, 13, 15, 70-71
Lake Superior District, 126, 127-130, 133, 135
Lake Superior Mining Company, 41
Lake Winnipeg, 20, 29, 71
Lake Winnipegosis, 20
Langlade, Charles de, 21
La Noue, Robutel de la, 20
La Potherie, 17
LaTour, Josette, 117
La Vérendrye, Pierre Gaultier de Varennes, 13, 20, 28, 47
L'Homme du Sault, 39, 143
L'Illinois (*see* Illinois)
liquor (*see* alchohol)
Little Deer, 79, 81
Little Rat, 79, 142
"Little North", 29
Little Vermilion (Crane) Lake, 50, 52
Logan, Robert, 79
Long Lake (Long Lac), 128, 156

McBeath, Adam, 119
McBeath, Mary, 119
McCargo, Capt. Robert, 94-95
McDonald, Duncan, 84
McDonald, John of Garth, 103
Macdonell, John, 59
McFarlane, Peter, 141, 142

McGillis, Hugh, 70
McGillivray, Archibald, 65
McGillivray, Elizabeth, 103-104
McGillivray, Joseph, 103
McGillivray, Magdalen McDonald, 33, 103
McGillivray, Simon, 66
McGillivray, Simon Jr. (son of William), 53, 84, 103, 144, Susan, 102-104
McGillivray, William, 3, 25, 32-33, 66, 84, 103, 104
McIntosh, Donald, 89, 139, 146
MacKay, Alexander, 94, 95
McKay, Alexander William, 95, 96-97
McKay, Charles, 97
McKay, John (HBC), 50, 79, 82-84, 98
McKay, Edna, 95
McKay, Nancy, 95
McKay, Col. William, 95
Mackenzie, (Sir) Alexander, 32, 49-50, 59-60, 70, 71,92, 94, 100-102
McKenzie, Daniel, 65, 71, 92, 100-101
McKenzie, George, 101
MacKenzie, Kenneth, 94, 100
MacKenzie, Louisa (w. of Kenneth), 100
McKenzie, Margarette Graves, 100-102
Mackenzie River, 49
McKenzie, Roderic (son of Daniel), 92, 101
Mackenzie, Roderick (Hon.), 92, 99, 100, 102, 109
McKenzie, Roderick (HBC master, Rainy Lake), 79, 92, 107
McKenzie, Roderick, Jr., 92, 120-121
McKenzie, Roderick, Sr., 36, 38-39, 92, 108, 117 ff., 139
McKenzie, Susan (see Taitt, Susan McKenzie)
McLellan, Archibald, 65
McLeod, Archibald Norman, 65
McLeod, Ernest Herbert, 156
McLoughlin, Dr. John, 39, 50, 53, 80-81, 84, 95, 96, 99, 144
McLoughlin, Marguerite Waddens McKay, 95-96
McPherson, Donald, 79, 81, 83
McTavish, Donald, 67
McTavish, John George, 65
McTavish, Simon, 25, 32
McTavish, Frobisher & Co., 100

Mackinac, Michigan, 15
Manitoba (province), 54
marriage in the fur trade, 37, 83, 92-95, 97-98, 104, 115-118
Marteblanche, Chief La, 28
Masta, Jean-Baptiste, 99
Masta, Pierre (teamster), 98-99, 142-145
Métis (*see also* Mixed-bloods), 37, 51-52, 83, 107, 108, 109
Michikan Lake Crafts, 164
Michilimackinac, 14, 15, 17, 20-21, 29
Michipicoten, 5, 20, 88-89, 99-100. 126-136, 149
Michipicoten River, 5, 126, 131, 132
minerals, miners and mines, 25, 41
Minnesota, 54
Missinaibi River, 5
missions and missionaries, 15-16, 17, 27, 28, 51, 83, 105, 121
Mississippi River, 3, 5, 52, 66
Mississippi Valley, 46, 47
Missouri River, 52
mixed-bloods, 37, 92, 94-7, 100, 103-4, 105-115
Monk, Murray (trapper), 153, 160
Montreal, 70, 71, 84, 86, 88, 93, 96, 98, 99, 114, l05, 109, 112, 116
Montreal-based fur trade, 3-4, 13-14, 15, 18, 21, 27
Montreal Department (HBC), 127, 129, l30
Montreal merchants/agents, 15, 17-18, 29, 30, 70, 77, 94, 97, 100, 103
Montreal River, 134
Montreal Treaty, 1701(Great Peace), 27
Moose Factory, 99, 129, 130, 132
Morrison, William 52-53
Moze, Henry John (HBC), 88-89

Nanook of the North (film), 157
New Brunswick District, 128, 130
New North West Company (*see* XY Company)
Niagara Peace Treaty, 29
Nipigon (*see also* Lake Nipigon), 13-14, 30, 71, 117
Nolin, Jean-Baptiste, 88
North American Fur Auctions, 153
North American Fur and Fashion Exposition, Montreal, 164
North American Fur Auctions (NAFA), 153, 159
North West Company, 3-5; 13, 25, 30ff., 47-51, 68-9, 72, 74, 79, 82-84, 86-89, 92-95, 97-100, 103, 105, 107, 14-6; amalgamation with HBC, 99, 103, 107; *see also* under competition
North West Company departments, 62
North West Company, Inc. (Northern Stores), 153, 159
North West Passage, 13, 46
Noyan, Jacques de, 14, 46

Ohio River, 52
Old Fort William (*see also* Fort William Historical Park), 3, 92-96, 107
Ontaio Trappers Association (OTA), 159
Osnaburgh House, 49, 71
Ottawa River, 27

Pacific Ocean, 13, 46, 49
Pacific Fur Company, 95
Peace River, 70
Peau de Chat, Chief Joseph, 39, 41, 108, 142
"pedlars", 48
Pembina, 53, 105
Pemmican Proclamation, 51
People for the Ethical Treatment of Animals (PETA), 159, 164-165
Perrot, Nicholas, 16, 17
Petit Vieux, l44, 145
Pic (*or* The Pic), 128, 146
Pigeon River, 3, 13
Pond, Peter, 49, 99
Pontiac Uprising, 29
Port Arthur, 3, 42
posts, 70, 73, 82-83, 85, 86-87, 88-90, 112-113
Postes du nord, 19-20
Pothier, Toussaint, 20, 21
Provencher, Joseph-Norbert, 83
provisions and provisioning trade, 69, 71, 81, 82 ff., 104, 106-110, 132-133

Quebec (city), 18
Radisson, Pierre Esprit, 16, 27-28
railways, impact on fur trade, 41-42, 137, 155
Rainy Lake (*see also* Lac la Pluie), 3-5, 19, 20
Rainy Lake (post and depot), 5, 46-55, 59-67, 70,
Rainy River, 3
Red River, 20, 51, 53, 71
Red River Settlement, 35-6, 51, 93, 94, 108, 116, 117
Revillon Frères, 154, 156
Revillon Frères Museum, Moosonee, 154
Richards, Thomas, 41, 129, 140
Rivalry (*see* Competition)
Robinson Superior Treaty, 40-42, 114,

135
Robinson, William Benjamin, 41, 135
Rocky Mountains, 48
Ross, Louis, 145
Royal Proclamation (1763), 29

Saguenay River, 27
St. Gabriel's Church, Montreal, 95, 97
St. Germain, Venant, 88
St. Joseph's Island, 90
St. Lawrence River, 16, 25-27
St. Lawrence Seaway, 58
St. Mary's River, 88
Saskatchewan River, 48, 49
Sault Ste. Marie, 15-17, 20, 27, 71, 89
Sayer, John Charles, 97, 98
seasonal round, 84-85, 107, 142-149
schooners, 94; *Isabel*, 131; *Otter*, 31, 71; *Recovery*, 141; *Whitefish*, 131
Selkirk, Thomas Douglas, Earl of, 35-36, 51, 83, 93, 95, 101
Semple, Governor Robert, 51
Seven Oaks, 35-36, 51, 93
Simpson, Frances, 36, 39
Simpson, George, 36, 52, 53, 110, 119, 121, 126, 128, 130, 146, 147
Sir Alexander Mackenzie and Company, 32
Smith, Donald (Lord Strathcona), 42
Solomon, Ezekiel, 29, 30
Songab, Margarette Ahdik, 97-98
steamships, 132
Stewart, Alexander, 117, 139
Swanston John, 135

Taitt, Daniel, 96
Taitt, James, 95-96
Taitt, Susan McKenzie, 95-6
Tanner, John, 32
textiles, (*see* cloth and clothing)

Thompson, David, 66, 71, 92, 93
Thunder Bay: area, 15; municipality, 3; port, 58
tobacco, 31, 79, 80, 82, 107
Tonquin, 95
Toronto portage, 17
trade goods,(*See also* alcohol, cloth and clothing, tobacco,) 14, 17, 16, 31-32, 39; 61-64, 72, 74, 78, 79, 82, 88, 94, 112, l32-3
trade routes, 4-5, 17, 26-27, 52, 68-9, 71, 74-75, 85, l30, l35, 148, l55
traders/wintering partners, 30, 34, 65, 70, 73, 94, 99, 103
trading, 78-85, 88-90, 94, 98, 111, l33-134, 144
transportation (*see also* canoes, boats, schooners), 30-31, 54, 58, 69, 70, 72-74, 78, 85-86, 88, 90, 110
Trappers (Native), 18, 115, 158, 161-164
Trappers (non-Native), 163-164
Treaty of Paris (1763), 48
Treaty of Paris (1783), 33
Treaty of Utrecht (1713), 19, 20, 46

Umfreville, Edward, 33
U.S. Indian policy, 52

Vermilion Lake, 52
Vezina (Visina) 107, 149
voyageurs, 14, 16, 63-4, 71, 83-85, 86, 92, 94, 98-9, 105, 107, 111, 112
Voyageurs' Highway, 5

Wadden (*also spelled* Waddens), Jean-Etienne, 94, 95, 99
Wadden, Véronique, 99
Warren, William, 33

weather (*see* climate)
Webseter-Ashburton Treaty, 52
Weyers, Mishaha (Latour), 105, 111-113
wild rice (*see* provisions and provisioning trade)
Winnipeg River, 3, 71
wintering partners (*see also* traders), 65
women in the fur trade (*see also* fur trade society and names of specific women), 14, 37, 39, 94 ff., 110, 117-122

XY Company, 32, 34, 36, 50, 83, 85

York Factory, 36

www.ingramcontent.com/pod-product-compliance
Ingram Content Group UK Ltd.
Pitfield, Milton Keynes, MK11 3LW, UK
UKHW062045180426
11947UKWH00030B/2059